# ANXIETIES OF INTERIORITY AND DISSECTION IN EARLY MODERN SPAIN

T0355649

*Anxieties of Interiority and Dissection in Early Modern Spain* brings the study of Europe's "culture of dissection" to the Iberian peninsula, presenting a neglected episode in the development of the modern concept of the self. Enrique Fernandez explores the ways in which sixteenth- and seventeenth-century anatomical research stimulated both a sense of interiority and a fear of that interior's exposure and punishment by the early modern state.

Examining works by Miguel de Cervantes, María de Zayas, Fray Luis de Granada, and Francisco de Quevedo, Fernandez highlights the existence of narratives in which the author creates a surrogate self on paper, then "dissects" it. He argues that these texts share a fearful awareness of having a complex inner self in a country where one's interiority was under permanent threat of punitive exposure by the Inquisition or the state. A sophisticated analysis of literary, religious, and medical practice in early modern Spain, Fernandez's work will interest scholars working on questions of early modern science, medicine, and body politics.

(Toronto Iberic)

ENRIQUE FERNANDEZ is a professor of Spanish literature in the Department of French, Spanish, and Italian at the University of Manitoba.

# Anxieties of Interiority and Dissection in Early Modern Spain

ENRIQUE FERNANDEZ

UNIVERSITY OF TORONTO PRESS
Toronto Buffalo London

© University of Toronto Press 2015
Toronto Buffalo London
utorontopress.com

Reprinted in paperback 2023

ISBN 978-1-4426-4886-9 (cloth)
ISBN 978-1-4875-5644-0 (paper)
Printed and bound by CPI Group (UK) Ltd, Croydon, CR0 4YY
Publication cataloguing information is available from Library and Archives
Canada.

Cover image: Portrait of Dr Joan Tomás Porcell at the age of thirty-six
dissecting the cadaver of a victim of the plague. From his *Información y
curación de la peste de Zaragoza y preservación contra la peste en general* (Zaragoza:
Viuda de Bartolomé de Nájera, 1565). Photo © Tarker / Bridgeman Images.

We wish to acknowledge the land on which the University of Toronto
Press operates. This land is the traditional territory of the Wendat, the
Anishnaabeg, the Haudenosaunee, the Métis, and the Mississaugas of the
Credit First Nation.

This book has been published with the help of a grant from the Federation
for the Humanities and Social Sciences, through the Awards to Scholarly
Publications Program, using funds provided by the Social Sciences and
Humanities Research Council of Canada.

University of Toronto Press acknowledges the financial support of the
Government of Canada, the Canada Council for the Arts, and the Ontario
Arts Council, an agency of the Government of Ontario, for its publishing
activities.

**Canada Council
for the Arts**      **Conseil des Arts
du Canada**

**ONTARIO ARTS COUNCIL
CONSEIL DES ARTS DE L'ONTARIO**
an Ontario government agency
un organisme du gouvernement de l'Ontario

Funded by the      Financé par le
Government      gouvernement
of Canada      du Canada      Canadä

# Contents

Contents

# Illustrations

# Acknowledgments

I want to thank the Social Sciences and Humanities Research Council of Canada (SSHRC) for awarding me a generous grant that allowed me to conduct the research for this book. In addition, the University of Manitoba offered me financial support through grants, teaching releases, and sabbatical leaves that expedited the writing process. A considerable amount of the research was done in the Biblioteca Nacional de Madrid, whose dedicated librarians and personnel I want to acknowledge. The members of the multidisciplinary group *On the Body*, which operates with the support of the Institute for the Humanities at the University of Manitoba, served as a very helpful sounding board for my initial ideas and drafts. Especially helpful were the commentaries and corrections by the anonymous readers to whom the University of Toronto Press sent my original manuscript for evaluation. They helped me to write a better book not only by correcting my mistakes but also by pointing out connections that I had not followed in my initial version. I want to thank Suzanne Rancourt, Senior Humanities Editor of the University of Toronto Press, for her interest in the book from the beginning and her efficient and expeditious publication process. I am especially indebted to those who proofread the manuscript: my wife, Lynne Fernandez, Judith Kearns, Brian Turner, Peter Fothergill-Payne, Karalyn Dokurno, and Barbie Halaby. Part of chapter 3 appeared as an article in Spanish in the *Bulletin Hispanique*: many thanks to Nadine Ly, the journal's director, who kindly granted me permission to replicate part of the article. The images reproduced here are courtesy of the Fondo Antiguo y Archivo Histórico of the Biblioteca de la Universidad de Sevilla, Spain; the Biblioteca Francisco de Burgoa, Oaxaca, Mexico; the Wellcome Collection, London, England; and the History of Medicine Division, National Library of Medicine of the National Institutes of Health, Bethesda, Maryland. Especially helpful was Michael J. North, Head of Rare Books & Early Manuscripts of the History of Medicine Division.

# ANXIETIES OF INTERIORITY AND DISSECTION IN EARLY MODERN SPAIN

# Introduction: Dissective Narratives

This book examines what I call "dissective narratives," texts written in sixteenth- and seventeenth-century Spain that resort to anatomical methods to expose the interiority of a fabricated Other that is to be sacrificed. I contend that dissective narratives are informed by an anxiety resulting from a widespread awareness of complex interiors in the oppressive ambience of the early modern Spanish state.[1] They are osmotic exercises that try to re-establish the balance between the inside and the outside – between the individual and the state – through the creation of dissective scenarios in which sacrificial victims have their interiors exposed. The narratives describe invasions of the inner body by methods akin to those typical of what Sawday has named "the culture of dissection." With this expression, he refers to the pervasiveness of anatomical dissection in the sixteenth and seventeenth centuries, not only as a medical technology but also as a discursive method of investigating psychological states and mental processes, which were deemed directly observable if the body was laid open. As Sawday writes,

> [T]he early-modern period sees the emergence of a new image of the human interior, together with a new means of studying that interior, which left its mark on all forms of cultural endeavour in the period ... Paradoxically, the very violence of dissective culture was a factor in the production of some of the more familiar structures of great beauty and vitality which we associate with the term "Renaissance" ... To deploy a phrase such as the "culture of dissection" is to suggest a network of practices, social structures, and rituals surrounding this production of fragmented bodies, which sits uneasily alongside our image (derived from

Burckhardt) of the European Renaissance as the age of the construction of individuality – a unified sense of selfhood.[2]

Dissection offered a new language of inner discovery in a period in which the curiosity about inwardness was so strong and so widespread that present-day critics speak of an early modern cultural imperative to be interior. The period was characterized by the growth of the inner realm, which acquired attributes previously associated with the outside world – such as vastness, infiniteness, and expansion – as if characteristics of the divine had been transferred to the human interior.[3] This inner enlargement is also related to what has been called the great process of internalization: many entities previously considered to have an independent ontological status in the outside began to be perceived as mental objects and moved inside human conscience. Concurrently, copious materials with which to furnish this expanding interior were made available by the exponential increase of new knowledge and its diffusion through the printing press.[4]

Although interest in interiority was particularly intense and pervasive in the period under scrutiny, I do not believe that interiority at large can be restricted to any given era. I disagree with some often-quoted recent studies that attribute interiority – and therefore consciousness – to human beings only after a certain century, thus turning previous generations into automata or zombies.[5] On the contrary, some form of interiority can be understood as a transhistorical characteristic of the human animal. Interiority's contents, however, and its perceived relation with the physical body and the external world are culturally constructed.[6] A definite aspect of this formation in early modern Spain is studied here within the wider debate on the emergence of the modern subject as the result of social and historical forces. Specifically, this book examines how the early modern subject constructs embodied interiority as a private locus on which it relies to claim individuation. This has to be understood within the wider subject of embodiment. Today, the term "embodiment" is widely used in many disciplines, from cognitive science to neurobiology and computer science, because it permits us to bypass Cartesian dualism through a phenomenological approach. In such an approach, being is presented as a process in which the physicality of the body is simultaneously subject and object, thus intersecting culture and nature. Also implied is a shift from the view of the body as a non-gendered, pre-discursive reality to an acculturated body created by its relations with the surrounding world. This body is then not limited to flesh and bone but includes habits, gestures, and behaviours, as well as the processes through which they are acquired and maintained.[7]

Dissection had a significant effect on the contemporary conception of interiority. On the one hand, it contributed to enlarging the perception of a private, embodied interiority. The popular anatomical manuals of the period abounded with images and descriptions in which the inner body was presented as a labyrinthine space of nooks and crannies, suitable for both conceiving and hiding ideas and feelings. On the other hand, dissection made clear that these bodily spaces could be broken into from the outside and their most private contents exposed. The result was that dissection could be called upon to both illuminate and obfuscate the same interior. This possibility of enlisting dissection in the service of two contradictory positions clearly helped increase the tension that lies at the centre of the anxiety of interiority. Capable of being instrumentalized in opposite directions, dissection played a role similar to the one Jessica Wolfe claimed for some of the new technologies of the period. Not only did they provide metaphors for politics, science, literature, and philosophy, they also served to express the anxieties triggered by a world perceived to be run by artifice and in which instrumentality mediated all the relations between men, and between men and nature. The term *machina*, in its double meaning of mechanical device and of contriving to deceive, encapsulated best this twofold perception of technology.[8] Similarly, I contend that dissection, also a technology, could be used to express the anxiety of an interiority that was deemed concurrently inscrutable and exposable. While it threatened the subjects with the punitive revelation of their inner secrets, it portrayed an inner body so complex and ambiguous, made up of so many organs, that it defied interpretation. The complex inner body portrayed by anatomical dissection was a *machina* in its two meanings: a machine and deceiving artifice. This body was made up of organs in the double Aristotelian meaning of *organon* as a body part and as an objectified instrument, a word that is etymologically connected to *ergon* (work).[9] In this second sense, bodily organs were suitable to be modified and instrumentalized by the person for operations of self-fashioning. However, since these organs could function autonomously and act on their own, they could churn out results different from those for which they had been enlisted by their supposed owner.

The dissective narratives I am about to examine are part of the manifestations of the culture of dissection in the literary realm. Although all of them are pervaded by the culture of dissection, they differ widely in style and content. They are inscribed in different generic traditions, and the dissected characters' reactions range from carefully hiding to easily revealing their interiors. Some resist, some are indifferent to, and some appear as if they comply with the dissection. In a few cases, the characters proceed to dissect themselves. Also varied are the inner contents exposed. Sometimes they conform to the law: what is found inside are orthodox thoughts that do not deviate from the positions endorsed by religious and civil authorities. The dissected subject is then proven innocent and the inspection unnecessary. On other occasions, unorthodox ideas are exposed that contradict the authoritative discourse. The subject is then found guilty and the dissection initiates punishment. Often, the interiors uncovered contain orthodox and unorthodox elements intertwined that exploit the contradictions and ambiguities of the authoritative discourses. In these cases, the guilt or innocence of the subject is unclear and the legitimacy of the dissective operation questioned.

The label "dissective narrative" is to be understood not as a genre but as an umbrella term that includes texts written within the formal conventions of different genres and traditions. Therefore, a unified poetics of dissection is not at work across these texts. On the contrary, a variety of ad hoc methods is used for adapting pre-existing bodily images to construct embodied interiorities and expose them to more or less dissective assaults. Because of this, the resulting narratives may take many shapes and meanings. Furthermore, the presentation of interiorities under assault is neither the only nor necessarily the main intention of these texts. In many cases, it is just one ingredient in a complex story, often serving as a thread within another theme of the plot. Such an elusive manifestation could indicate the subconscious resurfacing of an underlying anxiety of interiority. In other cases, intentionality can be posited and the dissection of interiorities occupies a deliberately central role in the story.

This book also deals with an early episode of humans becoming the target of science-power, in this case through the effects of early anatomical dissection as an incipient technology of bio-power. Sawday establishes the connection among anatomy, power, and punishment: "[T]he 'culture of dissection' also promoted the beginning of what Michel Foucault has analysed as the 'surveillance' of the body within regimes of judgment and punishment."[10] The role technology plays in this production of objectified data that can be examined in a representational format is already at work in the modus operandi of early modern anatomy. It opens the body to scrutiny by documenting its contents, by translating them into data that can be analysed. In this sense, anatomy is one of the early forms of "disassembly" of citizens into discrete data. Early modern Spaniards' awareness that their interiors could be so mapped constitutes the anxiety under examination here. Some aspects of this study also connect with the concerns behind surveillance studies. This relatively new field focuses on the "surveillant assemblage," or the convergence of once discrete vigilance apparatuses into a unified system that "operates by abstracting human bodies from their territorial settings and separating them into a series of discrete flows [that] are then reassembled in different locations as discrete and virtual 'data doubles.'"[11]

## Anxious Interiors and Sacrificial Victims

The anxiety of interiority results from the awareness of having increasingly complex, partly uncontrollable interiors whose contents can be exposed and become a liability.[12] Studied here is one of its manifestations, which I have called dissective narratives. They are more or less conscious attempts at assuaging this anxiety through artistic elaborations that permit displacements, projections, and substitutions comparable to the ones in dream work. A similar role of appeasing the anxiety caused by the perceived need to keep one's interior carefully concealed has been attributed to the literature of the period. Hillman writes about the abundance of opened bodies on the early modern stage: "It is as if early modern theatre, while at one level pushing somatic closure further than it had ever been, at another level provided a kind of safety-valve to relieve the pressure placed upon the body to be shut."[13] Similarly, the dissective narratives we will study accomplish their assuaging effect by putting forward sacrificial victims endowed with complex interiors. They are thus pre-emptive moves made inside the safety of surrogate selves that have been textually constructed for this scrutiny and follow a Girardian pattern.[14] However, these narratives follow the sacrificial model only on their surface. The victims may appear to behave like the bodies depicted in the contemporary anatomical books, which are passive and may even cut themselves open and hold their own layers apart to facilitate the inspection (for example, see Figures 5, 6, and 7 in chapter 1). In reality, they practise a form of pseudo-compliance with interpellating authority that, as will be seen, recalls the duplicitous confession and other methods of resistance characteristic of contemporary picaresque novels.[15] Because the characters that are presented to be scrutinized partake of elements of an authority and an alien figure, the dissective narratives may resemble some strategies of Greenblatt's self-fashioning.[16] Although the figures are created in the name of authority, as in Greenblatt's model, they exceed their original sacrificial function and subvert the authority in whose name they were created. But the dissective narratives are not self-fashioning narratives. They put too much emphasis on the negative and destructive aspect of the operation to claim that their authors' main objective is to construct a public persona or to mask their opinions.

The complex relation between self and Other, between hiding and revealing, between willingness and resistance that permeates dissective narratives is illustrated by the portrait of Dr Joan Tomás Porcell (see Figure 1). He was a Sardinia-born, Salamanca-trained doctor and reputed anatomist who taught at the University of Zaragoza. The portrait is included in his *Información y curación de la peste de Zaragoza y preservación contra la peste en general* (1565). During the outbreak of the plague in 1564, Dr Porcell was appointed the director of the Hospital de Nuestra Señora de Gracia in Zaragoza. In difficult circumstances and under the continuous risk of contagion, he courageously helped hundreds of victims of the plague. In addition, Porcell performed autopsies on five corpses of male and female victims to ascertain the pathology of the infection that was causing so many casualties. The book is the report of his findings.[17] Following the title page is the portrait of Porcell opening the corpse of one of the victims of the plague, as indicated by the abnormal lumps on its left flank. This portrait belongs to what Carlino has called "images of dissection in the Vesalian *maniera*."[18] By this he means the illustrations that became customary in anatomical books after the 1543 publication of Vesalius's *De humani corporis fabrica*, a book whose significance will be examined later. Among many other innovations, it included numerous engravings of anatomized bodies and, most important for the matter at hand, two portraits of Vesalius performing dissections. One is a torso portrait of a twenty-eight-year-old Vesalius dissecting an arm (see Figure 2). The other is a complex frontispiece that depicts him dissecting a body surrounded by an attentive audience in an anatomical theatre (see Figure 9 in chapter 4). These two engravings – attributed to Jan Calcar, a member of Titian's circle – have been profusely analysed because they exemplify important changes in the practice of anatomy. In previous depictions of anatomical sessions, the anatomists were portrayed reading aloud from a medical book while their assistants opened the corpses. This can be seen, for instance, in *Anathomia Mundini*, written by Mondino de Luzzi for his students in 1316. The title page of the Leipzig 1493 edition shows him reading aloud from a book at a pulpit while his assistant demonstrates the doctrine on a corpse. In the images in *De humani corporis fabrica*, Vesalius performs the dissection personally instead of relegating the task to an assistant. Significantly, the textbook is laid aside to indicate that now the main instrument of knowledge is the body and not the writings by Galen and other classical authorities.[19]

Although the portrait of Porcell is not of the same excellent manufacture as the engravings depicting Vesalius in the *De humani corporis fabrica*, it follows the same pattern (see Figure 2).[20] Similar are the general poses in which dissector and corpse face each other, the detailed features of the face, and the specific reference to the dissector's age when the portrait was taken – thirty-six in the case of Porcell. Missing are paper and a pen near the dissection table. However, he holds the knife he used to open the corpse in his right hand, his index finger fully extended over the back edge of the blade, as if holding a pen. His eyes, unlike Vesalius's, are not directed towards the spectator but engrossed in the dissection he is performing. He is so absorbed that he is unaware of being portrayed, or does not care to stop to pose. Furthermore, he does not appear to be interested in showing or teaching the audience but in finding a truth that continues to elude him. To open the body and extract the organs does not seem to be enough. His left hand holds a major organ, probably the liver or the stomach, which he seems to be about to cut open for further inspection. The corpse, as in the Vesalius portrait, appears to be that of a woman. The breasts are partially covered by a piece of cloth, although the strong muscles of the left arm and leg are masculine. Because the genitals are hidden, as was common in this kind of representation, the gender of the body is unclear, but that it is infected by the plague is evident by the abnormal growths or buboes on its side.

As in the dissective narratives studied here, this image depicts an operation to investigate a condition that, like the new forms of interiority spreading at the time, has its origin inside the body. As Sawday exemplifies with the tale of Medusa's head, somebody else's interior has to be opened and scrutinized because it is forbidden to examine one's own interior.[21] In the engraving, the idea of displaced self-investigation is encapsulated by the resemblance of Porcell to the recumbent corpse. Both figures carry their arms similarly bent at the elbow, as mirrored

1  Portrait of Dr Joan Tomás Porcell at the age of thirty-six dissecting the
cadaver of a victim of the plague. From his *Información y curación de la peste
de Zaragoza y preservación contra la peste en general* (Zaragoza: Viuda de Bartolomé de Nájera, 1565). Reproduced by permission of the Fondo Antiguo
de la Universidad de Sevilla.

images whose specular planes were separated by the edge of the operating table.[22] Also similar to the dissective narratives, the naked victim
displays contradictory signals of compliance and resistance. Its inex-
pressive, almost serene face shows indifference, as if it were unaffected
by – or even complied with – the gory procedure. However, its left
arm seems to be contracted by pain. The right hand trying to cover
the genitals is an empty gesture given the gaping abdominal cut, from
which the flaps of skin have been pulled back for an unhindered view
of the interior. Furthermore, one of the organs is displayed in the left
hand of Porcell, who, carried away by his zeal to find the origins of

2 Portrait of Andreas Vesalius at the age of twenty-eight. From the first edition of his *De humani corporis fabrica* (Basilea: J. Oporinus, 1543). Reproduced by permission of the History of Medicine Division, National Library of Medicine of the National Institutes of Health.

the contagious affliction, seems to be about to cut through the victim's organ into his own unprotected hand.

## Arrangement of the Chapters

The first chapter is an overview of the concept of embodied interiority, with an emphasis on the major transformation it was undergoing in those years. Different conceptions of what constitutes interiority, of its immaterial status, and of its relation to the materiality of the body had accumulated over the centuries. In the early modern period, the construction of interiority underwent a quantitative and qualitative change. Although this epochal shift is often associated with the inner turn that religious piety took in Northern Europe (the *devotio moderna*, the Mystics of the North, and the Protestant reform), its effects were visible everywhere, including Spain, and extended far beyond the original religious realm. Not only did allusions to an inner space increase – terms such as "interior" or "inside" became common on contemporary title pages, such as in Saint Teresa's *El castillo interior* (1577) – but now the allusions pointed to precise locations inside the body. Intestines, hearts, brains, and other organs became the seat of specific – often new – mental and psychological functions. This internalization matched the contemporary humoural psychology, which saw mental and psychical processes as the result of the interactions of fluids and their pressure on the organs. Concurrently, the new anatomical science confirmed the complexity of the inner body and its functioning. Along with the increase of interest in everything interior, its perception underwent an important change. In a period in which the modern state and the control of its citizens were emerging, the opposition of inside/outside became loaded with new meanings. The privacy of this inner realm, although always an ingredient of interiority, became fundamental. Consequently, the interest in strategies to hide one's interior and its contents grew, and with it the interest in revealing and deciphering others' interiors. In Spain, this reaches the category of an obsession and an art in the work of Baltasar Gracián. Although less explicitly stated, the system of blood and honour that regulated the behaviours of those in the higher echelons of society imposed a restraint of emotions that often translated into repression of their external manifestations.

Part of the first chapter is dedicated to how these factors played out in the specific case of Spain. In general, the pan-European pattern of increasing interest in interiority was followed, but some peculiar conditions existed. In Spain, the first European country to develop a modern state, older discourses that emphasized blood and religion continued to play an important role and became part of the new system. The resulting monolithic Spanish state grew a control apparatus more integrated and developed than that existing in any other contemporary country. The Inquisition was always a presence, a silent threat operating in the background. Its zeal and the specific ideas and groups it targeted fluctuated considerably over the years. Overall, this unpredictability exacerbated the anxiety of Spaniards, who could never be sure whether their thinking contained potential heresies of which even they were not aware.

Although this book does not intend to be an exhaustive study of dissective narratives, the following chapters include a significant selection of narratives to put the model to the test. The texts studied are written by four well-known Spanish writers of the period: Fray Luis de Granada, Francisco de Quevedo, Miguel de Cervantes, and María de Zayas. These writers have been chosen because they represent different generations whose combined lifespans overlap the most significant period of early modern Spain (i.e., the second part of the sixteenth and the first half of the seventeenth centuries). Their different personalities and careers provide a window into crucial aspects of the Spain of the time. They were practitioners of genres that are central to the literature of the period, and each one presents a unique combination of characteristics that makes him or her especially apt to demonstrate specific facets of the anxiety of interiority. Thus, Fray Luis de Granada helps exemplify how this anxiety took hold of people in the ranks of the Catholic church. Many of the symptoms described in his writing can also be detected in the works of Fray Luis de León, Santa Teresa de Jesús, San Juan de la Cruz, and San Ignacio de Loyola. Although these authors today are considered more significant for Spanish literature than Granada, he is the most suitable because only he combines several key factors that facilitate the study. Like the other religious figures mentioned, his life was punctuated by conflict with the Inquisition, but his high position in the Portuguese court removed him from the jurisdiction of the Spanish Inquisition, allowing him to choose how and when to react to the attacks of Inquisitor General Valdés. This circumstance allows us to examine how the posited anxiety of interiority evolved across the writings that Granada continued to produce in his long, industrious life. In addition, while the other religious writers tended to confine their production to one or two genres, Granada's copious literary output extends to a variety of genres, which results in the anxiety of interiority being expressed in varied forms. Finally, Granada is unique in that, unlike the other religious figures, he explicitly included anatomical dissection in his writing, thus providing us with firm grounds to ascertain how the new medical technology affected his perceived relation between the individual and a policing society.

Unlike in the case of Granada, I chose Quevedo and Cervantes in part because they are two of the most important writers of a period that they help define. Their writing offers specific manifestations of the anxiety of interiority that are unique in their sharpness and expressiveness. Quevedo masterfully applies the new discoveries and methods of anatomical dissection to the traditional image of the body politic, for which he takes advantage of satire's penchant for dismemberment. The results are poignant portraits of a society in which increasing individualism clashed with the tenets that kept it together. Anatomical discourse is not an explicit ingredient in Cervantes's writing. However, his carefully constructed characters present highly private interiors that are unveiled for the enlightenment of the readers with methods akin to dissection. I included María de Zayas because she is one of the rare cases of a woman writing with a feminist agenda and, most important for our purposes, presenting a gendered body with a distinct female interiority, which results in a highly specific kind of anxiety of interiority. This body is under continuous physical assault by the patriarchal order, which wants to access or control the reproductive organs of this body that it often ends up destroying in an orgy of near-dissective violence. Finally, I briefly include the case of Gracián since he is the acclaimed master in the construction of secretive interiors, as well as in their unveiling, a task for which he often resorts to dissective imagery. He also offers me the opportunity to lay the boundaries of my study since the kind of anxiety in which I am interested has been replaced in Gracián by what I call anxiety of performance.

Chapter 2 studies Fray Luis de Granada (1504–88). A deeply spiritual man of the church, he was the author of enormously popular books of prayer and an important player in Spanish and Portuguese high politics. His life exemplifies the importance that religion played in the construction of interiority and the risks of cultivating it in an increasingly policed intellectual and religious environment. In defence of this inner practice, he proclaimed that the human interior is God's work, and thus it cannot be suspected of harbouring anything but a reflection of God. To prove this point, he often put forward the testimony of the new anatomy. He appealed especially to discoveries that reinforced a view of the inner body according to the medieval image of man as a microcosm and the culmination of God's work. However, Granada's cautious argumentation was not enough to protect him from being accused of advancing forms of inner prayer and worship that resembled Protestant practices and other heresies of the day. After his two main spiritual treatises were included in the *Index of Forbidden Books*, he spent the rest of his life in Portugal, where his connections protected him from his enemies within the Spanish church. After this encounter with the Inquisition, his dissective narratives became more cogent in their effort to disprove that interiority could be dangerous. Without changing his basic line of argumentation, he adopted new strategies to prove the innocence of the interiority he postulated. In his later writings, Granada resorts to the figure of the martyr, whose interior, in spite of undergoing a cruel vivisection, does not reveal anything other than the truth of the faith she had willingly confessed to her interrogators from the beginning. A dissective narrative in this line is his defence of the Portuguese nun María de la Visitación, of whom he was a friend and admirer. In it, Granada presents her famous stigmata as a voluntary confession of the truth inside, while he portrays himself as a callous anatomizer/ torturer investigating this innocent interior. The confirmation by the Spanish Inquisition at the request of Philip II – at that moment also king of Portugal – that María de la Visitación had painted her stigmata and that the whole affair was a sham compelled Granada to recant in the final months of his life.

Chapter 3 is dedicated to Quevedo's concern with private interiority and its consequences for the survival of the body politic of Spain, which he considered to be seriously ill. Granada had lived in relatively tolerant times, but everything began to change in the second half of the sixteenth century. By the time Quevedo was born, the country had entered a spiral of decadence and become obsessively defensive against Protestantism and its political success. In some of his writings, Quevedo submits the contemporary body politic to a dissective process, mocking the dangers that the claims to its citizens' individuality imply for this collective body. For Quevedo, who believed in a hierarchical society, the individual interiorities of the different subjects acting as organs of the corporative entity of the state represented a danger for its survival. The unavoidable individual embodiment of the citizens and their claim to embodied interiority is dangerous for the body politic. In Quevedo's *Sueños*, in his picaresque novel *El Buscón*, and in some of his many shorter satirical compositions, the individual bodies of the lower classes are broken into a chaotic aggregate of parts that are inclined to further dismemberment and malfunction. Their inner organs, especially their digestive tracts, are presented as unruly and prone to all kinds of scatological accidents. These lower bodies replicate the chaotic role that they play within the body politic, whose survival they threaten. The other kind of interiority that Quevedo presents as a risk to the body politic is that of the *privado* or favourite of the king. In his parodic pamphlet *Visita y anatomía de la cabeza del Cardenal Armando Richelieu* (1635), Quevedo describes a fantastic trip by the famous anatomist Vesalius into the head of the ambitious cardinal. The head is presented as a monstrous growth on the body politic of France that endangers its very survival. By contrast, Quevedo's play *Cómo ha de ser el privado* exalts the figure of Valisero – an anagram for Olivares, the ruling *valido* in Spain – who is described as the perfect assistant to the king. Valisero dissolves himself within the body of the king and the body politic, to the point of sacrificing his individual existence.

The fourth and last chapter studies two of Cervantes's *Novelas ejemplares* and several of Zayas's *Desengaños*. In the *novelas* analysed, the same dialectics of resistance and submission found in previous chapters are present, even if no character is literally put under the dissective knife. Two of the best known of Cervantes's short novels, *El licenciado Vidriera* and *El coloquio de los perros*, are studied as dissective narratives. The picture they present of the human being is of an assemblage of precariously balanced organs subject to the same problems that plagued the mechanical artefacts of the time. The human being appears as a machine made of flesh that can be thrown out of balance intentionally or accidentally. Thus, Cañizares, the witch in *El coloquio de los perros*, has changed her interior to the point of achieving a demonic form of autonomy in which she is isolated from the rest of God's creation. She has turned herself into a clock that ticks on its own without keeping with astronomical time. The punitive conclusion of the story resembles a dissection performed in an anatomy theatre: her naked body exposed in the public square, her unresponsive flesh pricked with long needles by the curious bystanders. The case of the Glass Licentiate, in *El licenciado Vidriera*, resembles Cañizares's story in many aspects. Because of an imprudent regime of selfish learning and the accidental ingestion of a poisoned quince, young Tomás becomes sick. He partially recovers but develops a fixation with being made of glass. As if he were a walking anatomical figure whose outer layers are transparent, he has no reservations about answering the most delicate questions. His answers, however, are made up of stale truisms and bigotry, the products of years of selfish bookish learning. Tomás has become a talking machine, regurgitating the dry erudition and its implied prejudices that he has ingested as part of his excessive diet of self-fashioning.

Several of Zayas's *Desengaños* – *La inocencia castigada*, *El verdugo de su esposa*, *Tarde llega el desengaño*, and *Mal presagio casar lejos* – present jealous husbands who, suspecting adultery, murder their wives with cruelly elaborate methods that are not literal dissections but that share key ingredients with the dissective narratives studied. Zayas's heroines are affected by an anxiety of interiority resulting from their awareness of having interiors that are under scrutiny. Their interiority is, however, class- and gender-specific, constructed around their sexual/reproductive organs. Noblewomen's inner bodies were understood as synonymous with their female anatomy and as the foundations on which the reproduction – literal and metaphorical – of the noble order rested. Consequently, they were treated by the honour code as territories to be protected from any unsanctioned access. The result was an anxiety of interiority for the women, who were aware of the constant vigilance towards their bodies and of the consequences of being found guilty. Their situation was symbolized by the engravings of the contemporary anatomical manuals representing women in erotic poses whose sexual organs had been cut open for public display. Like the bodies in these images, upper-class women were eroticized objects exposed to the inquisitive male gaze. In addition, the horrific wounds that had been inflicted upon the sexual organs of the female bodies in the engravings symbolized the punishment that jealous husbands could enact upon women for sexual offences, real or imagined. Although none of Zayas's murdered heroines are literally dissected nor their female anatomies exposed, their bodies are subjected to cruelly elaborate torture and executions that resemble some dissective processes. As in the aestheticized images of anatomical books, the results of the husbands' revenge are beautiful corpses that are simultaneously abhorrent and appealing. More specifically, they resemble the so-called anatomical Venuses, which were ivory manikins intended as instructional aids for doctors and midwives. However, in Zayas's stories the post-mortem beauty of the executed wives' bodies also acts as in the case of the martyrs' incorrupt corpses and proclaims their innocence.

Chapter 4 includes an epilogue that is a brief revision of Baltasar Gracián's complex treatment of interiority. I explain why we must guard against the indiscriminate application of the term "dissective narratives" to any text dealing with interiority that resorts to anatomical imagery. I argue that his writings do not qualify as dissective narratives because they address a typically Baroque interiority that differs categorically from the previous cases. For him interiority is not a vague space that may harbour thoughts suspicious to the authorities and for whose atonement propitiatory victims are to be sacrificed. Interiority is a concrete entity that must be mastered to achieve personal success. The anxiety that interiority triggered with previous authors has been replaced in Gracián by an obsession with adequate performance, and the sacrificial victim has been supplanted by the figure of one's adversary in the quest for power.

The book ends with a recapitulation of the role that narratives of dissection play within the larger frame of the modern subject's formation. The fact that contradictory discourses, interiority, revelation of hidden truths, and an overriding anxiety are crucial ingredients of these narratives brings to mind the modern novel. However, dissective narratives should not be understood as heroic yet failed attempts at putting forward modern forms of interiority and the subsequent subjectivity. They are something more multifaceted and contradictory, the product of the anxiety of simultaneously embracing and rejecting the emerging complex interiority. This contradiction can be seen in the characters created to be dissected, which bear elements of the self and of an Other that are accepted and rejected at the same time. The conflicted nature of these narratives is also expressed in how the designated victims fluctuate between submission and resistance to the dissective process. Even when they appear to submit voluntarily, they interject obstacles that obscure their interiors. Eventually, the interiors they are compelled to surrender turn out to be made up of the same elements of the discourse in whose name they are investigated. Their building blocks, still recognizable, are taken from the predominant religious or political discourse but rearranged in forms that exploit – and therefore draw attention to – its arbitrariness, blind spots, and ambiguities.

**1**

# Dissection and Interiority:
# The Case of Spain

---

## The Conjoined Twins of Hispaniola

Interiority has traditionally been understood as a series of processes inside the body that imply an interaction between the material (or physical) and the immaterial (or psychological) – the last term used in the modern as well as in the etymological sense that refers to the soul, or vital spirit. Because of the opaque materiality of the body and the subtle nature of the inner processes, these are not visible to outside observers, who can gain access to them only indirectly through the subject's speech, actions, and gestures. In the early modern period, anatomy for the first time offered the theoretical possibility of side-stepping this problematic opacity and reaching directly inside the person through a systematic method of scrutiny. This privileged window to the processes of interiority had, however, evident limitations. First, the processes could not be caught in action, since dissections were carried out on dead bodies. On moral grounds, moreover, vivisection was not practised and, even if it were practised, the crude procedure could not be performed without entailing the rapid death of the dissected subject. Even today, though sophisticated techniques allow us real-time images of the inner body, direct access to the mind continues to elude us.

The imagination of the early modern period often chose to ignore these limitations and fantasized that dissection allowed for direct observation of interiority. The following historical case shows how, through a combination of ideological assumptions, the limited findings of dissection were construed as if they permitted access to some of the most subtle and inapprehensible aspects of interiority. In his *Historia*

3 (left)  View of the common torso and limbs and the two heads of conjoined twins whose abdomen and chest cavities have been cut open. Engraving, Italy, eighteenth century. (By permission of the History of Medicine Division, National Library of Medicine of the National Institutes of Health)

4 (right) Drawing of conjoined twins attached to the cover of a copy of the *Rerum medicarum novae Hispaniae: Thesaurus seu plantarum animalium et mineralium mexicanorum* (Rome: Vitale Mascardi, 1649). (By permission of the Biblioteca Francisco de Burgoa, Oaxaca, Mexico)

*general y natural de las Indias* (c. 1548–9), Fernández de Oviedo writes that on 10 July 1533, in the city of Santo Domingo, on the island of Hispaniola – present-day Dominican Republic – a woman named Melchiora, a Spaniard from Seville married to a man also from Seville, gave birth to a monstrous being.[1] It was made of two girls joined from the umbilical region upward to a point below the breasts (see Figures 3 and 4). The day after the birth, Fernández de Oviedo, accompanied by doctors and priests, went to see the monstrous being in his capacity as mayor of Santo Domingo and general chronicler of the Indies. He writes that the girls were not of the same size and that the right side of the larger girl was attached at an angle to the shorter side of the smaller. Although they were born with the same umbilicus, both were complete beings, with all the external limbs, and Fernández de Oviedo states that they would have been good-looking had they been two separate girls.

Administering the sacrament of baptism seems to have caused a serious theological problem because it was not clear if they were one person or two. The priest confronted the difficult issue by baptizing the conjoined twins as Melchiora and Joana, but when he baptized the second girl, he resorted to the ritual used when doubt exists about whether a person has been baptized before: "If you are not baptized, I baptize you" (Si no eres baptizada, yo te baptizo).[2]

Eight days after their birth the two girls died, and the consent of the parents to anatomize the body was sought and obtained in order to solve the mystery of the girls' identity as one or two souls. Oviedo gives a detailed account of the dissection, which he and other authorities attended:

When they had been placed on a table, the bachelor Johan Camacho, master surgeon, opened them in the umbilical region with a lancet in the presence of Hernando de Sepulveda and Rodrigo Navarro, doctors of medicine, and drew out all the viscera; and they had everything that is to be found in two human bodies, as follows: there were two sets of entrails, the intestinal tracts were distinct and separate, in each there were two kidneys and two lungs; each had a heart, and there was a liver and biliary apparatus for each; but the livers were joined one to the other but a furrow or line between the two clearly showed the part that belonged to each. After having opened them this way, it was seen that the umbilicus or navel, which from without appeared to be one, inside was divided into two canals or cords, and that each one of them went to its proper body or creature to which it belonged, although it appeared from without, as I said, to be only one. ([Y] puestas en una mesa, el bachiller Joan Camacho, óptimo cirujano, en presencia de los doctores de medicina, Hernando de Sepúlveda e Rodrigo Navarro, las abrió, con unas navajas por a par del ombligo, e les sacó todas las interiores; e tenían todas aquellas cosas que en dos cuerpos humanos suele haber, conviene a saber: dos asaduras e sus tripas destintas e apartadas, e cada dos riñones, e dos pulmones, e sendos corazones, e hígados, e cada uno una hiel, excepto que el hígado de la una e de la otra estaban juntos y pegados el uno al otro, pero una señal o línea entre ambos hígados, en que claramente se parecía lo que pertenecía a cada una parte. E así abiertas estas criaturas, pareció que el ombligo o vid, que en lo exterior era uno al parecer, que en lo interior e parte de dentro se dividía en dos caños o vides, e cada una de ellas iban a su cuerpo e criatura a quien pertenecía, aunque por defuera, como he dicho, paresciese uno solo.)[3]

Anatomical dissection had ascertained the existence of separate inner organs for each girl. From this evidence, the conclusion was drawn that two (departed) separate souls existed. Reassuringly, the chronicler ends by stating that there were two souls and that they "were sent to glorify God and to show His presence to those present and for future times" (para dar gracias a nuestro Dios e notificarse a los presentes y porvenir).[4]

Although instances of occasional dissections and autopsies have been recorded since antiquity, only after the implantation of modern anatomy did they become a widespread scientific practice. Beginning at the University of Padua in the fifteenth century, the teaching of anatomy – considered unnecessary for the education of doctors in previous centuries – spread to all other nations during the sixteenth century. Gradually, anatomy began to be taught not from Galenic textbooks but directly from dead bodies dissected in front of the students. At the same time, to help surgeons, midwives, and other members of the medical profession's lower echelon, sheets with detailed illustrations of the inner body were printed and made available at moderate prices. Some of these sheets allowed for the removal of layers to show inner organs. After 1530, one can talk of a real explosion of this kind of illustrated publication, which was popular not only among members of the medical profession but also among the public in general.[5] A milestone occurred in 1543, the year in which Vesalius's fully illustrated and groundbreaking *De humani corporis fabrica* was published. The book was an enormous success and was followed by an even more successful abbreviated edition a few months later. The main novelty of Vesalius's book was its numerous high-quality illustrations, taken from the many dissections he had done in the preceding years.[6]

The importance of Vesalius for anatomy and his impact on the history of medicine cannot be overemphasized. Certainly, corpses were opened by doctors in teaching contexts before, but their procedures were mere demonstrations of the Galenic text. As we saw, the common practice was that, while the professor read from the pages of Galen and other physicians of antiquity, an assistant opened the body to confirm what was written in the books, even if it was found that the physical evidence did not match the text, as was often the case. The differences were disregarded or attributed to pathologies. Vesalius criticized this modus operandi as being of no didactic or scientific value. His system of pushing the ancient text aside and placing the body at the centre of the research and teaching scene was revolutionary. Now what was found inside the body by the anatomist was what mattered, not the old texts. The findings were carefully committed to paper with the help of detailed drawings, for which the anatomists could enlist draughtsmen if their own drawing abilities were not sufficient. The capacity of the printing press to reproduce these images as engravings made them available to all readers in books in which the pictures were as important as, if not more so than, the text. If it is true that representations of the inner body could be found in earlier medical volumes, they were basic schemata that did not realistically represent the organs and their disposition. Vesalius not only dissected corpses, he invited his students to take part in the dissection since he believed that this practice was fundamental for the education of competent physicians, who should not limit themselves to repeating the inaccurate formulae of the old text but should have first-hand, accurate knowledge of the functioning of the body. Therefore, a radical change in the study of anatomy swept through Europe. The inaccurate Galenic anatomy – often based on the dissection of animals, not of human bodies – was not rejected immediately. Debates between the new anatomists and their Galenic counterparts became central to the life of the faculties of medicine in many universities. Over time, the Vesalian methods prevailed, and the development of scientific medicine in the nineteenth century is indebted to him.[7]

Anatomical dissection was also popular in Spain. Interest in the matter was widespread even before the publication of Vesalius's book. Many of the professors who taught medicine in Spain had studied at the University of Padua, the most advanced centre of anatomical research in Europe at the beginning of the sixteenth century.[8] As early as 1501, the University of Valencia created a permanent position for the teaching of anatomy, soon to be followed by the universities of Alcalá, Salamanca, Valladolid, Barcelona, and others. By the second third of the century, most Spanish medical universities were teaching anatomy according to the most modern methods based on dissection, proven by extant official documents that contain measures to guarantee dead bodies for regular dissections at the universities.[9] Another proof of the interest in medical and anatomical matters is that between 1475 and 1599, in addition to many ephemeral broadsheets difficult to account for, 541 medical books were published in Spain, many of them with some form of anatomical illustrations.[10] Anatomical books such as the Spaniard Valverde's profusely illustrated *Anatomía del corpo humano* circulated widely. Important for the popularity of anatomy in Spain was that Andreas Vesalius lived and worked in Spain as a physician of the Emperor Charles V, to whom he dedicated the *De humani corporis fabrica*. Vesalius was also held in great esteem by Philip II, who rewarded him with a pension for life and made him a count palatine.[11]

There is a widespread misconception that the Catholic church condemned the practice of anatomical dissection as some form of intrusion inside the body. The situation is quite the opposite. Pope Sixtus IV (1414–84) actually practised dissection during his studies in Bologna, and Pope Clement VII published an edict in 1523 expressly approving the practice of dissection for the study of anatomy. The myth of the church's opposition to anatomical dissections originates from the misinterpretation of the bull *Detestandae feritatis*, issued in 1299 against the practice of boiling the bodies of those who died in the Crusades.[12] This process was used to accelerate the separation of the flesh from the bones and to facilitate the prompt return of the bare skeleton to the homeland, where it could finally be buried, normally in a church. The bull was meant only to curtail this practice, not as a prohibition of dissection and other mortuary practices that entailed the dismemberment of the corpse. This is proven by Clement VI's decree of 1351 authorizing the division of French monarchs' bodies for their burial in separate places, as royal protocol required. Similarly, by the fifteenth century several popes had their bodies eviscerated and embalmed for burial. The opening of bodies for autopsies in the case of suspected foul play was common during the Middle Ages, moreover, as was the opening of deceased saintly individuals for preservation or to gather relics, such as the heart and other organs.[13] In 1551, Charles V commissioned an inquiry in Salamanca to investigate the religious implications of anatomy as practised by Vesalius, who was cleared by the board of any suspicions.[14]

Apart from its important medical and scientific significance, the culture of dissection was a factor in the contemporary awareness of interiority if only for the fact that it opened a new way to literally explore and map the inner body. Detailed drawings of the body – "paper bodies," as Carlino has named them – became compulsory in every anatomical book, thus contributing to the perception of bodies as entities with an interior that could be explored and mapped.[15] As Sawday wrote, "[l]ooking at the medieval delineation of the body-interior, what is most remarkable (to modern eyes) is the relative emptiness of the body cavity."[16] In addition, the application of perspective to anatomical drawings was valuable in fostering the awareness of physical inner space. The word that Durer used for perspective – *Durchsehung* (seeing through) – implied the sense of three-dimensional space. Leonardo da Vinci's frequent references to *parete de vietro* (glass walls) when talking about perspective point in the same direction. The vanishing point necessary in three-dimensional drawing implies the existence of the infinite, which, in the case of anatomical representation, is placed somewhere inside the body.[17] Unlike the two-dimensional sketches of skeletons from previous periods, the new representations emphasized that bodies were made up of multiple layers of organs that offered endless opportunities for concealed sinuses and the potential for secrecy.

## The Embodied Immateriality of Interiority

I have defined interiority as a series of psychological and physiological processes that have been traditionally considered as taking place inside the body. This working definition is intentionally vague so as to accommodate the reality that the processes encompassed under such an umbrella term change from period to period, even from author to author. Equally vague and eclectic is my decision to consider both psychological and physiological processes as constituents of interiority because I believe that it is impossible to separate them. Dyspepsia may be a digestive problem affecting the stomach, but its effects on a person's behaviour go beyond the specific organ where it originates. The tautology implied in my definition – interiority is what happens inside – reflects the spatial etymology of the term, which refers to the container (most precisely the part under its surface) instead of referring to what is contained within. The metonymy is shared by related terms such as "introspection," "inwardness," or "insight," which do not tell us what we are supposed to look for, only where. The use of this trope to refer to interiority is partially due to the inescapable complexity in ascertaining inner psychological processes and the consequent difficulty in classifying them. Indeed, terms such as "consciousness," "spirit," "memory," "feelings," and "imagination" are attempts at labelling an inextricable entanglement of subtle phenomena without exact limits that impinge one upon another. The slippery ontological status of these inner events is well reflected in Hume's famous statement that, when he looks inside, all he finds is "a bundle or collection of different perceptions, which succeed each other with an inconceivable rapidity, and are in a perpetual flux and movement."[18] An important part of the intractability of these events is that they are only subjectively observable. Since the subject alone has unmediated access to her interior, the most she can do to make it objectively available is to try to represent it in words as best as possible. Wittgenstein encapsulated this problem in his famous thought experiment in which everyone has a small box that contains a beetle, but nobody can look into anyone else's box, only in his or her own and then try to describe it.[19] This is the core of the intractability of the subjective or private quality of conscious experience or *qualia*, which can be sensed but not communicated in its original form.

My working definition of interiority is also intentionally vague about the exact nature of the interaction between the material or physiological and the immaterial or psychological. This vagueness allows me to pay attention to all the phenomena that constitute interiority as taking place within the opaque boundaries of the body, without the distinction of mental or phyical, thus sidetracking the conundrum presented by their very nature. Since antiquity, *anima* and its auxiliary *potentiae* – the vocabulary in use during the period under study – have been attributed to the mystifying status of immaterial substance or, put the other way around, embodied immateriality. In the *Corónica y historia general del hombre* (1598), the doctor Iván Sánchez Valdés de la Plata states in Aristotelian terms this traditional belief in the immateriality of mental operations: "The rational *anima* is not made up from matter and form because it is pure spiritual intellectual substance produced only by and from God, and not from the matter of inferior things" (El ánima racional no [es] compuesta de material y forma porque es pura substancia espiritual, intelectual, producida de solo Dios criada, y no sacada de la material de las cosas inferiores).[20] Equally, Isidore of Seville, elaborating on the Pauline image of the "homo interior," notes how the division of inside/outside coincides with the division of spiritual/physical: "The human being is a double entity, internal and external: the internal human being is the spirit, the external is the body."[21]

The mysterious interaction between the material and the immaterial inside the human being has often been explained by resorting to metaphors, such as that of the inhabitant of a house or state, a frequent one that will reappear in this study. Sabuco's treatise *Nueva filosofía de la naturaleza del hombre* (1588) offers a good instance of the image:

> The *anima*, which comes down from heaven, resides in the head, which is a divine member, able to move every part of the body, as Plato stated in his *Timaeus*, because reasoning and will are not located in a corporeal

organ such as the cavities in the cranium, nor coincide with the brains. The brains are only the servants in the house, who get and keep the spices for the prince to do with them whatever he likes. (El ánima, que desciende del cielo, mora en la cabeza, miembro divino y capaz de todos los movimientos del cuerpo, como dijo Platón en *Timeo*, porque este entendimiento y voluntad no están situados ni consisten en órgano corpóreo, como son las celdas de los sesos, que éstas sirven al ánima como criadas de la casa para aprehender y guardar las especies, para que el príncipe haga de ellas lo que quiera.)[22]

Other metaphors explain the interaction between the material and the immaterial according to a processual model that matches the humoural psychology of the period. In spite of appearing more sophisticated than previous explanations, humoural psychology is basically a metaphor in which the human body is portrayed as a complex vessel filled with liquids and equipped with its own heat-generating source in the stomach. According to this model, psychological processes, such as memory and imagination, depend on the evaporation of the humours and the subsequent vapours. The other ingredients in this concoction are the subtler natural, vital, and animal spirits that act like gases subject to the rules of physics in spite of their immaterial nature. Early anatomical science did not add much to this picture except to try to define precisely the exact location and size of the more or less metaphorical bodily spaces, like the four chambers or *ventriculi* in the brain, posited by this paradigm.

Although the very nature of the interaction between the material and the immaterial on which interiority relies has always been unclear, it has been considered to take place inside the body. In other words, interiority has always been conceived as embodied, although the exact location within the body and other details vary. Sometimes, the processes of interiority are understood to take place in specific organs – or empty spaces within the organs – such as the liver, the heart, or the head. At other times, they are understood to take place in less concrete locations, such as the breast, the entrails, or an indistinct inside that resembles a phantom limb in its throbbing yet impossible-to-locate existence.[23] In the Bible, emotion and thought are located in the innermost parts of the body; bowels and loins are loaded with remorse and other feelings. The innards of birds and other animals are also supposed to contain special knowledge, as the practice of the ancient haruspices presupposes. However, in recent centuries, an "aesthetic repression," in the words of Hillman, has affected this language of the entrails.[24] Descartes's notorious choice of the pineal gland in the brain as the place where that mysterious relation between the material and the immaterial takes place is but one more elegant variation of this assumption, which still exists today under different forms. Variations of the "Cartesian theatre" are somehow ingrained in our imagination. Freud considers the ego as the projection of the boundaries between the interior and the exterior of the human body. Originally, the child, subject to the pleasure principle, wants to internalize through eating all it finds pleasant while rejecting or excreting all that is unpleasant. The subject is then established as a spatial entity with clear boundaries to enlarge and protect.[25] When present-day researchers ask people where their sense of self is located, people tend to indicate somewhere in the head, slightly behind the eyes. They point to an imaginary empty space inside the head, even if they are aware that this empty space does not exist.[26] Children, too, when questioned, express a concept of the bodily interior as an empty space in which different elements – organs, food, feelings – are contained.[27] This intuition is so strong that spatiality continues to be embedded in the current vocabulary of the mind. Relatively recent terms, such as "subconscious" and "superego," or current definitions of the self as "a crossroad" or "position" rely on an implicit material-spatial element, even if the disciplines and people who coined them have been careful to distance themselves from dualism and its implications of an immaterial ingredient in the human being.

Although with many differences regarding the nature of the processes and their location, references to some form of embodied interiority can be found even in the earliest records. In his refusal of Ulysses's offer on behalf of Agamemnon, Achilles complains, "For hateful in my eyes, even as the Gates of Hades, is that man that hideth one thing in his heart and sayeth another."[28] More complex models of embodied interiority are implied in the old rhetorical formula used to refer to mental reservation *in foro interno*, or in the practice of memorizing a discourse by placing its contents in a mental house made up of diverse rooms and their corresponding furniture.[29] Indeed, appeals to the inside of the body are omnipresent because the existence of an inside to every surface is implied in Western thought. By defining place (*topos*) as a surface that encloses a body, Aristotle posits the existence of the corresponding interior.[30] In the resulting binary opposition inside/outside, the two poles are not of equivalent value. Inside is the favoured one, and, as such, it has been traditionally equated to truth, value, and meaning. Over the centuries this opposition has taken many forms, such as appearance versus essence in Aristotle, or the Stoic inward goods versus the inessential external elements. Christianity, as an inheritor of the classical traditions, has also emphasized the interior since the days of Saint Paul's opposition inner man/outer man.[31]

As is to be expected, the processes of interiority were equally conceived in early modernity as taking place inside the body and its organs. The idea that important truths literally hide within the body, inside the entrails, would have been perfectly reasonable for men and women of the period, who were accustomed to humoural medicine's emphasis on the physiological and material aspect of passions and desires.[32] As Maus observes of England, "in vernacular sixteenth- and early seventeenth-century speech and writing, the whole interior of the body – heart, liver, womb, bowels, kidneys, gall, blood, lymph – quite often involves itself in the production of the mental interior, of the individual's private experience." Memory, courage, and hatred were – and are – conceived as embodied processes located in the innards, the heart, the stomach, or the head. Furthermore, Hillman claims that the language of feelings as movements in the heart and other viscera "had not yet mutated beyond its corporeal referents" since it was not perceived as purely metaphorical, as is the case today.[33]

This perceived connection between interiority and bodily organs appears everywhere. In what is considered Spain's first dictionary, compiled by Covarrubias in 1611, the following example illustrates the use of the adverb *dentro* (inside): "Inside is an adverb to indicate location, Latin *intus*; inside my heart" (dentro es adverbio de lugar; *intus*; dentro de mi coraçón).[34] The work of Petrarch, the most influential voice in European poetry, abounds in passages in which human passions are located inside the body. The second line of the first poem in his *Canzoniere* contains the first of many references to his afflicted heart, breast, or insides: "of those sighs with which I nourished my heart."[35] Petrarch was developing a topos that can be found in Saint Augustine and the troubadours, among others. But Petrarch's enormous influence cemented the popularity of this language in any later poetical enterprise. His most renowned follower in Spain, Garcilaso de la Vega, often refers to an inner body that is so utterly explained that it even becomes visible.[36] The location of feelings and other mental processes inside the body is such a commonplace in early modern Spain that Cervantes, prone to making fun of literary conventions, occasionally parodied it. When Don Quixote explains to Sancho that Altisidora's words of love "roused more confusion than pity in my breast" (engendraron en mi pecho antes confusión que lástima), Sancho comically mismanages the poetic language of embodied interiority in his reply: "What a marble heart, what bowels of brass, and what a rough-cast spirit!" (¡Qué corazón de mármol, qué entrañas de bronce, y qué alma de argamasa!).[37]

## The Anxiety of a Private Interior

During the early modern period, not only can more references to interiority be found, but this interiority is endowed with new attributes. It begins to be perceived as more complex, tempting, and dangerous than previously thought. Most important, the concept of a proprietary interior became prevalent.[38] Although privacy had always been an important attribute, interiority was primarily understood as a shelter from the worldly turmoil and commonly used in religious practice; the "secrets" examined in this private space were mostly one's sins.[39] Accordingly, the inner space was considered less a part of the self than a void space where God could come.[40] This is evident in Saint Augustine, for whom the inner realm encourages contact not with oneself but with God. But in the early modern period, this inner space and its privacy began to be called upon mostly because they provided a personal locus, invisible from the surrounding world, as in Montaigne's much-quoted *arrière-boutique*. The contemporary infatuation with such secrecy is manifested in the many references to the fact that inner processes are invisible from the outside unless they are expressed in words, gestures, or actions. The practice of scrutinizing one's own and others' interiors becomes mandatory, often because it can give the subject an advantage against a mostly hostile external world.[41] One of the results is the frequent call to dissimulate. The need to hide one's thoughts becomes de rigueur for courtiers and worldly people alike, a trend reflected in the success of treatises on behaviour that advocate dissimulation through a constant control of gestures and words. The ability to read others' hidden interior also gains importance.

The obsession with hiding and discovering is also related to an anxious awareness that the private realm could hold dangerous contents. Consequently, this new interiority is more often described as ironic, pathetic, or even monstrous rather than heroic.[42] Its contents are seen as possible civil or political liabilities in a society in which the individual's thoughts began to fall under the surveillance of the emerging modern state. In this environment, the traditional inside/outside opposition becomes a vehicle for the emerging individual/social order disagreement, or put more concretely, the opposition of the incipient modern subject and its quest for autonomy to the equally incipient modern state and its keenness to control its citizens. A quote from Cervantes's ironic *captatio benevolentiae* in his prologue to the first part of *Don Quixote* illustrates how this private interior offers a space where power can be resisted. To refer to the reader's freedom to like or dislike his writings, Cervantes uses a Spanish proverb of the period: "under my cloak I kill the king" (que debajo de mi manto, al rey mato).[43] The reference to regicide reveals that the absolute liberty a private interior offers may include thoughts against the stability of the body politic. A less hypothetical case of the private interior as a threat to the new modern states is the famous "bloody question" under torture in Elizabethan England, which was what party the defendant would support if Papal or Spanish forces were to invade England. A religious allegiance to Catholicism, no matter how private, was considered a potential danger for the state that had to be investigated and punished.[44]

Not surprisingly, anxiety of interiority left traces in contemporary writings across Europe. An example is Montaigne's essay "Of Conscience" (book II, chapter 5), in which he states that, because those who have a guilty conscience tend to inadvertently reveal their guilt, one should have a clear conscience at all times. To make his point, he adduces examples from antiquity and his own time of people who uttered their secret crimes while asleep, revealed them in an episode of temporary insanity, or could not refrain from behaviours that raised suspicion. To illustrate the last case, he includes a personal anecdote. During the civil wars, a gentleman joined him in his travels. Although his new companion was careful not to reveal where his allegiance lay, Montaigne was able to ascertain that it was not with the king because the man could not refrain from showing his fear every time they went by cities belonging to the king's side. As Montaigne puts it, "[I] could read right into the very secret thoughts of his mind through his mask and the crosses on his greatcoat." In one of the jumps that characterize his essays, Montaigne moves on to the efficacy of torture to extract a confession. Although the pain inflicted may extract the truth, he observes that the fear and pain of torture make many confess to capital crimes they never committed. Although he does not state it, this effect invalidates the utility of keeping a clear conscience with which he began. The essay ends inconclusively with the story of a soldier who was accused by a countrywoman to have taken the little soup meat she and her children had to eat: "the general first summoned the woman to think carefully what she was saying, especially since she would be guilty of perjury if she were lying; she persisted, so he had the soldier's belly slit open in order to throw the light of truth on to the fact; the woman was found to be right." This case shows that truth, ultimately, resides inside. However, the soldier could have been innocent and then his brutal death would have been unjustified. The anecdote is especially unsettling because, as Montaigne writes about the gentleman who joined him in his travels during the civil wars, "[today] your enemy [is] indistinguishable from you by any clear indication of language or deportment, being brought up under the same laws, manners and climate."[45] Nobody is free from suspicion, and a clear conscience is not enough protection given that torture may make us reveal nonexistent crimes. Or it may find the proof of guilt inside us. But guilt or innocence is eventually irrelevant because the process used to extract the truth involves the irreversible destruction of the person.

## The Spanish Factor

Spain's peculiar development during the early modern period affected the interaction between the culture of dissection and the compulsion to be interior. The popularity anatomy enjoyed in Spain was mentioned earlier, and the inner turn was a pan-European phenomenon. Paige writes,

> Subjective interiority was too implicated in the new and ubiquitous technology of print, too bound up with the vicissitudes of a vocabulary evolving over many centuries, and too able to infiltrate the most seemingly incompatible positions – mysticism and scepticism, Protestants and Catholics, and others – to owe its existence solely to the activities of a specific national culture, class or creed.[46]

However, Spain, suffused by a mentality of protracted holy war – first against the Muslims, later against the Protestants – made of religious orthodoxy a matter of state to a degree unmatched in any other country. For the purposes of this study, the most important consequence was that citizens' religious beliefs became one of the main policing targets of the early modern state.[47] At the same time, or perhaps as a result, the interiority that can be traced in its citizens contains a stronger religious imprint than in other countries, as is the case in the dissective narratives examined in the following chapters. Although the narratives show an over-representation of sacred ingredients – such as martyrology and the devotion to the body of Christ and the relics – they are manifestations of the same encounter between the culture of dissection and the compulsion towards interiority that affected the rest of Europe. As Sawday correctly noted, sacralization was a characteristic of the European culture of dissection, but I think that it became a prevalent feature in Spain.[48] The reality is that, in spite of its unique historical development, Spain was affected by the inner turn and the culture of dissection.

Although Protestantism and its essential call for interiority did not put down roots in Spain, most of the factors that contributed to the explosion of interest in inwardness all over Europe did. This is the case with the call for a more private form of piety that began with the *devotio moderna* in the late Middle Ages. As will be seen in the study of Fray Luis de Granada in the next chapter, the books and ideas of Thomas à Kempis and the Mystics of the North circulated freely in Spain, at least in the first part of the sixteenth century. The same applies to Erasmus's works and the inwardness implied in his Christocentric understanding of religion.[49] Many other examples exist. Ignatius of Loyola's famed exercises relied on advanced mental processes that required inwardness. Furthermore, no part of the considerable amount of religious literature in contemporary Spain, not even that produced after the Council of Trent, can be discarded as formulaic writing or instructions for an external form of practice. Many passages in some of the most popular books of piety of the day, not only the ones by the mystics, contain calls to inwardness. It can even be held that Catholicism, unlike Protestantism, kept a more body-centric – primitive, some would argue – form of religious practice, especially with its development of the devotion of the body of Christ. This devotion becomes a soteriological space for believers to penetrate through the wounds inflicted in the Passion, the spiritual exercises of Saint Ignatius being a well-known case.[50] His exercises include four weeks of private contemplation of specific events of Christ's life, especially the Passion. Even if the activities occur under the direct supervision of a trained spiritual guide and are highly structured, they rely on a private mental space into which individuals have to retreat to change themselves. Unsurprisingly, the inner turn such a devotion demanded was deemed dangerous by some religious authorities, who believed the emphasis that the exercises placed on meditation in private was too close to the spirituality of Illuminati and Protestants.

Even if the Counter-Reformation curtailed what it saw as dangerously private forms of piety, it fostered changes that implied inwardness, although in a limited and controlled form. A well-known case is confession, whose importance was emphasized with the Catholic church's reinforcement of the sacraments after the Council of Trent. Confession was transformed into an individual practice that required a systematic exercise of self-scrutiny prior to the confidential narration of one's sins to the priest in a secluded area of the church. Before, confession was more a public act of social atonement and humiliation than this private act of inwardness. Although the old practice of confession also implied some turn inwards, the inner space it relied on was not a place of personal differentiation but a space to assimilate to a model and to the group.[51] Systematic inner scrutiny as instructed preparation to fulfil the renewed sacrament of confession was introduced only later. Many of the new – but also some of the old – confession manuals for laypeople literally included inner maps in the forms of graphics and tablets indicating how to search one's own conscience in a systematic way.[52] The exact role that confession played in the development of early modern interiority is still open for debate. On the one hand, the type of confession that the Counter-Reformation fostered implied only a directed and limited type of introspection since it was not a free enterprise of self-discovery, much less an affirmation of individuality. On the other hand, the thrust towards a systematic guided scrutiny that can be traced in the manuals for confessors between the Fourth Lateran Council and the Council of Trent has been recognized as a clear factor in the social control that characterizes the modern state and that Maravall connects to the "guided culture" of Spain during this time.[53]

If the compulsion to be interior in early modern Spain was analogous to what was happening in the rest of Europe, the power of the Spanish state and its means of policing this interiority was unique. Spain was exceptional among European nations because, between 1520 and 1640, royal power developed differently from what was happening in France and England, resulting in an incipient absolutism and a lack of constitutional restraints.[54] The importance that this absolutist state attributed to purity of blood and religious orthodoxy for its survival helps to explain the transition from the medieval Inquisition, controlled by the Roman church, to the Spanish Inquisition. From its original mission of overseeing the *conversos*, the Spanish Inquisition was gradually transformed into a formidable apparatus of censorship and thought control that reached all citizens and had access to the state resources to a degree unmatched in any other European country of the period. As Kamen states in his study of the institution, the Spanish Inquisition was "in every way an instrument of royal policy and remained politically subject to the crown."[55]

It would be reductive to understand the anxiety of interiority manifested in dissective narratives as a fear of having one's body scrutinized by the Inquisition in the sense of a literal dismemberment. Although they assume this dissective form, the narratives studied here are triggered by fear not of an actual physical invasion of the body but of having one's thoughts and wishes publicly exposed and consequently punished. The punishment and interrogation the Inquisition resorted to never included opening the body of the defendant or the convict. It is well documented that the torture sessions were far from an orgy of random physical violence and bloody procedures left to the whimsical, cruel creativity of the judges and executioners. Torturing procedures were actually rare. When they happened, they were brutal, yet the sessions were scripted; torturers had to follow rules that specified how many times and for how long the defendant could be subjected to a specific kind of torture, how the shedding of blood was to be avoided, and so on. Furthermore, the Inquisition intervened in relatively few cases, most of which ended not in executions or bodily punishment but in sentences of confinement in a convent or prison, extradition, and the seizure of property, this last being one of the main sources of financing for the institution. Appropriately, Kamen states that "the procedure of the Inquisition was calculated to achieve the greatest degree of efficiency with the least degree of publicity."[56]

A portrait of the modern Spanish state as a totalitarian, policed society oversimplifies the complex role played by the Inquisition. During the century and a half under examination, neither the subject of persecution nor the zeal with which it was pursued was uniform. Political preoccupation, although present in the religious control of the Spanish Inquisition since its inception, gained importance as it became clear Protestantism's success in Northern Europe had negative consequences for the Spanish crown. Ideas that had not caused major concerns at the beginning of the sixteenth century, such as Erasmus's scepticism about relics or his interest in vernacular versions of the Bible, became suspect. Even his least polemical works entered the ever-expanding *Index of Forbidden Books*, together with those of other initially unsuspected writers. The Holy Office's broad founding mandate of defending the faith gave much leeway for interpretation. Adultery and the breach of other sexual mores that today are only marginally connected to religion were often considered attacks on Catholic dogma. Over the years, not only did the ideas under scrutiny change but also the zeal with which they were prosecuted. Also, internecine disputes within the higher echelons of the Spanish church resulted in different factions with their own agendas controlling the Inquisition. As a result, certain ideas and groups that had been relatively tolerated until then were suddenly subject to in-depth scrutiny. Such unpredictability in the Inquisition, together with its secretive procedures including secret denunciations, acted as a con-formity-creating machine on the Spanish society. The situation is well expressed by what Bennassar has called a "pedagogy of fear," which implies an interiorized form of control and minding of one's words.[57] The anxiety the Inquisition inspired was in fact more important than its actual interventions. Not in vain did it have a vast network of secret informers, the *familiares*, who infiltrated all levels of society. Further-more, in many cases the denunciations to the Inquisition were brought by friends and family. People had to learn to mind their statements at all times. The Jesuit Father Juan de Mariana declared that the Inquisi-tion "has deprived us of the freedom to talk among ourselves; in every town, village, and hamlet, it has individuals ready to inform it of every-thing that goes on."[58]

Especially pertinent for the anxiety of interiority was the practice of self-denunciation. Since the inception of the Inquisition, yearly cam-paigns began with the Edicts of Grace, replaced by the Edicts of Faith after 1500. These campaigns included the appeal, under the threat of excommunication, to report neighbours who followed Judaic or Mus-lim rites, as well as anyone guilty of impious statements and acts. A Francisco Martínez Berralo was denounced and summoned to appear in an auto-da-fé in 1555 for having said that if so-and-so went to heaven, his own donkey, harness and all, should also go.[59] Most interestingly, people were also encouraged to self-denounce. Many self-denuncia-tions were triggered by the fear of being reported by somebody else if one did not confess voluntarily. Although self-denunciation did not bring absolution, it reassured the person that the death penalty would not be sought. However, other punishments, such as the confiscation of property, were not excluded. Lea mentions two husbands who accused themselves of having told their wives that they did not consider forni-cation a sin. The fear that their wives would report them made them confess.[60] The Edicts acted then as an opportunity to unburden the sense of guilt by reporting others and oneself. As Kamen states, "[t]he whole community conditioned itself into a state where denunciation of one's neighbour, often for the most trifling fault, was followed by

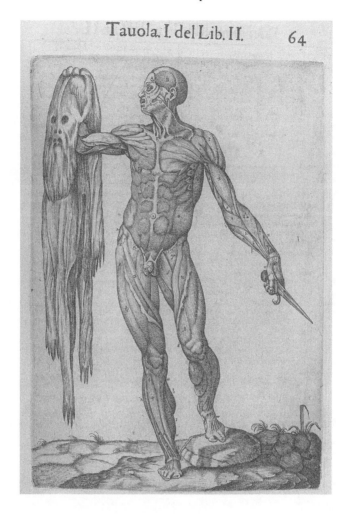

5 A self-flayed man holding his skin in one hand and a dissecting knife in the other. Engraving by Gaspar Becerra included in Juan Valverde de Amusco's *Anatomía del corpo humano* (Rome: Ant. Salamanca and Antonio Lafrery, 1560). (By permission of the History of Medicine Division, National Library of Medicine of the National Institutes of Health)

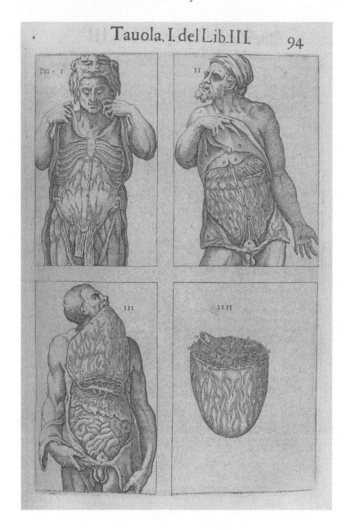

6  Men holding aside the skin that covers the central section of their bodies
and illustration of the omentum freed from the parts to which it is attached.
Engraving by Gaspar Becerra included in Juan Valverde de Amusco's
*Anatomía del corpo humano* (Rome: Ant. Salamanca and Antonio Lafrery, 1560).
(By permission of the History of Medicine Division, National Library of Medi-
cine of the National Institutes of Health)

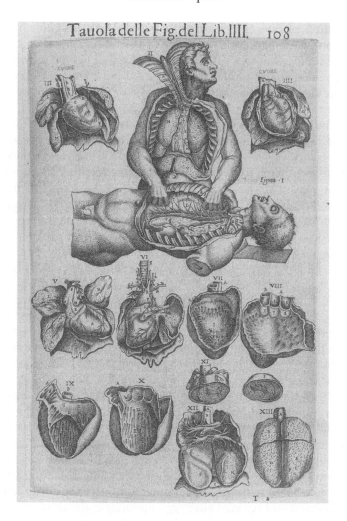

7 Man with an open thorax dissecting the same area in a cadaver, surrounded by projected images of the heart and other organs cut open. Engraving by Gaspar Becerra included in Juan Valverde de Amusco's *Anatomía del corpo humano* (Rome: Ant. Salamanca and Antonio Lafrery, 1560). (By permission of the History of Medicine Division, National Library of Medicine of the National Institutes of Health)

denunciation of oneself."[61] Some cases of self-denunciation reveal a near-paranoid state of mind, as the one of Catalina Zapata in Alcalá in 1564. She reported herself after remembering that twelve years before, without realizing the implications of her words, she had exclaimed, "You don't see me in misery in this world, nor will you find me suffering in the next."[62]

A curious resemblance exists between self-denunciation and the self-dissecting figures in some anatomical books of the period. The aforementioned *Anatomía del corpo humano* by Valverde contains several engravings taken from Vesalius's *De humani corporis fabrica*, altered in such a way that the corpses appear to be dissecting themselves (see Figures 5 and 6). These images, I contend, reflect the paranoia of denunciation and self-denunciation that the Inquisition had forced on Spanish society. This situation is particularly well encapsulated in one of the images. It represents a man, whose torso is cut open, performing the same operation on a dead body lying in front of him (see Figure 7). The act of simultaneously showing somebody else's and one's own interior is what happens in the dissective narratives analysed in the following chapters. Although these sacrificial figures submitted to textual dissection are fictional, they contain facets of their authors, such as thoughts they may have entertained but later discarded as untenable. As Montaigne wrote in his essay "Of Conscience," our enemies can be so similar to us in behaviour and formation that sometimes they are difficult to distinguish from ourselves. Because self-policing was mandatory in Inquisitorial Spain, mental sanitization ascertained whether or not one's thoughts and convictions could resist a thorough external scrutiny, although not even this assured impunity. To exteriorize suspicious thoughts in the form of dissective narratives served as a method of exploring one's otherwise opaque interior while obtaining some of the relief associated with voluntary confession and the punishment that these rehearsed and rejected alter egos undergo in the texts.

## 2

# Fray Luis de Granada's Ill-fated Defence of the Inner Man

## Fray Luis de Granada's Encounter with the Inquisition

Granada exposed the embodied interiority of Christian origins to the new discourse of anatomical science.[1] The results were dissective narratives that followed the martyrological pattern of innocence: no matter how crude and thorough the inspection was, only God's work could be found inside. The theme of undeserved scrutiny may be connected to circumstances of the generation to which he belonged. He was part of the cohort born in the early years of the newly created Spanish state. He and his generation were educated in the intellectually tolerant years of Charles V during the first half of the sixteenth century but had to continue to live during the second half in the religiously zealous period of the Counter-Reformation under Philip II. Any interest in the highly private religious experience of previous years became suspicious. Although Granada was not a mystic properly speaking, he has many characteristics in common with renowned Spanish mystical figures of the period, such as Saint Teresa or Saint John of the Cross, who were both a few years younger and respected Granada as an authority in matters of spirituality.[2] At the same time, his teaching reached a vast lay audience and he was, by far, the most popular religious writer of the day. His books went through dozens of editions in his lifetime and were immediately translated into other European languages. Granada's *Libro de la oración y la meditación* (1554) was the most published book of the century – more than 100 editions were published in the 100 years after it first appeared.[3]

Granada was not only a successful writer but also a prominent figure in the public arena. His reputation as a religious writer and a preacher put him in close contact with monarchs and other powerful figures who sought him out as confessor and adviser. In this capacity, he was an active participant in international politics, especially in his old age. The most significant episode of his life was his involvement in the infamous attack of the Inquisitor General against Carranza, the archbishop of Toledo, in 1559. In this notorious suit, Granada was also a victim. Two of his books were placed on the Inquisition's *Index of Forbidden Books* of 1559 because they recommended silent prayer and other practices that were considered dangerous.[4] In spite of this sentence, Granada offers the rare case of an individual who managed to withstand a formal attack by the Inquisition without being silenced for the rest of his life. During the twenty-five years between the inclusion of his books in the *Index* and his death, he continued writing in the safe haven of Portugal, from within the church and without completely abandoning his convictions. These later writings include dissective narratives that can be traced back to his awareness of the liabilities of the religious interiority he advocated. In some cases, his dissective narratives are a fully conscious effort on his part to justify his call for what he considered an orthodox interiority. In other cases, they can best be considered localized flare-ups or outbreaks of the anxiety of interiority within a text written with other general aims. In both instances, Granada's modus operandi is the same: he painstakingly takes apart embodied interiors within his texts to prove the harmlessness of the inner privacy and secrecy he champions.

Luis de Granada was born in the city of Granada in 1504, twelve years after the collapse of this last Moorish Kingdom of Spain.[5] His parents were Galician peasants who had moved to Granada to repopulate recently conquered territories. The premature death of his father in 1508 left him and his mother in a difficult financial position, but he thrived thanks to the support of the Count of Tendilla, who placed Granada as page to his school-aged children. This position allowed him to attend school and later enter the Dominican order at the age of twenty-one. In spite of his humble origins, he was an undisputable member of the *cristiano viejo* society because the peasant stock from Northern Spain from which he descended was a social group that could boast of their *limpieza de sangre* (purity of blood) since they had had the least contact with Moors and Jews. This was a social advantage not only in the recently acquired city of Granada, where Jewish or Muslim ancestry was common among many social strata, but also among the members of his generation, the first born in the monolithically Catholic state of unified Spain.[6]

Granada was born in the heart of a Spain that, with the conquest of Granada and the expulsion of the Jews, had put an end to the *convivencia* of earlier days, and this fact shows up in his writings, in which he is often a formidable polemicist and staunch defender of Catholicism against Judaism and Islam. But unlike many of his contemporaries, in spite of his zeal in defence of the Christian religion, Granada was against the use of violence for the conversion of Jews and Muslims.[7] His religious fervour was softened by the fact that he had been formed in the intellectually tolerant climate of the first half of the sixteenth century. He spent his formative years in the convent of San Gregorio in Valladolid (1529–34), where his education, apart from reading traditional religious texts, included works by many authors from antiquity and by contemporary humanist writers. He studied Erasmus and other northern intellectuals who would be suspected of Protestantism only in the second half of the century. Also part of the relative open-mindedness permeating his education was a striving to return to a more private form of religion. In the years that followed the *comuneros* revolt of 1521, the Dominican order, especially the San Gregorio convent where Granada studied, was under the strong influence of a form of affective spirituality with an emphasis on inner practices that would later be eradicated.[8]

Granada's career was typical of an intelligent, studious man from a humble family for whom the church was the only way to prosper. His intellectual abilities as well as his exceptional capacity as a preacher pushed him to ever-higher positions within the Dominican order and the church. Although he seems not to have pursued fame and power, his reputation gained him influential positions as confessor and adviser of powerful people. During the final thirty years of his life (1555–85), he lived in Portugal, where he was sent initially as the provincial of the Dominican order. There he became the confessor of the Queen Mother Catherine of Habsburg and the man of confidence of Cardinal Henry, who later would become the king of Portugal after the tragic death of Sebastian I at the battle of Alcazarquivir. Portugal also offered him a safe haven from the internecine fights of the Spanish church, especially after the 1559 Inquisitorial process against Archbishop Carranza, which also affected Granada. He maintained his powerful position in the Portuguese church and court until the end, even after 1584, when Philip II, taking advantage of the dynastic crisis opened by the death of Sebastian I, became the king of Portugal. Granada died in Lisbon four years later, in 1588, at the age of eighty-four.[9]

The most prominent aspect of Granada's successful yet relatively uneventful life is the amount of religious writing he produced and the popularity of some of his books. His learning, not limited to religious matters, was vast enough to allow us to consider him an erudite Renaissance man, although he was not a humanist properly speaking because he was not a creator of new ideas. He wrote in the medieval tradition of accumulating and commenting. He continuously looked back at the Fathers of the Church, Aristotle, and other figures of antiquity to find examples and authorities to prove the rightfulness of Christian doctrine. Often his most original contribution is limited to adding comparisons and metaphors from daily life to illustrate a well-known point of doctrine. He was not an original writer but a brilliant compiler of sources, which he conveyed in a clear prose peppered with vivid examples that could be understood by laypeople. This role of popularizer of complex religious matters was, however, dangerous because the church was concerned about the possible misunderstandings this kind of knowledge could cause among those not properly educated in the subtleties of Christian dogma.[10]

In the central decades of the sixteenth century, those who, like Granada, advocated the cultivation of spiritual interiority knew that they were promoting a legitimate aspect of Christian practice, but they were also conscious of walking a thin line that was getting thinner. If spiritual experimentation was acceptable, even fashionable, in the first half of the sixteenth century, any call to religious interiority became increasingly suspect as the century moved towards its second half. As early as the beginning of the century, certain forms of spirituality had been declared heretic, such as the one practised by the *alumbrados*, who were accused of quietist practices, that is, of searching for self-annihilation and subsequent absorption of the soul into God. One of the earliest cases was the Beata de Piedrahita, who claimed to hold colloquies with Jesus and the Virgin Mary and came under the scrutiny of the Inquisition in 1511. She had powerful protectors and was not fully prosecuted, but during the 1520s in Toledo, Valladolid, and Guadalajara, many other processes against *alumbrados* took place. In 1527, while studying at Salamanca, Ignatius of Loyola was brought before an ecclesiastical commission on a charge of sympathy with the *alumbrados* and of other mystical practices that bypassed the authority of the church to reach God directly. Later, the triumph of the Protestant Reformation meant that spiritual pursuits such as the aforementioned were identified with the more private approach to religion advocated by Protestantism. The well-known suspicions that the mystics Teresa of Avila or John of the Cross raised among the Inquisitors must be understood in this context, as must Granada's case.[11]

The interior practices that Granada wanted to promote in his readers were part of this old Christian lineage that had gone through a rebirth since the thirteenth century under the name *devotio moderna*. One of the most salient characteristics of this movement that originated in Northern Europe and spread to the rest of the continent was that it encouraged a more personal and intimate form of piety. *Devotio moderna* advocated a religious practice in which the faithful took their spiritual development into their own hands through a series of Christocentric meditations that incorporated the use of imagination to envision the life of Christ. It is significant that Granada's first extended work was the translation into Castilian of one of the founding documents of the *devotio moderna*, Thomas à Kempis's *Contemptus mundi*. With this translation, he put within the reach of the lay readership a hands-on manual filled with concrete instructions on spiritual practices that readers could follow on their own.[12] In addition to Thomas à Kempis, the influence of several other of the so-called Mystics of the North – the group of pre-Reformation religious writers who championed a more personal and spiritual form of faith – is also detectable in Granada, who often includes passages verbatim from Louis de Blois or John Tauler in his writings. Another clear influence in Granada is the Dominican Girolamo Savonarola, who advocated an interior form of piety connected to the *devotio moderna* that strongly influenced many Dominican monasteries in Spain during Granada's formative years.[13] Also easily detectable in Granada's writings are the ideas of Erasmus. In his study of the presence of Erasmus's ideas in Spain in the first part of the sixteenth century, Marcel Bataillon identifies many instances in Granada. Especially important for Granada, as for many of his contemporaries, was Erasmus's *Enchiridion militis Christiani* and its championing of an inner, truer religious practice. Also, Bataillon attributes Granada's frequent references to the Pauline *homo interior* to a direct influence of Erasmus's search for a more authentic form of piety.[14]

In spite of the influence of these writers, Granada was always careful to remain within the bounds of orthodoxy. He emphasized the importance of following approved Catholic doctrine, especially in areas where the Protestants dissented. When dealing with the role of grace in salvation, the authority of the church, or the importance of external practice, he introduced many caveats and clarifications. The radical step taken by the Inquisition in 1559 of banning his two manuals must be understood as an overreaction to a political and religious climate overheated by Protestant victories on all fronts. The Peace of Augsburg (1555) implied recognition of the Lutheran states in the former Holy Roman Empire. Philip II was struggling to subdue the Protestant rebellions in the Low Countries. In England, a hostile Elizabeth I was crowned in 1558 after the death of the pro-Catholic Queen Mary. The unfriendly international ambiance explains the conservative turn that political and cultural life took in Spain. In 1559, several events resulted in a surge of repression, such as the infamous prosecution of suspected Protestants in Valladolid or the decree prohibiting Spanish students from attending foreign universities. The same year, Inquisitor General Valdés attacked Archbishop Carranza, and the strict *Index of Forbidden Books*, in which Granada's manuals were included, was published.

Granada's encounter with the Spanish Inquisition deserves a detailed account because it was a defining event in his life. In 1559 the Inquisitor General and archbishop of Seville, Fernando de Valdés y Salas, took advantage of the temporary absence of Philip II from Spain to use his position as head of the Spanish Inquisition to attack the most powerful person in the Spanish church, the archbishop of Toledo, Carranza. Carranza's *Comentarios del catecismo cristiano* was denounced for containing dangerous heretical ideas ranging from Lutheranism to *alumbrismo*. The whole affair is today considered a case of personal animosity on the part of Valdés towards Carranza, a quarrel in which envy and professional rivalry were important factors. It involved the notorious arrest of Archbishop Carranza by the Inquisition and an embarrassing and complex prosecution that lingered for seventeen years, until it was settled in an intentionally ambiguous sentence proclaimed by Pope Gregory XIII in 1576.[15] What matters for this study is that, prior to his arrest, in his religious works Carranza had quoted and praised Granada, who was also his personal friend. This was enough for Valdés to have Granada's *Libro de la oración y la meditación* and *Guía de pecadores* scrutinized by his coadjutor, Bishop Melchor Cano. Granada's emphasis in his manuals on the superiority of mental or silent prayer over the preponderant form of vocal prayer was the main target of the inquisitorial censure, which considered these recommendations dangerously close to *alumbrismo*. In a period in which the importance of external worship was a Catholic tenet as contrasted with the inner private religiosity that Protestantism advocated, details discussed in Granada's manuals, such as the importance of not moving one's lips or closing one's eyes during prayer, were blown out of proportion. The silent intimate prayer advocated by Granada was considered especially dangerous since his manuals were aimed at people from all levels of society, including those not properly instructed in the subtleties of Christian dogma. The popularizing nature of his works is negatively reflected in Inquisitor Valdés's notorious dismissal of Granada's manuals as "contemplative stuff for the wives of carpenters" (cosas de contemplación para mujeres de carpintero), who could easily deviate from the church if they were left to their own forms of inner practice.[16]

The inquisitorial zeal was evidently not satisfied with the caveats and qualifications in Granada's manuals. For instance, in the first pages of his *Libro de la oración y la meditación*, Granada carefully qualifies the mental exercise involved in silent prayer and meditation: "The second recommendation is that while doing this exercise one should avoid excessive speculation of the mind, but one should instead use more of the sentiment and feeling" (El segundo aviso es que trabaje el hombre por excusar en este ejercicio [de la meditación] la demasiada especulación del entendimiento, y procure de tratar este negocio más con afectos y sentimientos de la voluntad que con el discurso y especulaciones de entendimiento).[17] Granada makes clear that he is not proposing a personal form of practice or religion, a qualification developed in an extended chapter entitled "Of avoiding any form of singularity" (Que se ha de evitar toda manera de singularidad).[18] However, these stipulations did not help the case of his books before the Inquisition. Apart from the detailed instructions on silent prayer and other mental religious exercises, his books contained passages that could be construed as dangerous if read with the narrowly scrutinizing eye of the Inquisitors. An example is Granada's reference to Saint Bernard's words on the need for not boasting about one's spiritual advances, quoted by Granada as "my secrets are for me, my secrets are for me" (mis secretos para mí, mis secretos para mí).[19] Similarly suspicious was Granada's use of Erasmus's well-known adage of the Sileni of Alcibiades – figurines whose exterior is unappealing but that are richly decorated on the inside. Granada compares these figurines to Christ, the prophets, and the saints, whose beauty was not public but hidden inside.[20] To make thing worse, *Sileni Alcibiadis* (1515) was also the title of a treatise by Erasmus in which he talks about the need for changes in the Roman Church.

Granada was in Portugal in 1559 when he discovered through friends that his books were about to be included in the *Index*. In August that same year, he decided to travel to Valladolid to see Valdés and try to stop this inclusion. Entering Spain was not without danger for Granada, given that he was a Spaniard and, as such, could be arrested by the Spanish Inquisition. However, he was well protected not only by his high position in the Portuguese court but also by his ties to Philip II's sister, Doña Juana, whose confessor Granada had been. Doña Juana, who was the regent while her brother was abroad, arranged for him to be granted an audience by Valdés. This meeting with Valdés did not solve anything. His books were already included in the *Index* and, as far as the Spanish Inquisition was concerned, the matter was settled. Granada returned to Portugal, where he would remain for the rest of his life, except for a few occasional trips to Spain and Rome for official business. He refrained from republishing his two books even though Portugal, where he lived, was a separate kingdom in which the Spanish *Index of Forbidden Books* had no effect. Only a few years later, after he had carefully expurgated all the passages that he considered problematic, he republished "corrected and amended" editions, as the new title pages read. The changes that Granada introduced in his books ranged from the elimination of the names and quotation of suspect authors, such as Louis de Blois or Erasmus, to the inclusion of many new caveats and clarifying paragraphs. Long excursuses were added in which he stated his position against Protestantism in subjects such as the importance of external practice or the need for good works to achieve salvation.[21] He also kept publishing religious treatises until the end of his life, nearly thirty years later.

## Granada's Dissective Narratives

Overall, Granada came out of this affair relatively unscathed, especially if one compares his case to similar ones in the same period, such as that of Fray Luis de León, who spent four years in prison after being reported to the Inquisition in 1571 for his translation of and commentary on the Song of Songs. Granada is a rare example of somebody who did not have to retreat completely from his previous tenets, even though his writings were condemned by the Inquisition. This exceptional situation was possible thanks to a combination of circumstances including the shelter that Portugal offered him, his powerful friends, and the Council of Trent's 1563 declaration that Granada's books stood in compliance with official dogma. However, Granada avoided public defiance and his demeanour was one of external compliance with the Inquisition, although he was deeply affected by having his two most popular books included in the *Index*. This was a heavy blow for a firm believer in the Inquisition, an institution to which Granada refers in his writings on several occasions as a most merciful and just tribunal. In his final book, *Introducción al símbolo de la fe*, Granada considers the Inquisition's methods to be "the lightest and softest punishment possible" (el castigo del Santo Oficio era el más breve y blando que pudo ser).[22] The suffering that the inquisitorial incident caused him is best illustrated by his own words in a letter to Carranza. Talking about his state of mind, and particularly referring to the interview he had with Inquisitor General Valdés in Valladolid, Granada writes, "I do not know what to say except *angustiae sunt undique* [distress surrounds me]; I would not like to go to heaven through Valladolid" (No sé qué me diga sino *angustiae sunt undique*, no querría ir al cielo por Valladolid).[23]

Granada kept opining and publishing on religious matters from within the church until his death, but his writings show the scars that Valdés's attack had left. Although Granada continued to exalt the role of interiority for religious practice, he included many clarifications to pre-empt further attacks. The inner space that he encourages readers to tap into is always presented as God's original manufacture and, therefore, as a naturally orthodox space that should not be suspect.[24] From his early writings, Granada repeatedly justifies tapping into the inner space not for its secrecy and autonomy but for its quietness, so conducive to spiritual work. In this "inner desert" – an expression common among mystical writers – there is the opportunity to reach God. To avoid the doctrinal dangers of having to elaborate on this direct access to the divine, he is careful not to expand on the nature of this contact.[25] As will be seen, he means to emphasize the innocence of this inner space by presenting it as a locus where nothing can be hidden. In order to do so, he also resorts to combining the light that the new anatomy has shed on every possible recess of the body with deeply rooted Christian metaphors that emphasize the harmony between the human being and the surrounding universe.

In his justification of the intrinsic blamelessness of this inner space, Granada enlists the old view of the whole universe as a manifestation of God, as His creation and, therefore, as something not separated from Him. In this view, so dear to the Middle Ages and still widely accepted in early modernity, the human being is part of God's creation, not a unique entity painfully separated from the rest of creation and its creator, isolated inside the body and surrounded by a hostile universe. The ruling principle in this image is harmony and hierarchy. The universe is presented as a continuum of space as well as time in which everything is intimately related to God and to all beings. This unity is reflected in the original meaning of "individual," which is not the modern sense of an autonomous self-sufficient entity that cannot be taken apart without being destroyed, but an older sense of being a part of creation that cannot be separated from its creator and the rest of creation. The human being, the lesser microcosm, follows the same patterns of space and time as the rest of creation because it is one more element of the great chain of being. As such, it is a central element in many of the totalizing diagrams that are included in the books of the period to illustrate the continuum of the chain.[26] This conception offers the human being no room for secrecy because the inner body can be read with the same hermeneutical tools used to understand the rest of the universe, which is God's open book. Furthermore, according to this fundamentally medieval view, there is no inside and outside in the human being or, more exactly, inside and outside are the same. Although soul – the inside – and body – the outside – are two different entities temporarily linked that take their separate ways after death, they are not conceivable as separate entities in the dualistic sense. Soul and body are form and matter and, therefore, inseparable according to Scholasticism.[27]

Granada's works abound in quotations from old authorities to support his image of a harmoniously united universe in which the humans and their interior were one more piece. The space inside the body cannot be different from the rest of the continuum of creation. However, he also resorts to the new knowledge of anatomy because, up-to-date as he was in the intellectual and scientific debates of the day, he was aware of its significance. Laín Entralgo, who has studied the anthropological aspects in Granada's works, concludes that Granada was familiar not only with the old Galenic sources but also with the new Vesalian anatomy, especially with Juan Valverde de Amusco's *Anatomía del corpo humano* (1560).[28] Although this familiarity with contemporary anatomical knowledge is detectable in some of Granada's early writings, by far the most extended treatment in his works are the several chapters on the subject in his final magnum opus, entitled *Introducción al símbolo de la fe*. The volumes of this true encyclopedic work of Christian apologetics appeared between 1582 and 1585, the final years of his life. Part 1 is an exposition of the complexity and harmony of all nature, from nonsentient beings to its highest point, the human being and the angels, as proof of the providence of God.[29] It contains a description of a human being that includes a detailed account of the body according to the old Galenic tradition and to the recent discoveries of anatomical dissection. This extended section has a more modern tone than other parts of Granada's book, which includes typically medieval subjects, such as monsters and chimerical beings. However, the content and location of this chapter make it integral to his argument for the superiority of Christianity. Granada places it at the end of his section on the universe. Following the order of the six days of Creation, he begins with the sun and then proceeds to the inanimate elements, the plants, the animals in order of their complexity, and finally the human being, the most accomplished aspect of creation because it is the closest to God.[30]

Seen in this context, the inclusion of the anatomical description of the human being's interior in *Introducción al símbolo de la fe* appears as one more point in Granada's traditional argument for the existence of God. But Granada's detailed account of the body, and especially of its interior, reveals an anxiety of interiority. Its presence becomes evident when we compare Granada's anatomical treatment of the human being with similar passages by other religious writers of the period, such as the Franciscan Juan de Pineda (1516–97). He was a contemporary of Granada's and also a successful preacher and writer of erudite religious books. Pineda's focus – the life of saints or sacred history – was much less dangerous during this period than the inner forms of piety Granada tackled. Consequently, Pineda had no problems with the Inquisition except some minor corrections to the content of his books, which were an unavoidable inconvenience for any contemporary writer.

Pineda's *Diálogos familiares de la agricultura cristiana* appeared in Salamanca in 1589, only four years after the last volume of Granada's *Introducción al símbolo de la fe*.[31] It is an encyclopedic religious work, similar in its catechist and apologetic intention to Granada's book. To prove the truth of the Catholic religion, Pineda includes all aspects of human knowledge, from the practical to the spiritual, from the theological to the scientific. The result is, like Granada's, a curious mélange that incorporates medieval preoccupations and methodology with sporadic signs of more modern concerns and practices.[32] Also like Granada, Pineda includes a detailed description of the human body to prove that such a marvellous work cannot be the result of chance, as Epicurus believed, but clearly is the hand of God. The first notable difference is that Pineda's book takes the popular format of the humanist dialogue or conversations among a fictitious group of friends that expand over several days. It is one of the interlocutors, the physician Filótimo, who in his long interventions explains the functioning of the human body in detail. Unlike Granada, Pineda does not convey a sense of urgency to prove his point. Moreover, Pineda's explanations of the marvels of the human body do not follow any order except that of the conversation and the topics at hand, all peppered with anecdotal excursuses. His approach lacks the forcefulness of Granada's systematic treatment of the human body, which follows a clear organization beginning with the bones and matching the order of exposition in the contemporary manuals of anatomy. Although Granada and Pineda are both familiar with Galenic and Vesalian anatomy, only Granada emphasizes that a qualitative change in the methods of anatomy has occurred thanks to the widespread practice of dissection. He is aware of the possibility of a real descent into the interior of the human being, as it had never been done before.[33] The description of the human interior through the dissective method is an integral part of Granada's exposition but not of Pineda's. The idea of the body's enhanced transparency is central to Granada's presentation of the human being, especially the openness of an interior to which anatomical dissection now permits first-hand access. Referring to the new anatomists, Granada emphasizes how they have opened the body for everybody to look inside: "[N]ot even the [study of the books] is enough [for them] but they go further and anatomize the bodies of the recently deceased so that not only the mind, but also the eyes may witness and judge the doctrine [contained in the books]" (Y ni aun esto les basta, sino pasan adelante a hacer anatomía en los cuerpos humanos recién muertos, para que no sólo el entendimiento, sino también los ojos, sean testigos y jueces de la doctrina).[34]

Granada stresses the transparency of the human interior by intertwining the anatomical material with old Christian imagery that implies openness to the outside. He begins the section dedicated to the anatomical description of the human being by referring to it as a microcosm or lesser world ("mundo menor"), the old image in which the inner perfection of the human being is a condensed reflection of all aspects of creation at the macrocosmic level. As Granada puts it, man – he always uses the traditional masculine form "hombre" to refer to the human being – is a microcosm "because everything that exists in the universe is also present in him in a smaller proportion." Man is therefore a mirror of what surrounds him, "a small map that the Supreme Maker drew, where everything that exists in the universe was represented not with images but by truth itself" (Porque todo lo que hay en el mundo mayor se halla en él [el hombre] aunque en forma más breve;

el hombre es como un breve mapa que aquel soberano artífice trazó, donde no por figuras, sino por la misma verdad, nos representó cuanto había en el mundo).[35] Inherent in the idea of the human being as a map, mirror, or open book is the transparency of this supreme divine creation, whose interior can be read inside out with the new methods of dissection.[36]

Apart from the simile of the human being as a microcosm that reproduces inside what is outside, Granada makes extended use of the image of the body as a house, temple, or castle in which harmony rules in spite of the diversity of the constituent elements: "The construction [of the human body] can also be compared to a tall building built on two columns, the legs supporting the whole building and the feet being the foundations" (Puede también compararse esta fábrica [del cuerpo humano] con la de una casa alta, armada sobre dos columnas, porque las piernas sirven aquí de columnas que sustentan todo este edificio, cuyas bases son los pies, sobre que ellas se sustentan etc.).[37] The cruciform design of churches has often been compared to the body of Christ on the cross, and the door at the side to the wound in his side. Granada's immediate source for this traditional image is, however, the anatomical treatises of the period. The metaphor of the body as a building constitutes a unifying theme across sixteenth-century Spanish anatomical writing, and it is present in Granada's main anatomical source, Valverde's *Anatomía del corpo humano*.[38] House and body are supposed to share the same numerical harmony of the universe in the Pythagorean cosmology. Vitruvius had stated that an aesthetically pleasant building had to follow the proportions of the different parts, and Cornelius Agrippa elaborated on this tenet in the early modern period.[39] Granada also connects the image of the body as a harmonious construction to its Pauline roots:

> In our body there is the brotherhood that Saint Paul so much champions, because all the members and senses serve each other, and all of them serve the common good that is the conservation of the whole [body], but in such a way that the lesser noble members serve the more noble ones. (En este nuestro cuerpo hay aquella hermandad que el Apóstol tantas veces nos encomienda, porque todos los miembros y sentidos sirven unos a otros, y todos al bien común, que es a la conservación del todo, mas esto con tal orden, que los menos nobles sirven a los más nobles.)[40]

He is referring to Saint Paul's Epistles to the Romans, 1 Corinthians, and Ephesians, which contain the metaphor of the temple of the church

as the body of Christ and the body of the Christian as God's temple –
"house" and "temple" being the same word in Hebrew.[41] An important
aspect of this view of the body and its interior as a house in the Pauline
tradition is that the image, while recognizing the variety of the constituents, emphasizes the possibility of integration and harmony through
equality and openness. Basically, the image of the body as a house is a
variation of the image of the body as a microcosm – that is, as a construction that repeats inside the order that is outside. The body is a
church or temple, and the church is made up of (Christian) bodies. Like
the image of the microcosm from which it derives, the image of the
body as a house emphasizes the idea that inside and outside are the
same.[42]

The emphasis on harmony and hierarchy in the image of the body as
a microcosm that reproduces the order of creation does not imply that
the human being was conceived as an immutable entity. As the rest of
the universe, the body is subject to all kinds of periodic changes and
contrary forces. Individual body organs are seen as influenced by the
movements of planets and stars, which produce imbalances and altera-
tions in human health and behaviour. Mutability in the functioning of
the body is exemplified in the abundant imagery of anatomical depictions in which limbs and inner organs are connected to the planets or the
signs of the zodiac. A variation of the same tradition is seen in diagrams
representing the changes of the body connected to natural cycles, such
as the seasons and months of the year or the hours of day and night.[43]
Granada's *Introducción al símbolo de la fe* attributes the evil behaviours
and thoughts to temporary external influences. Granada often presents
sin through the traditional Christian model of the arousal and satisfac-
tion of sexual desire, which stand for all other iniquities. In the chapter
entitled "Order of this spiritual monarchy and war of our adversaries
who resort to lust" (Orden de esta espiritual monarquía y guerra de
nuestros adversarios en esta parte concupiscible), Granada gives an
explanation for the existence of sin that corresponds to that of disease
in humoural medicine. Sinful tendencies are an overpowering of the
*potentia sensitiva* by the mounting pressure of the passions:

> But when passions and sensual appetites are strong, they blind reason and
> disturb will, which are diverted. We can see an example of this in people
> suffering from dropsy, who, in spite of knowing the damage that drinking
> does to them, are compelled by their thirst to drink because their thirst
> diverts their will, which makes their reason to approve of it and order the

members to do it. (Mas cuando las pasiones y apetitos son vehementes, ciegan la razón, y trastornan la voluntad, y llévanla en pos de sí. El ejemplo de esto vemos en un hidrópico, el cual sabiendo cuánto mal le hace el beber, todavía puede tanto este apetito que lleva tras sí la voluntad, la cual hace que el entendimiento apruebe esto y dé sentencia que así se debe por entonces hacer, y así lo ejecutan los miembros.)[44]

Man's interior and its functioning are easily explicable and readable for Granada; they operate by the same principles that affect the rest of the universe and are always visible because, even in apparently hidden spaces, the same universal laws are at work. As Granada puts it, quoting Psalm 138:15: "Not even one of my bones was hidden from You when my body was formed in the entrails of my mother" (Ninguno de mis huesos hubo escondido a Vuestros ojos cuando mi cuerpo se formaba en los secretos del alma del vientre de mi madre).[45] Sin is a temporary malfunction of the system, an imbalance of the passions that, like the humours, are affected by the movements of the outside world.[46]

## The Compliant Transparency of Martyrs

In the anatomical manuals, Granada found material to represent the human interior as an entity that contained nothing except God's work, no matter how thoroughly it was inspected. Also notable in Granada's writings is a striking trait present in some illustrations of the anatomical manuals: the dissected body assumes an attitude of compliance with the dissective operation. This trait grows from a convention that the illustrations in contemporary anatomical manuals inherited from the animated skeletons of the medieval *memento mori* and *danse macabre*: the dissected bodies were portrayed not as corpses but as if alive, casually standing or sitting, often surrounded by architectural or bucolic decorations, and engaged in their daily routines. Most striking in these animated figures is, as Sawday puts it, "the extraordinary degree of cooperation which they seem to display in 'submitting' to the dissective process."[47] The engravings of the self-dissecting or self-anatomizing bodies are the epitome of this cooperation. In them, a human figure holds a knife that has been used to cut open its own interior in one hand, while the other pulls aside the layers of muscles and other organs to allow the onlookers to peek into the deepest spaces inside the body. One of the best-known self-dissecting figures appears in Valverde's

*Anatomía del corpo humano,* a self-flayed male figure that has removed the skin of his body with a knife still held in his hand while the skin hangs from his other hand (see Figure 5 in chapter 1).[48] As Sawday also has pointed out, this compliance of the anatomical plates' cut-up bodies is also present in the contemporary religious discourse. He detects a tendency to represent the Passion of Christ as the near-dissective dismemberment of a sacrificial figure offering himself so that the faithful can reach salvation through his interior. This type of sacrificial representation is best exemplified in the devotion of the Sacred Heart of Jesus, which became prominent during the Counter-Reformation.[49] The theme also appears among Spanish religious writers, as in Fray Juan de los Ángeles's *Diálogos de la conquista del reino de Dios* (1595):

> The surgeons do an anatomy on the bodies of those who die of unknown causes, not unlike what was done to the body of Christ, which a soldier opened with a lance. He discovered His heart and that love [for mankind] had taken possession of it, and this love was the cause of his death, because water and blood ran from it as it were still alive. (Y como los cirujanos suelen hacer notomía del que muere, cuando de su muerte no hallan causa, así la hicieron de Cristo; que uno de los soldados le abrió su pecho con una lanza y descubrió el corazón, y echóse de ver que el amor que dél se había apoderado era causa de su muerte, porque salió dél agua y sangre, como si estuviera vivo.)[50]

Another version of the religious discourse that presents a similar compliance of the victim is martyrology. The torture described in martyrological narratives not only shares many of the gruesome methods of anatomical dissection but also relies on the martyrs' sacrificial abandonment to the hands of the executioner. The martyrs' compliance with the process of martyrdom – often symbolized by representation of the martyrs holding the same instruments used by their torturers – resembles that of the self-dissecting figures in anatomy books and in sacred anatomy. This is the case with the depiction of Saint Bartholomew in *The Last Judgment* fresco of the Sistine Chapel: a figure that bears the features of Michelangelo holding the knife of his martyrdom in one hand and his flayed skin in the other, a representation that, appropriately, has been compared to the self-flaying figure in Valverde's *Anatomía del corpo humano.*[51] Granada's *Introducción al símbolo de la fe* narrates several lives of saints that follow the martyrological pattern: a traitor who reports the future martyrs to the authorities, the voluntary confession of the martyrs' Christian faith, the threat of torture, and so on. It also includes the martyrs' refusal to recant their faith in spite of the enticing offer of indemnity, the cruelty of the torturers, and their impotence in front of the martyrs, who, in spite of being children in many cases, remain firm in the midst of the cruellest and most refined tortures. Often, the victim is so unaffected by the torment that the torturer begins to doubt whether the irons or similar instruments of torture used are hot or sharp enough, sometimes resulting in a comic situation in which the torturer is burnt or hurt while testing the instruments.[52] Any attempt at finding anything but the martyrs' faith is futile given that what is inside is evident on the outside through their words and behaviour. Their beliefs do not need to be forcibly extracted because they are already confessing. Appropriately, Granada compares the bodies of the martyrs to transparent reliquaries and monstrances.[53]

Granada's inclusion of a large martyrological section in *Introducción al símbolo de la fe* responds to the apologetic intention of his book, in which he alleges the testimony of the supra-human fortitude of the martyrs as divine proof that Christianity is the true faith. The old Roman martyrology was undergoing a rebirth towards the end of the sixteenth century, becoming a formidable propagandistic weapon used by Protestants and Catholics in their confrontation. Both sides resuscitated this ancient genre by adapting it to the contemporary wars of religion. Followers executed by the other faction, often after gruesome tortures, were identified with the early Christian martyrs under the Roman emperors. Martyrologies in the form of books or pamphlets, often illustrated with eye-catching engravings, were an excellent propagandistic tool proving the righteousness of one's cause and the cruelty and wickedness of one's opponent. The Protestants were the first to use this form of propaganda with John Foxe's fully illustrated *Book of Martyrs* (1554), soon followed by other titles, such as *Catalogus testium veritatis* by Matthias Flacius (1556) and *Histoire des martyrs persécutés et mis à mort pour la vérité de l'Evangile* by Jean Crespin (1556–97). The Catholic side did not fall behind in this propagandistic war. In the final decades of the sixteenth century several books included not only the stories of the martyrs of antiquity but also numerous cases of Catholics who had been tortured and executed by the Protestants. To this category belong the *Martyrologium Romanum* by Baronio (1586) and the *Flos sanctorum* by Rivadeneira (1599–1601).[54]

*Introducción al símbolo de la fe* is also part of this revival of martyrology as a weapon for propaganda. Granada includes both martyrs of antiquity and Catholic victims of the Protestants. He presents the endurance of those who underwent the cruellest tortures and deaths as proof that the Christian (Catholic) religion was the true one. But these accounts also double as dissective narratives that emphasize complete disclosure of an interior in which nothing but God is present. Granada's narration of the martyrdom of Thomas Ford, an English Catholic executed under Elizabeth I in 1582, offers a good example. Ford and two other Catholic priests were taken to the authorities and asked to confess that they were part of a political conspiracy against England, to which Ford replied, "Your accusations are false. The true reason of our death is our Catholic faith … as God, who can see inside all hearts (Ps 7:10) and will unveil what is hidden in the dark, knows" (Ficción es lo que nos acusáis de traiciones. La verdadera causa de nuestra muerte es la religión católica … Esto ve nuestro Dios, que escudriña los corazones (Ps 7:10), y revelará lo escondido en las tinieblas).[55] Because the authorities usually could not extricate a satisfying confession from martyrs, they resorted to torture. Following the generic pattern, the more cruelty and violence applied, the more exasperating the lack of results. In addition, as often happens in the martyrological model, the perceived obstinacy of martyrs leads to an orgy of dismemberment that concludes with the destruction and dispersion of the body. This is the case in Granada's narration of the martyrdom of the Jesuit Edmund Campion, who had been executed in England a few years earlier:

> The Calvinists asked him to pray with them but he refused and denounced their false religion. Then he told all the Catholics that were present that they should pray the Credo when he was about to die, so that although he was unable to proclaim his faith by word of mouth, they would do it for him. Then the cart that held him under the rope was removed and he hanged, but before he died, his natural parts were cut off, he was opened with a knife, and his heart and intestines were removed and thrown into a fire. The body was quartered and the quarters and his head were boiled in water, and finally nailed to the doors of the city to be displayed. (Entonces los calvinistas comenzaron a pedirle que rezase con ellos, lo cual él no quiso hacer, abominando su falsa religión, mas pidió a todos los católicos que allí estaban que, en el punto que él estuviese muriendo dijesen el Credo, para que la fe que ya no podía confesar con su boca la confesasen los innumerables católicos que estaban allí presentes. Y desta manera hurtando a la carreta los pies debajo, quedó ahorcado, y antes de que expirase … le cortaron sus partes naturales y abriéndolo por medio con un cuchillo, le

arrancaron el corazón y las tripas y las echaron en el fuego, y le cortaron el cuerpo en cuatro cuartos, los cuales junto con la cabeza cocieron un poco en agua hirviendo, y así los pusieron con clavos hincados en las puertas de la ciudad.)[56]

Campion's martyrdom becomes a dissective process that fails to retrieve anything but his unwavering Catholic faith, which he not only willingly confessed at the beginning of the process but unstoppably continued to proclaim, even after death and dismemberment, through the mouths of the other Catholics present.

## Sor María de la Visitación's False Stigmata

Granada's interest in the martyr as a person who cannot but confess the presence of God in her interior is evident in a religious scandal that brought him much grief at the end of his life: his support of the Portuguese nun María de la Visitación, whose visions and stigmata were later proven to have been falsified. To appreciate the importance of this scandal fully, one must understand its implications in the strained political relations between Spain and Portugal at the time. After the dynastic crisis provoked by the death of King Sebastian I, Philip II used military force to seize the vacant Portuguese throne. The strong nationalistic faction had another candidate for the crown and regarded Philip II as a foreigner in spite of his having a claim to the Portuguese throne because his grandfather had been the Portuguese king Manuel I. The situation was further complicated by *Sebastianismo*, the belief that King Sebastian I had not died at Alcazarquivir – his body was never recovered – and that he would eventually return. The Portuguese church was involved in all the political intrigue surrounding these events, especially the Dominicans, who, unlike other orders, were committed to the nationalistic factions that opposed Philip II.[57]

The Dominican Granada, although old and ailing, was so close to the Portuguese royal family that he could not but be involved in politics. On the one hand, over the years Philip II had seen the Spanish Granada's position in the Portuguese court as an asset and had used him to obtain information to undertake diplomatic missions. In 1568, Philip II had tried to use Granada for his political intrigue by asking him to influence the election of the counsellors to advise the regent Queen Catherine, who ruled Portugal during King Sebastian's minority. Two years later, Pope Pius V sent Granada a letter asking him to influence young King Sebastian in choosing a consort who would benefit the pope's and, presumably, Philip II's interests. Later, when Cardinal Henry became king, Philip II sent him Granada as a secret ambassador. He was able to disguise the true nature of his mission as a private visit because he was an old friend of the cardinal's.[58] On the other hand, Granada seems to have served as a faithful adviser to Queen Catherine and to Cardinal Henry before and after he became king. Granada had been the confessor of Queen Catherine, King Sebastian's mother and regent, and the confidant of Cardinal Henry, great-uncle of King Sebastian I. After his great-nephew's death, Cardinal Henry reluctantly ruled as king of Portugal for a short period (1578–80), but his age and his position within the church prevented him from marrying and leaving an heir to the throne. Granada's position became more complicated when in 1580 Philip II was proclaimed king of Portugal. The position of vicar general of the Dominican order was vacant at that time, and the person elected for the position was Fray Antonio de la Cerda, an unpopular candidate appointed by the Duke of Alba and considered, therefore, pro-Spanish. Soon a letter from the pope appeared in the court replacing de la Cerda with Granada, who had been opposed to de la Cerda's nomination. The letter was easily proven a forgery perpetrated by the faction opposing Philip II. The whole affair infuriated the monarch, who blamed Granada for it. Overall, the role that Granada played during this dynastic crisis is uncertain. Torn between conflicted allegiances, he seems to have acted according to his own dictates in some instances and in contradictory directions in others.[59] It is in this complex context that the political implications of Granada's staunch support of Sor María de la Visitación can best be understood.

Statements made by visionaries of the period were politically significant since they contained negative forecasts of contemporary events, especially military enterprises. Their prophecies were often appropriated as arguments by the different political factions vying for power at the court. Also, the providentialist view of Spain in international politics as God's arm acting in history made these visions more influential. Several cases can be mentioned matching this pattern in the sixteenth and seventeenth centuries. In the same period in which Sor María became famous, the ex-soldier and visionary Miguel de Piedrola repeatedly forecasted the demise of Spain. In his letters, he referred to Madrid as a corrupt Babylon about to be punished. He was investigated in 1578 by the Inquisition. Later, after being involved in a murder, he was arrested and sentenced to confinement in a monastery. Also famous was Lucrecia de León, who at the same time , inspired initially by Piedrola, made bleak predictions criticizing some political decisions. Eventually, Lucrecia was also arrested. The political influence of visionaries, especially religious women, continued well into the following century, in which Sor María de Ágreda was the political and spiritual adviser of Philip IV for over twenty years.[60]

María de la Visitación (born María de Meneses in 1551) was a Dominican nun of noble descent who began to have visions and stigmata in 1577. She claimed that the blood marks in her forehead were caused by a crown of thorns that had appeared during a vision she had had of the battle of Alcazarquivir, in which her brother had died, together with King Sebastian I and many young Portuguese noblemen. In 1583, she became the prioress of her convent, her visions – and especially her stigmata – giving her an international reputation.[61] As opposed to the strained thaumaturgy of the Carmelites, who supported Philip II, María de la Visitación was seen as epitomizing the excesses of the Dominicans, who, as mentioned, opposed the annexation of Portugal by Spain.[62] Her family connections to King Sebastian I and the failed Alcazarquivir expedition, some statements attributed to her in which she supported *Sebastianismo*, and the maybe not-so-coincidental fact that the nationalistic Portuguese faction had chosen the five stigmata of Christ as their banner – in connection to the *quinas* or five shields of the Portuguese coat of arms – made her a political force that Philip II, inclined as he was to believe in miraculous events, could not ignore. In May 1588 he sought her blessing for the Spanish Armada, which was about to set sail to England. Seeking her approval was probably a gesture to involve the Portuguese in an enterprise with religious implications comparable to those of King Sebastian's failed expedition to Morocco. Three months later, after the Armada was defeated and a Portuguese nationalist rebellion against his rule broke up, Philip II's treatment of Sor María de la Visitación changed radically. The monarch was informed that the nun had prophesied that he had no legal right to the throne of Portugal and that many misfortunes would befall him unless he renounced the Portuguese throne.[63] Urged on by Philip II, the Inquisition moved to take a closer look at Sor María de la Visitación. The stigmata on her hands were closely examined and proven false, and Sor María de la Visitación confessed that she had fabricated visions and levitations.

Granada, in the final months of his life – he would die in December of the same year – was directly affected by this scandal because he had been one of Sor María's strongest defenders. His support is recorded in the positive report he wrote in 1587 and sent to Sixto Fabri, the Master General of the Dominicans, after visiting the nun in her convent and examining her wounds, together with her confessor Gaspar d'Aveiro.[64] But Granada's support went further. He published an extended document entitled *Historia de Sor María de la Visitación*, in which he narrates her life in the most encomiastic tone.[65] As a pious exemplary biography intended to confirm the Christian faith of its readers, it took a hagiographic pattern, illustrated with anecdotes extolling her many virtues and saintly behaviour.[66] Granada includes other visionaries to prove that similar miraculous events had been constant in the history of Christianity. He adduces not only visionaries from the Old and the New Testament, but also more recent cases, such as Saint Francis of Assisi. Then he changes subjects and narrates in detail the lives of two female martyrs from the Roman period, Saint Cecilia and Saint Catherine of Alexandria, as the most pertinent antecedents for the case of María de la Visitación. He explains how their torturers, after having resorted to the cruellest torments without managing to make their victims confess anything but their resilient faith, were overtaken by rage and ended up boiling and decapitating Saint Cecilia and dismembering Saint Catherine of Alexandria under a wheel of knives. Even these extreme forms of dismemberment as a search for a hidden truth were fruitless. When, finally, Saint Catherine was decapitated, only the whitest milk came out of her body.[67]

That Granada saw Sor María's stigmata as a trial similar to martyrdom is also evident in a second report he wrote. In it, he refers to the intrusive physical examination of her stigmata that her confessor and he performed as a "martirio" (martyrdom).[68] Granada presents himself both as an anatomist and as a Roman torturer who painfully and unnecessarily tries to penetrate her body to extract an inner truth that is already obvious on the outside. Granada also presents the part of the book containing the visions of Sor María as a confession, like the martyrs' voluntary confession of their Christian faith in front of their Roman judges, "since it was very painful for this virgin to write because of the wound and nail that she has in her hand, and the prelate ordered her to describe all the matters [of her visions] in detail to her confessor, who was to write them down faithfully as he heard them from her" (porque

era muy penoso a esta virgen escribir por su mano, por razón de la llaga
y clavo que en ella tiene, dióse esta orden por el perlado que ella diese
cuenta a su confesor de estas cosas, el cual las escribe fielmente de la
manera que las oyó a ella).[69]

The connection between martyrdom and stigmata is clear in the section in *Historia de Sor María de la Visitación* in which Granada lists other
visionary saints. He chooses to conclude with an extended exposition
of the case of Saint Catherine of Sienna as Sor María's most poignant
and pertinent predecessor. Catherine of Sienna, whose image was often
represented in churches and religious books, was a Dominican nun,
like Sor María, and the quintessential model of the stigmatized saintly
woman during the Middle Ages and the Renaissance. Her stigmata are
implicitly compared to the tortures of martyrdom because they are the
product of a love for Christ so intense that she shares the pains of his
Passion. Like the wounds of Christ, especially the one left on his side by
the Roman soldier's spear, her miraculous lacerations are paths to the
interior, where the possibility of true salvation resides.[70] As the etymological meaning of the word indicates, stigmata are external signs or
marks that stand for something else. They point to an interior process
of suffering exteriorized by the miraculous wounds, which are not due
to any external causes but open from the inside. In martyrdom, the
wounds are imposed from outside and confirm an inner truth already
confessed by the words and behaviour of the martyrs at the beginning
of the process. In the case of the stigmatized person, the wounds are the
result of an inner truth that spontaneously breaks out through the body
to confirm that the saintly behaviour has a real internal cause.[71] Granada
describes this openness of Sor María by resorting to the Pauline image
of the house:

> As Solomon says in his Proverbs, he who walks straight, honestly and
> without fear is   like a house that is open on all its sides, so that anybody
> outside can see that inside there is nothing hidden. Consequently, those
> who come to talk to Sor María de la Visitación – even those who before-
> hand distrusted the divine nature of what is happening to her – come out
> not only convinced but also as devout believers; and because of her virtue
> and truthfulness, they can clearly see that in such an open heart there can-
> not be deceitfulness but only purity and simplicity. (Porque, como dice el
> Sabio [Salomón], quien anda simplemente anda confiadamente, sin temer
> mal de nadie, es su vida y ánima ... como una casa abierta por todas par-
> tes, donde quien está de fuera ve cuanto hay dentro de ella, sin haber cosa

escondida o solapada. De donde resulta que todos cuantos la ven y hablan con ella, aunque hayan antes dudado de sus cosas por ser tan grandes, salen de ella no sólo desengañados sino también edificados y devotos, porque como la virtud y la verdad tenga tanta fuerza ven claro que en aquel pecho tan abierto no hay doblez ni fingimiento sino pureza y simplicidad.)[72]

The five stigmata are central to Granada's argument for the veracity of her case. These portentous wounds are the most direct and palpable signs of an inner, divine possession that is also revealed by her pious humility, her visions, and the miracles she performs. María de la Visitación's stigmata are external, but they reach deep inside. As Granada clarifies, "she claims that her wounds are deep because she feels greater pain inside than outside, and that they would open if somebody put pressure on them; and the pain is all inside, and on the outside the burning is such that she does not allow anybody to touch them" (Y las heridas que en estas partes tiene, dice ella que parecen ser penetrantes, porque siente dentro mayores dolores que de fuera, porque, si en ellas tocaren recio, le parece que se abrirán; y el dolor todo es de dentro, y en lo de fuera tiene tan gran ardor, que no consiente tocarle nadie). The stigmata point to the invisible internal process of her divine possession by hurting or bleeding on significant occasions in an unmistakably revealing pattern: "Every Friday the wound on her side bleeds five small drops that form the exact form of a cross; every drop is round, slightly bigger than a lentil, and she collects them by putting on her wound a piece of very thin cloth that she has folded in four, and every layer is soaked in her blood, so that every Friday four such cloths are produced" (Todos los viernes le salen de la llaga del costado cinco gotas de sangre, puestas por orden en una perfectísima figura de cruz, y cada gota de sangre es redonda poco mayor que una lenteja; y para recogerlas pone ella encima de la llaga un lienzo, el más delgado y más usado que puede hallar, doblado con cuatro dobleces, los cuales todos penetran estas cinco gotas y pasan de parte a parte, de modo que cada viernes salen cuatro paños de éstos). And even more revealing of her interior is that "on the day of the Exaltation of the Cross of the year of 1584 iron nails began to grow inside the stigmata that pierce her hands, and these nails have been growing since then" (el día de la Exaltación de la Cruz del año de 1584 comenzaron a nacerle clavos en medio de las manos y llagas que pasan de parte a parte, y han ido creciendo hasta agora).[73]

Granada was, however, painfully wrong in his assessment of María de la Visitación. In August 1588 her whole case crumbled when the Inquisition took a more in-depth look at her at the insistence of Philip II. The stigmata in her hands were carefully examined and, after being soaked in tepid water, they were found to be painted. Incriminating testimony was added by nuns of her convent who declared that they had peeped through a hole in the wall of her cell and seen her paint the stigmata and prick them to obtain blood to paint crosses on the pads. Finally, María de la Visitación confessed that everything had been a sham. The whole case was proven to be the concoction of an insecure woman who craved attention and influence. María de la Visitación was condemned to perpetual solitary confinement in a convent outside Lisbon. The verdict was publicly read in the cathedral of Lisbon and in all the churches of the city, and copies were sent to many European courts because of the international fame of the "Portuguese nun," as she had come to be known.[74] The scandal was of such proportions that the pope deposed the Master General of the Dominican order, Sixto Fabri. Granada, who had been her staunch supporter, found himself in a difficult position, to the point that the affair seems to have affected his already delicate health and precipitated his death, barely four months later.

In his final days, a blind and ailing Granada wrote an admission of guilt for his prominent role and his credulity in the scandal. This document, probably the last he ever wrote, is "Sermón contra los escándalos en la caídas públicas" ("Sermon against the Scandals Caused by the Mistakes of those Holding Public Positions"), in which Granada undoes the discourse of inner transparency that he had championed for so many years at such a great personal cost. After extolling the Inquisition for not having being duped by this treacherous nun whose falsehood was finally uncovered, he tries to excuse his gullibility by quoting a decree of Pope Zephyrinus (199–217 AD). This decree claims that one should not be so distrustful as to suspect the intentions of a person whose exterior acts are all positive, given that, after all, only God can scrutinize the heart of man.[75] The final words of the quotation are a clear echo of Psalm 7:10: "Deus scrutans corda et renes" (God who scrutinizes hearts and entrails). Granada had used this passage repeatedly in his works in the sense that nothing inside the human being is to be feared because it is God's product, no matter how deeply the inside of the body is scrutinized. Now, in this apologetic document, he uses the psalm in the opposite meaning, to admit the practical impossibility of knowing what truly is lurking inside a human being in spite of the external signs.

## Granada's Failed Defence of a Divine Interior

One must be careful not to make of Granada a tragically failed prede-cessor in a linear narration of progress in which the modern self is the unavoidable result. He is not a forebear of modernity who celebrates the autonomous inner self in the intransigent times of Counter-Reformation Spain, nor a proto-hero of modern individuality whose efforts were thwarted by the Inquisition. He epitomizes an old form of religious interiority that had been a tolerated component in the piety of the Christian church since antiquity but that became a liability as a result of the inner turn brought along by Protestantism. This old interi-ority is mostly a form of introspection that examines how closely one follows a list of precepts that emanate from God, and it includes a series of techniques – such as the silent repetition of prayers or the vivid men-tal picturing of biblical scenes – that can be used to reach certain mental states. However, it is difficult to deny that a religious interiority such as the one represented by Granada is somehow a predecessor of modern interiority. Religious interiority, understood as the construction of an inner space of scrutiny, claims and expands the same bodily real estate – heart, bowels – that will be claimed later for the more complex opera-tions of the modern self. It also has been argued that all that has occurred between this old religious interiority and the new forms of modern interiority is a terminological replacement in which the law of God is renamed the rule of reason. At the very least, it must be recognized that an enhanced awareness of mental space was in part the result of the religious emphasis on cultivating a systematic and cerebral form of praying.[76]

Distancing Granada from us is his writing style, enshrined in Scho-lasticism and armoured with endless quotations from the Fathers of the Church and their commentaries on biblical passages. Through this thick foliage of the conventions of contemporary pious literature, mod-ern readers have problems identifying an authentic voice that may tell them much about Granada himself. However, sieving through his writ-ings, one can catch glimpses of an anxiety of interiority expressed within the limited conventions of religious writing. What reveals Granada's anxiety of interiority is not so much the content of his writ-ing as subtle variations in his treatment of a pre-established Christian theme, his choice of a specific topic, or his repeated use of certain images. This is the case, for instance, when he enlists the recent discourse of anatomy to harmoniously unite the inside of the human being and the rest of the world. Granada introduces an extended chapter on the new anatomical discourse as one more testimony to his otherwise conventional corroboration of the existence of God, the creator of a complex machine. But, indirectly, Granada is also anxiously dissecting and exposing the same interior whose cultivation brought him so many problems. The complex bodily interior that is unveiled is selectively presented to prove the greatness of its creator but also as an example of transparency in spite of its complexity. Older images of religious origin, such as that of the body as a house in the Pauline tradition, are mixed with the discourse of anatomy to demonstrate the transparency of an interior in which nothing except God's work can be found. Similarly, the traditional discourse of martyrdom used by Granada as part of his Christian apologetics is enlisted in its dissective capacity. The martyrs provide him with a canonical example of an interior that can be scrutinized, pierced, and torn to pieces, but in which only God's truth is to be found. Furthermore, the dismembering process of martyrdom is proven unnecessary because the contents of the martyrs' interiors are already visible on their exterior. Another variety of this kind of voluntary, even unstoppable confession of the interior is shown in the figure of the stigmatized, whose stigmata break out from the inside, inverting the direction of the wounds inflicted by the torturer in order to search inside the martyr's body.

Granada's basic line of defence was denying the more complex forms of interiority by excluding them as erroneous or subsuming them within an older, simpler paradigm of exclusively religious interiority. He appealed to the old concept of the unity between the inner sphere of the human being and the rest of creation outside, thereby denying the risks inherent in the new forms of interiority. By doing so, he was trying to escape backwards, to ignore the gap that had begun to open between the created universe and the interior of the human being as an autonomous locus of selfhood and conflict. His was a fundamentally outdated and reductionist view of the human being's interior, one that lacked the capacity to account for the emerging forms of interiority.

# 3

# Quevedo and the Interiority
# of the Body Politic

## Quevedo's Dissective Satires

Francisco de Quevedo is not a forerunner of the modern form of autonomous interiority that relies on one's own reason as the ultimate authority. He was suspicious – even dismissive in the case of the lower classes – of an autonomous subject. Furthermore, his belief in an absolutist monarchy of divine roots as the best government is incompatible with the independence that represents modern subjectivity. His sharp tongue and criticism of those in power, even if they cost him dearly, do not qualify as the systematic attitude of distrust towards external forms of authority that characterizes the modern intellectual who dwells in politics. He has been called a *bufón culto* (learned jester) of the ruling class who often served as a subsidized pen.[1] However, Quevedo was well versed in discourses that dealt with the subtleties of the inner realm: his sonnets play with the interiority characteristic of the Petrarchan poetic voice, and his metaphysical poetry displays an equally subtle perception of the self that has often been compared to John Donne.[2] Also, not only his solid knowledge of Christian doctrine but also his lifelong study of Stoicism – especially of the works of the contemporary Catholic neo-Stoic intellectual Justus Lipsius – equipped him with the vocabulary to deal with interiority.[3] The dissective narratives studied in this chapter reflect his deep knowledge as well as his distrust of interiority, which he considers a platform for antisocial behaviour. He constructs intricately grotesque characters and subjects them to anatomical inspection and dismemberment through parody. Their inner organs are exposed as sick members of an ailing body politic.

Quevedo's distrust of the human interior as a place where self-interested, socially dangerous passions run amok was the antithesis of Granada's optimistic trust in the human interior as a harmless space to experience God. This difference in outlooks can be partially explained by the changes that took place over the nearly eight decades separating their lives. Born in the politically successful early years of the Spanish state and its expanding empire, Granada was educated in the optimistic humanism of the first part of the sixteenth century. Quevedo, in contrast, was born in 1580 and is often seen as a product of the Counter-Reformation, the generalized *desengaño* (disappointment), and the beginning of the financial and military collapse of the Spanish empire. Quevedo, like Granada, was deeply immersed in Christian doctrine. He held the degree of doctor in theology, wrote profusely on religious matters, and even started a religious career. But Quevedo's view of the role of religion was different from Granada's because Quevedo lived at a time when the earlier open experimentation with private forms of devotion had been replaced by a restrained religious practice that distrusted unregulated inwardness. Accordingly, religion for Quevedo, who believed that the monarchic state was a natural extension of the same divine order that underpinned the cosmos, was more important as a meta-discourse to legitimize this order than as a path to introspection.

From the time he was born, allegiance to the monarchy was strongly stamped on Quevedo. He first saw the light in the royal palace in Madrid, where he spent his childhood. His parents were low nobility of northern descent and served the royal family in their daily life. Quevedo's father was secretary to Maria of Spain, daughter of Emperor Charles V, and his grandmother and his mother were ladies-in-waiting to the queen. Although he was not a member of the high nobility, he knew many of them and probably had some personal access to the king and the queen. This intimate contact with the royal family was a rare asset in a period in which the Spanish kings were becoming remote, inaccessible figures rarely seen in public. Although Quevedo left the court when he began his advanced studies, the story of his life is one of repeated return to the court. Whenever he returned to Madrid, he stayed with family members or noble friends who lodged him, and, at some point, he even owned a house in the city.[4]

In spite of, or maybe because of, his proximity to the court, he was painfully aware that the political reality of the contemporary court was far from the heavenly order that a divinely inspired monarchy was supposed to incarnate. He witnessed first-hand the corrupt trading of power among courtiers, the insolvency of the profligate crown, and the disastrous military campaigns that characterized the ineffectual rule of the later Spanish Habsburgs. These shortcomings did not affect his belief in the monarchic system because, as he often points out in his writings, the reason for the failure was not the system per se, but the men and women behind it – himself included – who did not live up to the high demands of the divine model. In spite of the many bitter disappointments of his political career, Quevedo remained a fervent monarchist. When he disagreed with political decisions, he made it clear that the decision was the fault of the king's favourite. However, Quevedo recognized that the kings, despite the divine origin of their positions, were plain human beings. The king is both the remote, semi-divine head of the body politic and simultaneously the human being that his parents and other members of the family were charged with helping in daily life. His father's professional duties included dealing with the tailors and other purveyors to the royal family. In his writings, Quevedo often mentions that the king is, after all, only a human being. Such is the case when he notices that kingship is sometimes due to such a fortuitous factor as "the premature labour and the impatience of the belly of their mothers" (1:598; Quien debe la majestad a las anticipaciones del parto y a la primera impaciencia del vientre).[5] This is one of several issues in which Quevedo's personal position seems to be one of simultaneous approval and derision, revealing a difficult, unstable accommodation of apparently untenable contradictions. Similarly, while in some of his writings he defended the value system of a highly static society that relied on blood, in others he mocked the situation and appealed to the equality of all humans. In these writings, he uses the Christian tradition to justify a hierarchical society with the king as its head, as well as to deride this order, appealing to the strong egalitarian drive of Christianity.

For Quevedo the monarchic system and fixed social order it ruled over was the incarnation of divine order on earth. The view of the political order as a reflection of its divine counterpart is an old concept long embraced by Christianity. Saint Augustine writes that the social order relies both on every member of society having his/her definite place within it and on each member having his/her immutable nature and function. These two attributes contribute to what he calls *pax corporis* or social harmony.[6] Quevedo briefly expresses the same idea in his *Migajas sentenciosas* by playing on the double meaning of the word *estado* (state/

estate) as the political unified nation and as the social status or position of a person or class: "A state is when all the people live together according to their estate" (1:1092; Estado, convivencia propia de cada uno en su estado).[7] At least in theory, no social disharmony can exist in this order in which personal identity and social position are one and the same, as reflected in the famous expression "soy quien soy" (I am who I am), which encapsulates the idea that one's identity is based on one's social position and on the obligations and duties attached to it. This belief seems not to agree with Quevedo's relentless pursuit of high position and honour. But he did not see a contradiction between his undeniable personal ambition and his defence of the established order: he deemed upward social mobility acceptable for noble individuals of exceptional value – like him – who were entitled to develop the full potential of their noble blood in pre-eminent offices.

Quevedo considered that aspirations to higher positions were, however, an evil when they became a widespread desire that affected all social classes, especially the lower ones. He did not approve of what he saw as a dangerous generalized trend towards *medrar*, that is, to better one's social standing by resorting to money and deception.[8] On many occasions, he lampoons this social disease in passages that qualify as dissective narratives, namely, narratives resorting to anatomical vocabulary to expose the interiority of an Other that has been textually fabricated for such a purpose. The characters to dissect are based on real persons and on prototypes of the period whom he re-creates as grotesque figures ruled by the opposite of the self-control advocated by the Christianized doctrines of neo-Stoicism. These characters are guided by an uncontrolled drive for personal success, to the point of disregarding the natural, divinely inspired social order and, in some cases, even of threatening the semi-divine king. To perform these dissective operations, Quevedo chooses two opposing types in the social order: the *pícaro* and the *privado*. Their extreme positions at the bottom and the top of society respectively make them well suited to exemplify socially destabilizing drives. The *pícaro* is used to lampoon the social ambitions of the lower classes. At the other extreme of the social scale, the royal favourite or *privado* is used to mock the hubris in an individual citizen who aspires to be crowned king. Between these extremes, other members of the body politic – judges, soldiers, tailors – are exposed to similar dissective operations that denounce and deride their aspirations.

I should advance a peculiarity of Quevedo's narratives: although apparently the dissections are practised on private bodies, the body

politic is really the one under the knife. Quevedo is using allegorical
conceit, making the relation of private citizens' organs and their whole
bodies stand for some of the tension between the body politic and its
unruly constituents.[9] For instance, the pamphlet examined later dissects
the head of Cardinal Richelieu as an abnormal, parasitic limb that is poi-
soning the French body politic. Another mechanism Quevedo uses to
extend his parallels of individual bodies to the body politic is to group
them into corporations. Masses of lawyers, tailors, and pimps are
gathered in scenarios such as Doomsday and Hell, where they are collectively dismembered, so revealing their abusive and parasitic relationship as a group to the rest of the body politic. Finally, attention is paid to
cases in which dissection and dismemberment are applied to isolated
individuals but in such ways that their unruly interiors are shown to
replicate their dysfunctional behaviour as members of the body politic.

   Although Quevedo resorts to dissective methods in many of his writings, he does it most frequently in his satirical writings. This can be
attributed to the fact that dismemberment is a fundamental ingredient
in satire, which Northrop Frye compares to anatomy in his classification of genres. Satire takes pleasure in reducing a body or entity to a
grotesque accumulation of assorted parts.[10] This feature of satire is
present in the etymological origin of the word, the Latin *satura*, which
means a potpourri of dissimilar elements.[11] Dissection – in the sense
that Sawday understands it, namely, as a discursive activity that helps
investigate psychological states and mental processes inside the body[12] –
offered Quevedo a highly embodied language to parody threats to the
established order in the concrete imagery and crude realism that he
mastered. Especially, it allowed him to present the widespread obsession with social climbing as unchecked bodily pressures and as an inner
disease.

   Like many educated people of the time, Quevedo was familiar with
anatomical dissection and its most popular texts. This shows in some of
his works, especially in his *Visita y anatomía de la cabeza del Cardenal
Armando Richelieu*. Also like many contemporary writers, in his writings he compared the search for hidden truths behind the appearances
of society to the medical dissective practice of looking inside the opaque
surface of the human body. The appeal of this method as an epistemological tool for Quevedo is fully revealed only in the context of a Spain
obsessed with death as the definitive *desengaño*. The anatomists' crude
removal of the skin and flesh to show a gory reality of bones and bloody
tissues closely resembled death's ability to dissolve skin and flesh in the

tomb and show the ultimate reality. In his religious treatise *Providencia de Dios*, Quevedo talks of the "pious cruelty of anatomy" (la piadosa crueldad de la anatomía) that allows us to know the hidden physical reality inside the human body and makes the "dismembered dead body serve as a lesson for the living" (1:1455; el muerto despedazado fue docta y útil lección para los vivos).[13] His writings abound in passages that contain direct allusions to dissection. Sometimes they include references to the process of cutting the flesh to look inside, as in his *Migajas sentenciosas*, where a sharp blade is compared to the sharpness of a friend's eye in detecting character flaws (1:1054). Other passages make indirect references to the epistemological process of looking for the truth inside. In *El sueño de la muerte*, he derides those who pretend to be made up of honour and compares them to puppets, whose inside is made up of "old rags and sticks" (1:184; andrajos y palillos). Quevedo's inclination to use the image of dissection goes so far as applying it also to his own body. Sometimes he singles out organs of his body for rhetorical purposes, as when, to guarantee the truth of what he is describing, he begins his first-hand narration *Grandes anales de quince días* by clarifying, "I am offering my eyes to be read, not my ears" (1:730; Doy a leer mis ojos, no mis oídos).[14] In his metaphysical poems and in his religious and Stoic writings, he systematically presents his diseased old body as a lesson for the reader.

Quevedo extends the dissective method to explore the truth not only inside human bodies but also inside objects or situations. In this sense, the title and content of his satirical work *El mundo de por dentro* (*The World Inside*) refers to the idea that the truth hides under the surface. He often uses the words "lo interior" (that which is inside) and "lo retirado" (that which is secluded) to refer to a truth that can be accessed only by going beyond the exterior layer of appearance. The validity of the method of looking inside for truth is for Quevedo so universal that he sees it acting not only in human history but also in the history of salvation: in his *Política de Dios*, Quevedo explains how an old prophecy from Moses's days was fulfilled by the drops of water and blood that Longinus's last spear thrust extracted from inside Christ on the cross, thus confirming that he was the true Messiah (1:640).[15]

## The Dissection of the Body Politic

To represent society as a body whose organs correspond to the different social classes and their functions is an old metaphorical practice that permits one to address abstract social relations in a concrete form. Also, this image exposes society as a whole to a dissective treatment, a possibility that Quevedo exploited for its parodic potential. His textual dissections of the body politic are not attempts at destroying or subverting the image or the conservative system it was often used to portray, but are rather the logical next step in the literary evolution of this metaphor. In its long history, the image of the body politic had been enriched with the subdivision of organs into smaller units or the addition of new ones altogether. Not did only the functioning of the organs become more specific and detailed, but also the relationship among the organs became more complex, and sub-narratives dealing with the relations among the parts or even within each part had developed. Through this gradual complication, the allegory of the body politic grew ripe for dissection.

The image of the body politic Quevedo had access to at the end of the sixteenth century was a rich stockpile of varied materials and meanings accumulated over centuries. To appreciate this wealth fully, a brief account of its origin and evolution is necessary. At the core of this image, the contradiction between the unity and multiplicity of a single organism made up of separate entities, such as the human body or a state, acts as an archetype that is able to express otherwise untenable concepts.[16] This makes the body politic so flexible that it can represent the whole universe as a body, or the opposite – the body as a microcosm that contains the many diverse elements that constitute the universe, as was the case in Luis de Granada.[17] This flexibility allowed the image to be innovatively recombined and adapted to changing political scenarios over the centuries. Not surprisingly, it is transcultural: it appears in the *Rig Vedas* and the *Mahabharata*, and it is fundamental to the system of castes in India, in which the different castes (warriors, workers, Brahmins) are identified with separate body parts of Brahma, who stands for the whole cosmos. The same kind of anthropomorphism is present in the representation of deities such as the four-armed Shiva Nataraja, who brings the universe into existence in his dance.[18] In the West, the Stoics were among the most influential users of the image. Typical formulations are Cicero's, who in *De officiis* warns his readers of the danger if every member in the body tries to appropriate the well-being or the health of the other parts (2:22). Similarly, in *De ira*, Seneca asks, "What if the hands should desire to harm the feet, or the eyes the hand?" to indicate that universal *concordia* must prevail among individual members of the body politic (2:31).[19]

The Stoic formulation of the body politic does not differ from the Christian view except in specific points and, even then, only in a question of degree, such as the emphasis that the Roman Stoics placed on the personal subduing of passions for the well-being of the state. In fact, many of the Stoic treatments of the image were later subsumed within the Christian appropriation of it. Somehow independent of the Stoic traditions is Saint Paul's brief yet highly influential formulation of the church as the body of Christ. This formulation originates in the Greek political vocabulary of the period, and Saint Paul transferred it into a religious context. Curiously, the image gradually returned to its original political meaning in the following centuries.[20] Before the twelfth century, the body of Christ as a metaphor for a group was mostly used to refer exclusively to the Christian community or the church. But because Christendom and society were often interchangeable terms, the Pauline image of the church as a body lost its religious specificity. It began to be applied to other collective entities and, eventually, to the state.[21] After the twelfth century, the core of the image – a body made up of parts – also underwent a rich development that expanded on the diverse, often contradictory, latent meanings.[22] Aquinas made it more pliable for political use by combining the *corpus mysticum Christi* with elements of Aristotle's concept of the state as a body. According to Aquinas, the church was not only a representation of the mystical body of Christ but also a body in itself, whose diverse members constitute a unity in spite of their different natures. This is stated in a fundamental passage reproduced here because it exemplifies how the image of the body politic, while still remaining faithful to its religious origins, became more anatomically complex:

> In the natural body is found a quadruple union of the members to one another. The first is according to conformity of nature, because all members consist of the same like parts, and are of one *ratio*, even as the hand and foot of flesh and bone; and thus the members are called one in genus or species. The second is through the binding of them to one another by nerves and joints; and thus they are called one by continuity. The third is according as the vital spirit and forces of the soul are diffused through the whole body. The fourth is according as all members are perfected by the soul, which is numerically one in all the members. Moreover, of the said unions, the first is not union in the absolute sense, because that in which is this union is not numerically one as in the case of the three following;

because through faith in and love of the numerically one thing believed and loved, they are united; likewise the Holy Spirit, one in number, fills all.[23]

Thomas Aquinas made the trope of the body politic especially appropriate to the description of the inchoate medieval states that originated from the breakup of the Roman Empire, which derived their legitimacy from the union between church and state after Constantine became the first Christian Roman emperor. It was a flexible tool for political argumentation and was argued by both sides in controversies as diverse as the relationship between rulers and the pope or the primacy of one form of government over another. In spite of its many variants and applications, it always kept its original ambiguity regarding the hierarchical relationship between the head and the rest of the body. This permitted the use of the image to defend the head's priority over the other members or, in its corporatist interpretation, to present governance as a communal enterprise in which the parts have a voice. The head was often used to represent the interest of the totality of the body and identified with the king, while the different members of the body represented the social groups that made up the body politic. Many thinkers in the Middle Ages maintained that the head or leader of the body politic was entitled to power over the parts in the name of the common good, for which they adduced both Aristotle's traditional idea that the good of the many is preferable to the good of the individual. On the other side of the debate, John of Salisbury's *Policraticus* was – or at least was understood to be – a defence of the corporatist image of the monarchy in which the king is compelled to rely on, and even to consult with, the various members that make up the kingdom.[24]

During early modernity, the image of the body politic was used both by liberal and by absolutist monarchists to defend their positions. Erasmus uses it to argue for a strong yet limited monarchy in a treatise he dedicates to Charles V, while Machiavelli deploys it to argue in favour of a *governo misto*.[25] Eventually, the analogy of the body politic came to be seen as an inappropriate way to represent the reality of social relations, and it was displaced by the image of a machine whose parts were bound together by a social contract.[26] Hobbes's *Leviathan* (1660) is considered to be simultaneously the swan song of the image of the body politic and the harbinger of the image of society as a machine. Hobbes presents the body politic not so much as a living organism as a self-contained machine. In his introduction, he famously compares society to watches and mechanisms that move by themselves through springs and other contrivances. Finally, by the eighteenth century, the image of the body politic was no longer productive.[27]

In Quevedo's lifetime, the image was at its peak: it had accumulated an immense repertoire of variations and meanings, and it was still considered a valid tool to represent societal relations. An exhaustive study of its use is beyond the scope of this book, but a few examples may help us to understand how frequently and creatively Quevedo used it. The frequent appearances of the body politic in his writings range from brief references to the king as head or the ministers as hands, to fully developed allegories that combine some traditional elements into new formations. A specific technique to which he resorts is to rework it through a peculiar return to its origins, namely, to the body of Christ. For this, Quevedo rereads events in the life of Christ in ways that emphasize his embodiment and then translates them into the discourse of the body politic. For instance, in his political treatise *Política de Dios* (1:541), he quotes the passage of the Gospels in which, in the middle of a crowd, Jesus feels that somebody has touched his tunic. Quevedo interprets this passage as a political lesson for the king, who has to be attentive to the slightest touch on his body, namely, on all his kingdom's subjects and territories.[28]

Quevedo's treatment of the body politic resorts both to the corporatist and to the hierarchical traditions of the image, often simultaneously. As a staunch defender of the absolutist monarchy, he uses the narrative to point out the supreme position of the king. At the same time, he appeals to the corporatist tradition of the image and its emphasis on the mutual dependence of all the parts, although, following Aquinas's example, he is careful not to extend this interdependency to a call for equal dignity of the parts.[29] In his *Marco Bruto*, Quevedo expresses the paradoxical connection of the king with the rest of the body politic through the concept of shared health: "The king is the head and his subjects are the members. The subjects hurt when the king hurts. If an apoplexy affects the brain, the feet die and the hands tremble" (1:841; Del rey, que es cabeza, son miembros los vasallos. Cuando los vasallos se quejan, el rey les duele. Apodérase una apoplejía del cerebro; muérense los pies y tiemblan las manos). In many passages he resorts to health to symbolize not only the unity of the body politic but also the need to implement the appropriate measures to keep it healthy. So he compares those who do not allow the doctor to bleed their arm to rid them of fever to states surrounded by enemies whose citizens do not want to pay tributes to arm troops (1:613). In another passage, referring to the consequences of the Diet of Worms – which took place in the German city of Worms in 1521 – he makes a pun of the double meaning of the word "diet" as a selection of food and as the general assembly of the estates of the Holy Roman Empire. The sick German Protestant states, writes Quevedo, had not benefitted from their "diet" or from their bloodletting (i.e., the wars; 1:256).[30]

The treatment of the body politic as sick or in need of medication and healing, as in the examples just quoted, is part of a strong tendency towards the pathologization and medicalization of the image in those days. As a matter of fact, the health of the body politic has been part of the image since its inception. The harmony of its members (*pax corporis* or *concordia corporis*) was understood as health, and the lack thereof as sickness, which, according to the Galenic paradigm, resulted from one or more members not collaborating with the rest or from the infiltration of elements alien to the body. As the image of the body politic became more and more complex, and more organs and specific functions were added, the potential for malfunction and disease grew exponentially. In his study of the image of the body politic in early modern England, Harris sees a perceptible increase in its depiction as suffering from ailments due to imbalances of an ontological nature or triggered by the intrusion of external (i.e., foreign) elements. As for the reasons for this increase, he suggests new medical theories, especially the change from a humoural to an ontological model of disease, the new political order, and the Neoplatonist tendencies in the contemporary political and medical discourse.[31] Whatever the reasons, the representation of the body politic as sick became popular in many European countries. In Spain, this popularity manifests itself, for instance, in the writings of the *arbitristas* and of other writers of political treatises, such as Jerónimo de Ceballos's *Arte real para el buen gobierno de España* (1623) or Pérez de Herrera's *Curación del cuerpo de la República o remedios para el bien de la salud del cuerpo de la República* (1610).[32]

Also part of the tendency towards medicalization was the application of anatomy to the image of the body politic, which was dismantled into its constituent parts whose individual functioning – or, most often, malfunctioning – was scrutinized. The procedure could be used to argue either in favour of or against the survival of the current political order depending on the intentions behind the procedure, be it to heal the sick body or to reveal that it was incurable because its anatomy was that of a monster. In other cases, the dissection of the body politic was part of a larger text whose purpose was not political but philosophical or artistic. In these texts, the justification or the discredit of the political situation was not the central issue. This is the case in John Donne's *Devotions upon Emergent Occasions* (1624).[33] Donne, practically a contemporary of Quevedo's, was struggling with the concept of man as a microcosm, which he found too optimistically uncomplicated for the disorderly chaos that he saw in the human being. He thought that the cause of this disorder was precisely the multitude of different elements and organs that constitute both the human body and the body politic.[34] In his dissective analysis of the human being, he jumps continuously from the physical body to the body politic, presented as a multitude of discordant elements barely held together by a central authority: "And since the brain, and liver, and heart, hold not a triumvirate in man, a sovereignty equally shed upon them all, for his well-being, as the four elements do, for his very being, but the heart alone is in the principality, and in the throne, as king, the rest as Subjects." His interest in emphasizing the disharmony of the parts makes Donne choose a sick body, often his own, for these dissective analyses. While talking about how diseases and poisons may affect the liver, the head, or the heart, he extrapolates the devastating consequences to the political body: "And yet this is also another misery of this king of man, the heart, which is also applicable to the kings of this world, great men, that the venom and poison of every pestilential disease directs itself to the heart."[35]

Dating from the same period, Shakespeare's *Coriolanus* (1623) describes how the survival of Rome was threatened by the dismemberment of the body politic resulting from the struggle between patricians and plebeians after the fall of the Etruscan monarchy. At the beginning of the play, the senator Menenius tries to calm the populace, furious because the authorities have withheld stores of grain. He tells them the fable of the belly, an old story that can be traced back to Plutarch and Livy.[36] Its plot is simple: all the organs of the body conspire against the belly – here symbolizing the Roman senate – which they accuse of being idle and not contributing to the common well-being of the body. But as the belly is not fed, the whole body falls into a state of debility because it does not receive the nutrition the belly provides. The traditional moral of this well-known fable is that distress may overcome the whole body if there is disharmony. The innovation in Shakespeare's treatment is not his interpretation of the fable but his detailed description of the parts and their functioning. Not only is the stomach given a voice and depicted as a complex entity, the other organs and limbs appear as separate entities that are further fragmented. Especially notable is the case of the plebeians, who are metonymically represented as a many-headed beast, as tongues, and as other body parts to emphasize the lack of class unity. In *Coriolanus*, the body politic explodes into a multitude of disarranged, fragmented parts, and the individual bodies of its members are also displayed as a chaotic entity made up of parts that act on their own. The traditional image of the harmonious body politic is completely subverted by a detailed dismemberment of its parts and by a kind of *mise en abyme* in which each part is shown to be made up of other parts equally subject to disharmony and disintegration.

### The Disorderly Lower Members

As in Shakespeare's *Coriolanus*, in Quevedo's writings the lower classes are portrayed as disjointed entities whose body parts lack harmony. This harsh depiction is clearly part of Quevedo's condemnation of the proclivity for undue social climbing, which he considered affected all the social groups of Spanish society. For Quevedo, the lower members embody the Stoic concept of the *vulgus*, the ignorant mass who, lacking the self-discipline that lineage, resources, and education had bestowed upon the upper classes, are bound to follow their most basic instincts. In myriad witticisms, puns, and jokes, Quevedo represents the lower classes and sections of the middle classes as a grotesque accumulation of body parts subject to the most basic functions and instincts. They are a conglomerate of disjointed organs that, thinking only of their short-term financial interest, lack the organization and discipline required for their long-term well-being and for that of the rest of the body politic. Scatological passages abound in which the lower members of society are portrayed as unable to control their bladders, stomachs, and other organs. It is as if, through their incontinence, these citizens' individual inner organs mirror the unruly role that their class plays within the body politic.

Quevedo's famous *Sueños*, the fantasies depicting the social decay of the Spain of the period, abound in similar passages in which dismemberment is central. This is not forced into the text; instead, it is the direct legacy of two related themes that inform the *Sueños*: the narration of dreams and the descent into hell. These ancient themes were not only alive but, as will be seen, had been rejuvenated by the new anatomical science. The oneiric element is an obvious ingredient of the *Sueños*, present not only in their titles but also in their basic structure of narrated dreams, or rather, nightmares. Dreams often contain images of dismemberment since it is commonly present in the subconscious. Similarly, the narrations of the descent into hell present bodies taken apart as some of the punishments and horrors of the underworld. Furthermore, the *Sueños*, being a satire, thrives on the genre's traditional reliance on dismemberment. A similar combination of dream, satire, and descent into hell is characteristic of one of the *Sueños*'s most influential sources: Lucian of Samosata's *Dialogues of the Dead*. In Lucian's famous satirical work, bodies that have lost their integrity play a central role. For instance, the narrator derides the vanity of the strongest athletes and the most beautiful women, who have been deprived of the skin, flesh, and muscles of which they were so proud; they are reduced to skeletons that are barely held together.[37]

The first *Sueño*, *El sueño del juicio final*, is a social satire that uses the scenario of the resurrection of the dead on Judgment Day. Quevedo describes how, after the blast of the proverbial trumpet, the corpses that time had dispersed are gathered as a prerequisite for the rebirth of the flesh announced in Christian doctrine. He is astonished, however, at how every resurrected soul collects its dispersed limbs and organs with such precision that "nobody mistakenly put on the legs or other members of their neighbours" (1:126; nadie por yerro de cuenta se ponía las piernas ni los miembros de los vecinos). In spite of the thoroughness of the reconstructive process, some of the resurrected bodies come to the Last Judgment intentionally missing extremities or other parts of their bodies that could be held as evidence against them. For example, those who sinned with their eyes, as with the lecherous, do not want to appear in front of the judges with the instrument of their sins on their faces. The same happens with the greedy, who do not want to reattach their hands, and with a long list of sinners who reject the organs that were the main instruments of their sins. The extreme case is that of women who sinned with the beauty of their bodies, who cannot but regret having to present them in front of the tribunal.[38]

Although the dismantled bodies in Quevedo's Doomsday and in other hellish scenarios of his *Sueños* are those of individual subjects, they are often gathered in clusters that match the traditional division of the body politic into professional groups. The clusters are the result of the peculiar way in which sinners are made to pay for their sins in the afterlife scenario Quevedo fancies: they are punished collectively, not individually, according to their predominant sin, which is always a direct consequence of their trade in life. So all the tailors are thieves because they surreptitiously kept part of the fabric which their clients had provided. The grouping of sinners in hell according to their function in society results in a travesty of the body politic, which is normally arranged by the professional function of their members. In Quevedo's dream, hell is a grotesque political body rebuilt by grouping the members according to their shortcomings in fulfilling their professional duties. The different punishment chambers are organized using this criterion and form a perverted, upside-down body politic. Its head is Satan, who rules it from its lowest point. In a comic deflation, Quevedo gives us an anti-Dantesque image of a Satan who lives in proto-bourgeois comfort. He rules hell not from a cavernous throne chamber or a frozen lagoon but in a cosy small study or cabinet ("camarín"; 1:162).[39] There, in the intimacy of private life, he is surrounded by interesting sinners and their peculiar body parts. During Quevedo's visit, Satan proudly shows him some of the rarities that he keeps in his study, such as the old maids, whose virginities have mummified naturally. Satan is presented as one of the proto-collectors who gathered disparate objects in their *Wunderkammern*, *studioli*, or *gabinetes de curiosidades*. These places served to keep curious objects classified on shelves and cabinets so they could be properly admired by guests. This typically Baroque practice, to which much scholarly attention has been paid, anticipates the origin of the modern museum.[40] On the one hand, the cabinets indicate an interest in re-establishing order through organized display in an ever-expanding world being flooded by strange objects from Asia and America and by new ideas that threaten the old order. Collectors arrogate to themselves the role of gods among the objects that make up their collections. God was the first collector when he created Eden and made Adam its (failed) keeper; similarly, Noah's ark is the first attempt at organizing and preserving a collapsing world. On the other hand, Baroque collectors tended to emphasize the exceptional and the monstrous in their cabinets, as if reflecting the worrisome abundance of exceptions in a supposedly ordered universe.

In Quevedo's satirical dream, Satan behaves like a collector who gathers and proudly displays sinners whose recalcitrant nature makes them impervious to fire, along with body parts, such as the virginity of old maidens, that remain eternally incorrupt, as if they were holy relics. But these are only a minimal portion of his vast collection, which comprises the many damned souls he has carefully distributed according to their sins to different rooms of hell. This classification has allowed him to instil order in an otherwise chaotic and dysfunctional Spanish society. Symptomatically, he has organized the citizens according to their failure in life to comply with the divinely inspired social order. However, even Satan is not without reproach in his role as monarch of hell. He has retreated to this room to live conveniently distant from the rest of his kingdom. In a comic deflation, to access him in his cabinet one has to confront not a dangerous monster but a servant who acts as a polite butler. In the intimacy of this room, Satan, surrounded by his gallery of curiosities, does not act like the sovereign that he is; rather he acts like a wealthy private citizen who prefers the comfortable normalcy of private life to the difficult task of overseeing the disorderly body politic of hell. This image is a clear criticism of a king who prefers to remain in the comfortable life of the court and shed his duties while ruling through a *privado*.

A similar image of social disorder, of a dismembered body politic in which its members do not perform their assigned duties, is present in *El Buscón*. Like the *Sueños*, *El Buscón* offers a panoramic view of the lower and middle classes of society, but here Quevedo does not group them in a Doomsday or hellish scenario. Instead, the sequential narration of Don Pablos's attempt at social climbing makes the different types of Spanish society parade in front of the reader: the lowest levels, personified in Don Pablos's family and other equally low characters; and the middle classes, personified in the masters he serves. The body politic is in the background of this picaresque novel even when it seems to be dealing with individual bodies. From the beginning, dismemberment is entrenched in the ignominious professional activities of Pablos's family: his mother visits the gallows at night to gather body parts for her potions; his father is a barber who vainly euphemizes his job as "shearer of cheeks and tailor of beards" (95; tundidor de mejillas y sastre de barbas).[41] Barbers were also the lowest echelon of the medical profession. They practised bloodletting and other basic surgical operations and often were called to help in the dissections with the mechanical aspects of opening the bodies.[42] Even Pablos's younger brother is made to participate in this economy of dismemberment. He steals money from his father's clients while they are being shaved, an operation which Don Pablos describes as "extracting the marrow from their pockets" (9; sacaba el tuétano de las faldriqueras). Later in the novel, his uncle, the executioner of Segovia, is introduced. His job includes hanging limbs of his victims along the roads leading into the city. He actually applies this treatment to Pablos's convicted father, whose execution is the most literal case of dismemberment in the novel. His uncle also encapsulates the relationships of Pablos's family to the body politic, characterized by an attack on its integrity. Their demeaning professions – barber-thief, witch, executioner – imply assaults on the citizens' bodies. Correspondingly, the punishments they receive are assaults on their own bodies, as in the case of his father's execution and, to a lesser degree, in the public flogging of his mother and his younger brother. They are sick limbs that at some point are publicly severed from society. Because his uncle is the executioner and his father is executed, Pablos has the dubious honour of being doubly involved in the disintegration of the body politic.

Body parts appear in *El Buscón* as the result of literal dismemberment, as the ones aforementioned, as well as in tropes. Some metaphorical cases are nearly literal, as when Pablos and his *pícaro* friends are arrested in Madrid. When the officers try to grab them, they are left holding only rags that come apart in their hands because the *pícaros'* clothes are made up of poorly patched together fragments of once expensive clothing. A similar symbolic case is the description of the courtship practices in the convent of Seville. Because the bars that secured the windows of the nunnery allowed the suitors only partial access to the bodies of nuns and novices, Quevedo describes their courtship as a process that parodies the Petrarchan poetic fragmentation of the loved woman's body. This idea of fragmentation is reinforced by the use of a culinary term to refer to the interlaced lovers' bodies as a potpourri ("pepitoria") of parts: "a hand here, a foot there, in another place there were parts such as we eat on Saturdays: heads and tongues, but brains were missing" (293–4; una mano y acullá un pie, en otra parte había cosas de sábado: cabezas y lenguas, aunque faltaban sesos). Finally yet importantly, dismemberment is implied in the metaphorical descriptions of some characters as an incongruous accumulation of non-human ingredients *à la Arcimboldo*, such as the celebrated description of the Dómine Cabra.[43]

As in the *Sueños*, the disintegration of the body politic is always present in *El Buscón*, even when it deals with individual bodies. The techniques through which the individual dismemberments reveal their collective connotation vary. One is narrating them in ways that parody famous or sacred texts by describing similar operations performed on bodies that are traditionally recognized as symbolically collective. A few instances can clarify this technique. During Pablos's dinner with his uncle the executioner and his friends in Segovia, it is implied that the meat pies consumed ("pasteles de a cuatro") contain the flesh of

Pablos's father or other executed convicts. This turns the dinner into a mock Last Supper that includes a grotesque communion with a sacrificial body.[44] This jocular allusion to the body of Christ serves to insinuate the body politic into the scene because the body of Christ is the historical origin of the image of the body politic, as we saw. Similar religious allusions are used to introduce the presence of the body politic in episodes of the novel in which dismemberment is symbolic rather than literal, as when the officers rip off the clothes of the *pícaros* during their arrest, echoing the removal of Christ's clothing by the Roman soldiers before the crucifixion. This also occurs in the passage of courtship in the Seville convent, which contains a clear reference to the religious practice of dividing up the corpses of martyrs and saints to serve as relics. Here, the lovers' adoration of the body parts of their loved ones living behind the grilled windows of a convent is explicitly compared to the way the faithful piously adore the relics ("hueso de santo") behind bars in the churches. Similar overtones are present in Pablos's mother, who steals body parts and clothes from hanged convicts. Her collection includes the ropes, which she expressly associates with the so-called second-class relics – those that have been in contact with the bodies of martyrs.

Parodic references to the dismemberment of the bodies of Christ and the saints are only one of the ways in which individual bodies are connected to the threatened integrity of the Spanish body politic in Quevedo's writings. The connection can take different forms, as in the many passages in which he lampoons those who resort to cosmetic enhancements and modifications to hide bodily imperfections or the ravages of age. Natural or artificial bodily parts are present in these passages, including his interlude *La ropavejera* (The woman who deals in used clothes). This character taken from daily life sells not only used clothes but also false teeth, shoes with high heels, and similar contraptions that she calls "chunks of persons" (2:569; retacillos de personas). In this and similar passages in Quevedo's writings, the reader encounters the old woman who wants to look young and beautiful through the use of cosmetics, padding, and false teeth, the bald or white-haired man who wears a wig or dyes his hair to look younger, or the prostitute who deceitfully pretends to be a virgin. Quevedo sees the practice of changing or disguising one's true nature as a collective obsession that has gripped Spanish society. He is especially irritated by those who want to hide their humble origins to improve their social position and the way they embellish their true nature with pretentious clothes, luxuries, and even the purchase of titles of nobility. All these transforming practices are not only instances of vanity, foolishness, or dishonesty, but they also constitute a widespread practice of destabilization of the social structure through a falsification of categories such as age, marital status, or class. For Quevedo these are ontological realities and, as such, essential for the maintenance of the social order in a body politic where each member must occupy the position into which he or she was born.[45]

Don Pablos's effort in *El Buscón* at disguising his lowly origins in order to climb to high social positions is presented as the epitome of this form of deception. The readers laugh at the ingenuity he and his colleagues show in their attempts to be taken for gentlemen and at the disastrous results of their schemes. Deceptive transformation reaches its apex when, near the end of the novel, Pablos joins a theatrical company. Access to the company's costumes, together with the theatrical abilities he learns, enables him to impersonate all members of society, including the king, who is a stock character in the company's repertoire. The theatrical company is a smaller remake of society that has been hastily "patched" together ("zurcido" as it is literally described), a term that also applies to the patchwork of texts by other companies they perform on stage. Pablos also composes and sells love poems that are made-to-order compositions praising specific body parts of his customers' lovers: "some wanted a poem praising her eyebrows, others wanted a poem to her eyes, or sonnets to her hands, or a short poem to her hair" (286; unos por coplas de cejas, y otros de ojos, cuál sonetos de manos, y cuál romancicos para cabellos). The company is a travesty of the real social order: it is an upside-down world in which the actresses' husbands sell their wives to other men, rogues play the role of emperors and kings, and Pablos thrives with the noble-sounding name of Alonso. Eventually, he becomes the director of the company, which, in its inversion of values, resembles the organization of hell described in the *Sueños*. However, the theatrical company is too unstable to last: the owner of the company is arrested because of his many outstanding debts, and the body politic based on deception that is the company "was *dismembered*" (289; nos *desmembramos* todos; emphasis added).[46]

The danger that the unruly lower members imply for the Spanish body politic is best epitomized in Quevedo's passages presenting the *pícaro*'s inner organs acting on their own. On several occasions, the *pícaro*'s hunger is described as if his stomach and intestines had agency. Pablos refers to the hunger he suffered when he lived with the stingy Dómine Cabra as "my innards cried for justice" (121; mis tripas pedían justicia). When he finally eats after being rescued from the Dómine's house, he speaks of "the celebratory bonfires that my happy intestines ignited" (131; las luminarias que pusieron las tripas de contento).[47] Most notorious are the instances in which the malfunctions of Pablos's intestinal tract result in diarrhoea and vomiting, as when Pablos violently expels the enema back into the face of the old woman who applied it to him. One night he is so scared by the trick that his fellow Alcalá students played on him that he cannot refrain from soiling his bed. Other lower characters are also affected by similar incontinence, such as the inmates of the prison to which Pablos and his colleagues are taken, who continuously break wind and soil their clothes. The inability of all these members of the humblest social strata to control their intestinal tracts replicates their disorderly behaviour as lower organs of the Spanish body politic. The consequences of their unruliness are detrimental not only for themselves but also for the rest of society. In the words of Kamen, "the mobility of the poor, the rising tide of beggary and vagrancy … make poverty spill out of its old restricted channels and flood over so as to threaten the security of the upper classes."[48]

## The Ambitious Interiority of the *Privado*

The *privado*, *valido*, or royal favourite (similar to the *pícaro*) is often presented in Quevedo's writings as a limb affecting the integrity of the body politic. However, the treatment of these two figures differs. Whereas scatological urges pressure the *pícaro*'s lower organs, subtler humoural disorders affect the *privado*'s higher organs. Ambitious thoughts and aspirations build up inside his head and heart, the organs that best represent his elevated position in the body politic. Also different is how Quevedo faces the dissection of the *privado*, who is always analysed as an individual, never as a social group gathered in collective scenarios. This individualized treatment matches the unique status of the *privado*, whom the king has singled out to hold the highest political position.[49]

Quevedo's most extended exposition of how the interiority of the *privado* may endanger the body politic is his short satirical pamphlet *Visita y anatomía de la cabeza del Cardenal Armando Richelieu*. It was written in 1635, a few months before Spain declared war on France. In this political satire, Quevedo lampoons the powerful favourite of Louis XIII, Cardinal Richelieu, whose head becomes the fantastic scenario of a journey of exploration. To this end, Quevedo brings Vesalius – the father of modern anatomy, who had been dead since 1564 – back to life and makes him literally walk inside Richelieu's head through his ear.[50] Upon his return, Vesalius's prognosis is that the conspiratory activities that go on inside the ambitious cardinal's head are infecting the whole body politic of France, turning it into a deformed monster with two heads: the natural one, King Louis XIII's, and a hydra-like overgrowth, Richelieu's.[51] Quevedo's choice of target for this pamphlet must be understood as a consequence not only of the war that had broken out between France and Spain but also of Richelieu being a threatening political figure. He was the most notorious representative of the *privanza*, which had developed simultaneously in several monarchies. The defenders of an absolute monarchy had problems coming to terms with the existence of a figure so dangerously close to the king.[52]

The presence of a *privado* was not exclusively a French or Spanish phenomenon; it extended to several European states during the first half of the seventeenth century. Bérenger has identified the contemporary emergence of the *privado* as a pan-European institution that began in the early seventeenth century and disappeared after 1660. Mazarin and Richelieu in France, Lerma and Olivares in Spain, and Buckingham in England are the most famous cases, but *privados* ruled in other countries in the same period. Bérenger rejects the traditional interpretation that this pervasiveness of *privados* was a consequence of the period's kings having exceptionally indulgent or weak characters that made them inept or disinclined to take on the traditional tasks of the monarch. A better explanation is to see the widespread phenomenon as a new political development that resulted from the increasingly complex state machinery.[53] This situation seems to match the situation in Spain. Philip II was the last of the monarchs who tried to handle the enormous task of ruling a modern state alone. Appropriately, he went down in history as a king who personally took care of all the affairs of his vast empire. He is often depicted as continually immersed in endless minutiae and red tape, to the point that it prevented him from fulfilling other important tasks of a monarch.

Another reason often given for the *privado*'s emergence is that it coincided with the development of the doctrine of reason of state, which required the monarch to have a double for the pressing state affairs that he could not resolve with the sure-handedness expected of a Christian ruler. In Spain, the anti-Machiavellian tone prevails in many political treatises dealing with the limits in *simulación* and *disimulación* permissible in a Christian monarch. Prudence is always recommended, and some forms of reservation are accepted, but lying is not acceptable, especially in matters pertaining to faith or justice.[54] Since the *privados* were not anointed persons, they served as expendable buffers between the kings and the indignities of daily government.[55]

Spain's institutionalization of the *privado* figure in those years results from the same conditions existing in the rest of Europe, a few peculiarities apart. Because the Spanish monarch's inaccessibility and seclusion in the court was strictly enforced, the function of the *privado* became even more relevant than in other countries.[56] In his detailed study of the *privanza* in Spain, Tomás y Valiente shows that only in the first half of the seventeenth century did the figure of the *privado* take a form distinct from its many medieval antecedents or from Philip II's royal secretaries. The institutionalization of an almighty *privado* is a reaction of the Spanish high nobility against the rising merchant class and, at the same time, a privatization of the public sphere, which falls under the control of the *privado*'s family or clan.[57] In Spain, the theoretical discourse around the *privanza* is more complex and abundant than in the other European countries. For instance, it is the only country in which the concept of the *privado* as the friend of the king is fully developed.[58] The peculiar nature of the *privanza* in Spain is evident also in the different treatment of the favourite in English and Spanish theatre. The Spanish theatrical tradition treats the favourite as a tragic figure, a tendency that goes back to medieval ballads and, especially, to Don Álvaro de Luna, the *privado* of John II and constable of Castile, executed in 1453. Accordingly, many *comedias* in which the *privado* plays a central role deal with the theme of the fall from fortune. Overall, Spanish dramatists are more inclined to depict a positive, even flattering image of the *privado* than their English counterparts.[59]

Quevedo's adult life coincided with the tenure of the two most powerful *privados* in Spanish history: Francisco de Sandoval y Rojas, Duke of Lerma, the *privado* of Philip III; and Gaspar de Guzmán, Count-Duke of Olivares, *privado* of Philip IV and an influential figure in Quevedo's life. Pedro Girón de la Cueva, Duke of Osuna and Spanish viceroy in Italy, although not technically a *privado*, should also be included.[60] Quevedo himself was a kind of *privado* of the Duke of Osuna in Italy and, to a much lesser degree, of Olivares in the initial years of their relationship. The importance of being the *privado* of a powerful person is best explained in the definition of the word *privado* in the 1611 etymological dictionary by Covarrubias, which emphasizes the individuating effect that this relation caused: "To be a *privado* means to be favoured by some lord who, by choosing him, makes him different from the others."[61] But although in his writings Quevedo praises the absolute submission to the authority figure that has singled one out as *privado*, he also points out the need to oppose this figure under some circumstances. He gives the individual some autonomy from authority when a higher moral order is at stake. This critical stance is reflected, for instance, in his *Migajas sentenciosas*, in which Quevedo advances an interesting etymology of the word *privado* that differs from Covarrubias's: "*Privado* is he who, in private and when nobody else is present, because of the respect due to the figure of the prince, is able to oppose the will of his lord when he is unfair" (1:1085; Privado es el que sabe y puede privadamente y a solas, por el respeto debido a príncipes, oponerse a la voluntad injusta de su príncipe).[62]

A highly idealized example of this complex relationship between the *privado* and the prince is presented in Quevedo's play *Cómo ha de ser el privado*, which he wrote towards the end of the 1620s. In this period, he was on excellent terms with the *privado* Olivares, of whom the play is a clear exaltation. The fact that the action takes place in Naples barely hides the fact that the main characters are Philip IV and Olivares, whose name is easily discernible as an anagram of the Marquis of Valisero.[63] Quevedo's writing of the play coincides with the resurgence of interest in the dramatic treatment of the *privado* brought about by the public execution of Rodrigo Calderón in 1621. Although technically not a *privado*, Calderón had been the right hand of the Duke of Lerma. His dramatic fall and ensuing execution as punishment for many years of public embezzlement triggered a revival of the tragic figure of the *privado* in Spanish poetry and theatre. Even Quevedo wrote a poem dedicated to Rodrigo Calderón regarding his fall from fortune.[64]

Under these circumstances, it was obviously tempting for Quevedo to write a play about the figure of the *privado*. Also tempting was the fact that the traditional treatment of the *privado* in Spanish drama dealt with the fall from fortune or the importance of friendship, which are subjects dear to neo-Stoicism. *Cómo ha de ser el privado* includes these two themes in its conventional plot. The king is enamoured of a lady-in-waiting, but thanks to the advice of Valisero, manages to control his passion and renounce her for the good of the state. In a parallel secondary plot, two suitors compete for the hand of the king's sister: one of them is a monarch from a Catholic country, and the other is a prince from a Protestant country. Once again, Valisero's good advice is pivotal in convincing the king to give his sister's hand to the Catholic suitor.

This parallel plot is not far from the events of the Spanish court at the time, corresponding to the famous incognito visit of the Prince of Wales in 1623 and to the possibility that he might marry Philip IV's sister, Doña María, who finally married the Catholic king of Hungary in 1626.[65]

Although *Cómo ha de ser el privado* follows the traditional treatment of the *privado* as a tragic figure, the play is not properly speaking a tragedy. It ends not in the favourite's fall and execution but in a happy ending thanks to the *privado*'s advice. The tragic element comes from Valisero's reluctant acceptance of the onerous position of *privado* and, especially, from the death of his only son. Valisero agrees to be *privado* only out of duty, not personal ambition. From the beginning of the play, Valisero is in control of his erotic impulses, unlike the king. During the play, the reader witnesses how Valisero has to tame another passion traditionally confronted by the Stoics: the grief arising from the premature death of a beloved person. When he is told of the death of his only son and heir, he launches a Stoic tirade against fortune and then resigns himself to his fate. He will continue to fulfil his duty of serving his king without looking for recompense other than the self-rewarding exercise of virtue. Valisero is presented as a Senecan figure, once again a barely veiled reference to Olivares, who had lost his only son in similar circumstances and also was so interested in Stoicism that he was sometimes celebrated as a modern Spanish Seneca.[66] The stoic control of passions is central in the play. Valisero, who is fighting his *luctus*, also has to teach the king to control his passions, specifically the king's love for the beautiful lady-in-waiting Serafina. The king is aware that he is in a battle with himself: "I am fighting with my own eyes / they want to look at her / but my reason is restraining them" (2:605; Con mis ojos batallo / los ojos quieren mirar / la razón los ha enfrenado). One of his most valuable strategies is to develop self-knowledge. Comparing his royal person to a ship, the king describes the use of a sounding line to probe the depths of his feelings and not run aground or be bogged down in an ocean of love (2:630). Finally, thanks to the advice and example of Valisero, the king claims victory over his passions: "today I will cry victory / if I can subdue my passions" (2:600; podré decir que hoy victorioso he sido / si mis afectos modero).

In other writings, Quevedo spells out the important role that the *privado* plays in the king's fight with his nature. For instance, in his *Migajas sentenciosas* he says that princes are, like everyone else, servants of their own natural passions, and the choice of a favourite is similar to the choice of a doctor (1:1088). The *privado*'s role at the king's side is like that of a doctor who monitors the king's passions, which according to the Stoics are the result of an imbalance of the humours. Passions are disease-like pressures inside the body that have to be kept at bay if one wants to follow a higher virtue.[67] In *Cómo ha de ser el privado*, this concept of the passions is best expressed by the *gracioso*, Violín, who, as is traditional in the *comedias*, talks about the same issues as the noble characters but at a correspondingly lower level. Violín embodies the *vulgus*'s inability to control the passions, an inability expressed through his bodily functions; he depicts the inner corporeal pressures not as passions and vapours but as defecation when he jokes that he feels an uncontrollable need to give birth to his twin – his stools – buried in his intestines. He finishes the joke with the anecdote of a person who died in a similar situation from exerting excessive pressure on the intestines (2:617).

As well as a doctor who heals the embodied king of his passions, *Cómo ha de ser el privado* presents the *privado* as the king's friend. This relationship is described in highly embodied terms when the king offers the position of *privado* to the Marquis of Valisero:

> How could you, Marquis
> You who are my favourite,
> Be against us becoming
> A unity in our friendship
> So that in this our friendship
> King and counsellor may become
> A single being and will
> Between two breasts divided?
> (¿Cómo, Marqués, siendo vos
> mi privado, estáis opuesto
> a que se haga un compuesto
> de la amistad de los dos,
> y con estrecha amistad
> estén el rey y el valido,
> y en dos pechos repartido
> un ser y una voluntad?)                                    (2:596)

The king appeals to the classical theme of the unity of friends in his invitation to Valisero to join him in a shared body. The result is a singular entity made up of two separate individuals fused into a *compuesto*, a word that implies alchemy, especially amalgamation of noble metals, and was commonly applied to the indissoluble union of body and soul – "este compuesto de cuerpo y alma" (this compound of body and soul), writes Quevedo in *La cuna y la sepultura* in reference to the human being (1:1205).[68] Although the king does not mention the hierarchical difference in the nature of the parts making up this new compound entity, Valisero brings it up in his speech of acceptance: he compares himself to an atom that receives light from the king, who is the sun. With these words, Valisero agrees to the union, but he stipulates that he will always be in a position inferior to the king's in the new common body. The creation of this corporeal unity matches Hillman's observation about Shakespeare, who "seems to have imagined human relations through corporeal existence," since the characters in his plays conceive relations such as friendship "in terms of entering or being within their bodies, or having one's own body inhabited or possessed by another."[69] As a result of this union, during the rest of the play Valisero acts as if he has given up his own self to be absorbed into the king's body, of which he has become a mere organ. This renunciation of his self is also expressed in the presentation of him as if he were dead in life. Thus, when he is forced to take an award of 12,000 ducats from the king, Valisero accepts the money with the condition that he will use it only to build his own tomb, given that his only heir is dead (2:628).[70]

The *privado*'s need to become a dead body walking reappears in different forms in Quevedo's writings. In his *Política de Dios*, Quevedo states, "An Arab says, sir, that the king must be like an eagle: he must be surrounded by dead bodies, but not be a dead body" (1:570; El rey, señor, – dice un árabe –, ha de ser como águila, que ha de tener cuerpos muertos alrededor y no ser cuerpo muerto). In the same book, John the Baptist is presented as the ideal *privado*: "John the Baptist was just the voice [of Christ], and that is the ideal for a minister, who is mere voiced air, nothing else" (1:623; Fue el Bautista voz, Señor, eso ha de ser el ministro, la voz formada, y dala el ser quien la forma. Es aire articulado, poco y delgado ser por sí sola).[71] The *privado* has to become bodiless. Quevedo indicates that all the *privado*'s limbs and organs, especially those that symbolize the possibility of action, quit being his own to become something the king has loaned to him: "This is the king's duty: to give his people what they are missing, and this happens when he gives somebody eyes and ears so that this person can see and hear on his behalf" (1:618; Éste es el oficio del rey, dar a los suyos lo que les falta, esto se hace cuando el príncipe da sus ojos y sus oídos a otro para que vea y oiga por él).

This lengthy exposition of how the ideal *privado* is characterized in *Cómo ha de ser el privado* was necessary because the figure of the *privado* contained in *Visita y anatomía de la cabeza del Cardenal Armando Richelieu* is the exact opposite. In this pamphlet Richelieu is denigrated as the worst sort of *privado*, one who cannot control his own passions, especially his ambition to make himself king. Instead of demonstrating Valisero's praiseworthy self-denial, Richelieu is governed by an ambition that turns him into a monstrous outgrowth, a protruding second head on the body politic of France. The pamphlet is dated 12 October 1635, a few months after the French king Louis XIII declared war on Philip IV.[72] It is just one of the several anti-French pamphlets circulating at that time in Spain and is part of the hostilities of the war in the form of propaganda against an enemy presented as intrinsically evil and grotesque.[73] *Visita y anatomía de la cabeza del Cardenal Armando Richelieu* describes a fantastical journey inside a living being. This is a narrative sub-genre with ancient literary roots in the biblical story of Jonah swallowed by a marine monster and in a similar story by the Hellenistic writer Lucian of Samosata (already mentioned), whose influence on Quevedo is well known. This kind of trip is connected to the descent into hell because hell, in its earliest forms, is the stomach of a monster, as represented in the medieval legends of Hellmouth or the jaws of hell.[74] A more recent predecessor of this type of journey is the story of how Alcofribas entered the body of Pantagruel, as well as Xenomanes's anatomization of Fastilent, both by Rabelais, whose name is mentioned in Quevedo's pamphlet.

Another likely influence on Quevedo's *Visita y anatomía de la cabeza del Cardenal Armando Richelieu* is the Spanish poet Luis Barahona de Soto's extended poem *Primera parte de la Angélica* (Granada, 1586). This famous poem, also known as *Las lágrimas de Angelica*, is based on the love between the giant Medoro and Angelica in *Orlando furioso*. Quevedo, who wrote a burlesque version of *Orlando furioso*, likely knew Barahona's poem.[75] In the fourth canto of Barahona's poem, the heroic Zenagrio fights with the ogre Orco, a character similar to Góngora's Polifemo, to liberate Angelica and Medoro from the island where the ogre keeps them captive. In the battle the ogre swallows Zenagrio, who descends into the stomach of the monster uninjured because in his childhood he had been immersed in the waters of hell by a fairy. From the stomach he proceeds to explore the entrails of Orco, which are human except for their enormous proportions. Zenagrio describes the organs in mostly Vesalian terms, depicting their functioning according to the humoural medicine of the period. So he observes the flow of the different humours that control the bodily functions and the temperament of the ogre. He notices the black fluid of cholera rising as Orco is enraged when he realizes that Angelica does not love him. Possessed by wrath, Orco begins then to swallow trees and enormous rocks. Zenagrio avoids being crushed by escaping to the area of the heart, where he is safe only because air enters to be mixed with the blood. Then he intentionally obstructs the pipe through which the air comes into the cavity of the heart. Orco begins to feel that he is suffocating and, in an attack of maddening rage, rips open his breast and stomach with his own hands. Zenagrio survives and Angelica rescues him from inside the dead monster.[76]

Barahona, a medical doctor, probably got the ideas for his poem from anatomy books circulating in Spain that analysed the human body as a house or castle. Although using the image of the body as a house in medical writings was mostly a medieval practice, in Spain it survived well into the sixteenth century. Many Spanish anatomical manuals of the post-Vesalian era were still medieval in their predominantly Galenic content. Moreover, Spanish manuals that contained the most recent anatomical knowledge had a tendency to use outdated imagery and describe the body as a microcosmic entity organized in the form of a fortress, polis, or state. Some of them resorted to dream narrations to present allegories of the body. The earliest of the contemporary Spanish anatomical treatises to use this trope for the description of anatomy is *Libro de anatomía* (1542), by Luis Lobera de Ávila, a surgeon of Charles V. The book includes a dream in which the human body is described as a castle defended by different captains, who are organs such as the stomach and the liver, whose orders other organs follow. Similar but much more developed is the dream contained in the *Libro de anatomía del hombre* (1551) by Bernardino Montaña de Monserrate, also a physician serving Charles V. The book contains a dream narrated in the form of a dialogue between the Marquis of Mondéjar and his doctor; in it the human body – in this case a woman's – is presented as a tower or fortress that serves as a royal palace to shelter a princess: the *anima rationalis*. The different activities in the fortress are identified with the functioning of the organs, which are aimed towards both the defence of the fortress and the creation of a new fortress in the womb. The allegorical imagery in this book is much more detailed than in the previous one. For instance, the head is described as a vast library in which books are shelved in different rooms according to their subject matter, an image that reappears in *Visita y anatomía*.[77]

Other possible influences on Quevedo's *Visita y anatomía* are several treatises published towards the end of the sixteenth century that are, properly speaking, not medical but present the human body using the image of a republic: Miguel de Sabuco's *Nueva filosofía de la naturaleza del hombre* (1582) or Iván Sánchez Valdés de la Plata's extensive *Corónica y historia general del hombre* (1598). The latter has chapters with self-explanatory titles such as "How similar man is to a building" and "How man resembles a kingdom, and a city, and the ruling of a city or any people, and their buildings and fortifications" (En que declara cómo el hombre concuerda con muchos edificios; En que declara cómo el hombre es semejante a un reino y a la gobernación dél, y a una ciudad y a cualquier pueblo y a la gobernación de cualquier pueblo y a sus edificios y posturas de edificios y guarniciones). However, the most interesting book in this category is *República original sacada del cuerpo humano*, published in 1587 by Jerónimo Merola, professor of medicine in Barcelona. This book uses the analogy of the body as a state to demonstrate that the existence of a hierarchical order in society is a natural and necessary phenomenon. Following the Platonic conception of political order, Merola defends the idea that those who obey the rulers do so because it is in their own nature to be in a subordinate position. Accordingly, chapter 25, entitled "How royal policy is represented in the body," derogatorily refers to *democratia* – in the negative meaning of "demos" as the masses – as what happens when the hands, the spleen, or other lower organs want to rule instead of the higher organs.[78]

Finally, one direct influence on Quevedo is the nearly contemporary satirist Trajano Boccalini (1556–1613), who published Menippean satires about Spain between 1612 and 1614 in Venice, which Quevedo most likely read during the years he lived in Italy (1613–19). Some of Boccalini's satires are similar in tone and setting to *Visita y anatomía*, especially the one in which famous doctors of antiquity are summoned by the gods to cure sick empires and kingdoms. Followers of Boccalini published similar anti-Spanish pamphlets in the same period, such as *Esequie delle reputazione di Spagna*, printed in 1615, in which the corpse of the reputation of Spain is dissected by famous anatomists. The doctors find several organs affected by an illness that has spread throughout the nation. The intestines are deemed too long and unfit for normal digestion, making the Spaniards so hungry that they have to go to the New World for riches to satiate their gargantuan appetite.[79]

Quevedo's *Visita y anatomía* has many similarities to the aforementioned texts, as detailed analysis reveals. To understand this complex pamphlet better, it is best to divide it into three parts according to their content. The first narrates a fictitious meeting at the University of Montpellier, which was famous for its medical studies. The meeting is under the guidance of Jacques de Billy, abbot of Saint Michel and a renowned humanist who had died nearly fifty years before the pamphlet was written. Present are a group of famous doctors and learned men, most of them also dead by the time the pamphlet was written. The meeting resembles the official consultations that took place when a contagious disease or an epidemic threatened a city or a country.[80] The words "visit" in the title and "exorcism" in the first lines of the pamphlet (1:903) point to the interventions performed by religious authorities when widespread psychosis or heresy were suspected in a community. In these cases, the Inquisition sent envoys to inspect specific towns or extended areas, especially the countryside, which was considered to be more prone to such deviation because of its remoteness. The term "visit" was also used to refer to the general inspections of territories of the Spanish crown by royal envoys. That these administrative and fiscal examinations conjured up anatomical associations can be seen in a commentary made by a colleague of Juan de Ovando, who in 1567 was commissioned to lead a visit for the council of the Indies: "Normally [Juan de Ovando] dealt with all business entrusted to him by anatomizing it, creating new skeletons and proposals until he found all their heads; then he would study the heads and master them."[81]

The attendants at the meeting deem the body politic of France to be affected by the "French disease" (mal francés), a pun that plays with the name often used in Spain to refer to syphilis. They conclude that the disease, which infects the whole body, has to come from the head. Since the king cannot be suspect, the head of the powerful favourite Richelieu is believed to be responsible. Given the gravity of the situation, Vesalius volunteers to examine the cardinal's head, but the first difficulty is to find it, because it is not where it is expected to be, namely, on top of Richelieu's body. After several puns on how Richelieu "has lost his head" – i.e., he has lost his mind – to the point that even he himself does not know where it is, Jacques de Billy announces that the head is in Rome. The head being in Rome is attributed to Richelieu's similarity to the Roman god Janus, who has two faces looking in opposite directions, an allusion to Richelieu's double alliances in the wars between Protestants and Catholics and to his occasional alliances with the Turks.[82]

The aberrant outgrowth that is Richelieu's head is harmful for both the natural head – the king's – and the whole body politic of France. The monstrosity of this head is made obvious in the unnatural autonomy it has developed from the rest of the body politic, which allows it to roam freely in Rome to pursue its own interests. This conspicuous autonomy is the opposite of what is expected of the ideal *privado*, like Valisero, who was discreetly subsumed within the body of the king, or like John the Baptist, who limited his existence to being just a voice. If Richelieu does not have a body, it is not a consequence of having given up his own interests to be at the service of the state, as was the case with Valisero. Richelieu's lack of a body is the atrophy resulting from his exclusive dedication to ambitious plotting. He is an example of what, in his "Carta al cristianísimo Rey Luis Decimotercio," Quevedo calls "cerebros desvelados" (1:889; restless brains). Richelieu, reduced to a bodiless thinking head, is the epitome of ambitious men who live only to concoct intrigues.

The second and longest part of the pamphlet contains Vesalius's report to the committee after coming back from his trip to Rome. He relates how, to enter Richelieu's head, he pretended to bring news affecting Richelieu's ambition to depose the king of France. When Vesalius was still at a considerable distance from Richelieu's head, he was absorbed, together with many other nonsensical stories and lies, by the cardinal's ear, which acted as a Charybdis that engulfed all kinds of rumours.[83] Once inside the head, Vesalius encountered three rooms or chambers where the mental *potentiae* – memory, will, and reason – run their operations. The operations taking place inside these chambers, which the fictitious Vesalius relates to the committee upon his return, are parodic developments on the humoural psychology of the period. According to the predominant theories, the ventricles acted as containers in which the humours, and other liquids and gasses, were mixed and boiled. Their ethereal by-products constituted the base for the elusive mental processes. Juan Huarte de San Juan, in his famous *Examen de ingenios para las ciencias* (1574), is specific about the number, location, and function of these empty spaces: "Four ventricles are required so that the rational soul can ponder and philosophize: one on the right side of the brain, the second one on the left, the third one in the middle of these two, and the fourth one at the back" (Son menester cuatro ventrecillos para que el ánima racional pueda discurrir y filosofar: el uno ha de estar colocado en el lado derecho del celebro, y el segundo en el izquierdo, y el tercero en el medio de estos dos, y el cuarto en la postrera parte del cerebro).[84] The existence of chambers in the brain described by Quevedo's Vesalius also conforms to the new anatomical knowledge discovered and illustrated by the real Vesalius and his followers. The anatomists had established the existence of cavities in the head, but not all agreed on the number of cavities, three or four, or on what happened in those empty spaces, because the results of the dissections were inconclusive.[85]

Quevedo makes Vesalius visit the three chambers inside Richelieu's head lantern in hand, as if he were going through the circles of hell. To Vesalius's surprise, the head of Richelieu is not empty, as he had initially thought – a pun based on the Spanish expression for dull people as those who "no tienen sesos" (have no brains). Quite to the contrary, he finds plenty of matter that, upon further inspection, turns out to be not brains but a turban folded in a way that resembles coiled brains. This turban is a jocular allusion to Richelieu's alleged secret alliance with the Turks. Vesalius reports also that all kinds of liquids flood the chamber. This matches the natural fluids that, according to the anatomical treatises of the period, were found when a head was dissected.[86] In the case of Richelieu, however, the liquids are a by-product of his perverted mind, such as a lake made up of tears that he is ready to shed whenever he feels the need to deceive somebody. The lake of tears inside Richelieu's head echoes the lakes of hell, and it is one of the many elements in Vesalius's report that reveal the hellish nature of Richelieu's head. The three rooms where the *potentiae* operate seem like dungeons in which Richelieu is being tortured by his own ambition. This is a punishment similar to the one suffered by Judas, who, as Quevedo writes in his *Política de Dios*, was the worst *privado*, "because a demon has possessed him and taken hold of his entrails, his heart, and the most intimate part of his mind" (1:592; porque el demonio que lo poseía había entrado en sus entrañas, el que poseía el corazón de Judas poseía lo retirado de su mente). Similar to the manner in which Judas, Brutus, and Cassius – the three traitors to their natural leaders often denounced by Quevedo – suffer their deserved punishment by being eternally devoured by Satan in Dante's hell, Richelieu is receiving punishment in life inside his own head. This is his own private hell, where he lives in the tormenting solitude of his voluntary separation from the rest of the body politic, which is the tangible embodiment of the divinely

instituted order. His wilful separation entails a renunciation of the ben-
eficial effect of the divine order and leaves him at the mercy of the
involuntary operations of his own inner passions.

Richelieu's strong passions make the *potentiae* operate contrary to
their nature. Thus, his memory is paradoxically ruled by forgetfulness,
as evidenced by his ingratitude towards those who helped him reach
his high position. The chamber in which Richelieu's damaged memory
operates is described as a chaotic library whose books contain many
underlined passages that Richelieu considered worth remembering.
The most annotated volumes are Rabelais's *Gargantua and Pantagruel*
and *Les paraboles de Cicquot, en forme d'advis, sur l'estat du roy de Navarre*.
By emphasizing Richelieu's interest in Rabelais's stories of the two
giants, Quevedo alludes to the monstrous nature of the cardinal.[87] *Les
paraboles de Cicquot* (1593), a book attributed to a jester and adviser of
Kings Henry III and Henry IV, was considered to be a parodic version
of Machiavelli's famous treatise.[88] A maxim is inscribed on the walls of
Richelieu's cranium stating that those ministers who want to depose
their kings should flatter the populace and, once they have gained
power, should mistreat it. Given the presence of political maxims in
Richelieu's memory, the medical committee decides that they should
summon Montaigne, the reputed authority on the Machiavellian art of
ruling according to aphorisms.[89]

The private library inside Richelieu's head reflects the significance, as
well as the wariness, associated with the possession of books and the
practice of private reading at the time. As Eisenstein and others have
shown, the abundance and the affordability of titles that the printing
press initiated were integral to the development of early modern individuality. After the popularization of printed books, reading in the privacy of one's well-furnished personal library or study supplanted the
collective reading aloud of costly codices and manuscript books.
According to Roger Chartier, "in the course of the sixteenth and seventeenth centuries in Western Europe, reading, for the literate élite,
became the act par excellence of intimate, private, and secret leisure."[90]
The negative effects such a habit might entail are emphasized in Quevedo's pamphlet. It clearly parodies Montaigne's secluded library
tower on his estate in the Périgord, the privacy that he repeatedly
claimed to enjoy when he retreated to consult his books, and his habit
of decorating the ceiling of the room with his favourite maxims in Latin
and Greek. That such isolated absorption might have deleterious consequences is a commonplace epitomized by Don Quixote's insanity,

triggered by his excessive reading of the many fictional books in his library. If in his case the results are mostly laughable and inconsequential adventures, in another they may be dangerous for the republic. The immoral Machiavellianism that Richelieu extracted from the ill-reputed titles he chose to peruse in his private library proves it.

The chamber in which Richelieu's *voluntas* or will operates is reddish and swollen, a condition attributed to a contagion from the red colour of his cardinal's hat. As was the case with the other *potentiae*, his will is distorted by his ambition, which has taken over and rules according to the Latin maxim "sic volo, sic jubeo, sic pro ratione voluntas" (1:99; thus I wish it, thus I command it, thus is my will in place of my reason).[91] Will and reason are so entangled that his ambition to be king hampers the moderating effect of reason. The chamber also contains the blood-covered bodies of those whom Richelieu ordered secretly murdered or publicly tried and executed. Quevedo explains their presence in the chamber where the will operates by resorting to a pun on the Spanish expression "tener voluntad" (to have ill will towards somebody). Finally, the chamber where his reason resides is suffused "with a viscous acrid fluid that flowed from his memory through orifices and windows" (se alimentaba manando por unos orificios y ventanillas un alimento viscoso y acre de su memoria) and by a resident demon called "Yo me entiendo" (1:908; I am the only one to understand what I mean).[92] His sick reason is spinning in an endless loop of ambitious, faulty lucubration, using the customary connectors of scholastic logic, such as *ergo, sequitur, probo consequentiam, nego maiorem*, etc.

*Visita y anatomía* ends with the decision reached by the committee: Richelieu is suffering from *morbus regius* (king's evil or scrofula), a disease similar to jaundice and often associated with envy and ambition because one of its symptoms is a yellowish complexion.[93] He is so sick that he cannot be cured, and his disease is so contagious that it may infect the king's brother, Gaston d'Orleans, and the Queen Mother, Maria de Medici. The only cure is not medical but political. But because it is well known that the king hears and sees only through the ears and eyes of Richelieu, denouncing him to the king is useless, as has been proven on previous occasions. The pamphlet comes to an abrupt end with the committee adjourning the session without a decision on which line of action to implement, except the vague advice that Richelieu should be commended so highly that the king may become jealous and depose him.[94]

The image resulting from Quevedo's pamphlet is that of a Richelieu at the mercy of physiological processes that take place inside his head, described as a pump that absorbs and expels through the ears and that transfers liquids and vapours among its chambers according to differences in pressure and temperature. The image combines the Christian-Stoic dislike of the body with the emerging perception of it as an ordinary physical object and not as a microcosm.[95] Not only the body but also most of the mental functions are *exteriora* in the Stoic sense of the conditioned elements in embodied existence that are beyond our control. Except for the most elusive parts of mental operations involved in the nebulous workings of the soul and its free will, not all the other operations of the mind are properly ours since they are physically rooted in the flow of humours, which follow mechanical laws.[96] Richelieu's head is a complex machine, but it is neither a clock-like organism that sings the praises of its creator with its complexity and precision nor, much less, a microcosm whose perfect functioning reflects the divine order, as was the case in Granada's optimistic description of human anatomy.[97] Trapped in a dooming complexity, this body is mechanical not in the objective sense implied in the Cartesian body-machine, or in the sense of the glorified machine of modern technology, but in the sense of a mechanical contraption made of flesh, prone to passions and decay, and subject to the blind, meaningless rule of physics. This rule dooms it to repetitive movements, like the hydraulic automata of the period, which are examined in the next chapter.

## Embodiment and the Interiority of the Body Politic

Quevedo dismisses the idea of an autonomous subject that is based on the private sense of interiority fostered by individuated embodiment. He denounces such interiority not only as defective but also as dangerous for the survival of the idealized social and political order he championed. For him, the sense of privacy and uniqueness that brews within the opaque boundaries of one's skin is not sufficient to posit a universally valid selfhood, independent from the external social order. The necessary submission of all members to the social order implies renouncing the alluring delusion of autonomy that individual embodiment promotes. No matter how seductively real and compelling the phenomena that occur inside the body may feel, they cannot be taken as absolute truths or inform action. As well as "gut feelings" and passions, higher mental operations must also be distrusted. Intellectual hubris is fostered by choosing and committing to memory apposite passages from private reading in the seclusion of one's personal library. Richelieu's head, which contains such a library, is ruled by unbalanced humours. In a continuous state of disarray, it operates through a continuous suction and expulsion of words and ideas through the ears and the eyes, which resembles the scatological bodily functions that characterize the out-of-control behaviour of the populace.

In spite of his extended and creative use of the image of the body politic, Quevedo sees the embodiment implied in it as categorically different from the embodiment of the human being. Like the human body, the body politic is made up of distinct organs – the individual citizens – but its interiority is neither the result of their interactions nor the combination of the interiorities of its members, nor yet subject to them. The interiority of the body politic is one of a superior order and, thus, supersedes that of its constituting members and their interactions. In addition, unlike the human body, which is impelled by its organs and their production of humours, the body politic should not act in a mechanical way as the result of the pressure of social groups. For the body politic to function as Quevedo envisions it, citizens' interiorities are to be treated as dangerous surpluses resulting from their inevitable individual embodiment, as potentially toxic by-products that have to be sacrificed at the altar of the order that must encompass heaven, earth, and human society. For Quevedo, this "natural" order represents a higher truth than the inner pressures that the human organs generate, no matter how alluring and real they feel.

Such a necessary renunciation is part of the same characterization of human nature as flawed found in the Christian and other traditions in which Quevedo was immersed. This sobering view, so masterfully developed in his metaphysical poetry, is now enlisted to protect the body politic against its own members' claim for autonomy. The members must practise self-renunciation to counteract the alluring delusion of individual autonomy. This task may take on different forms depending on the position of the subject within society. Although everybody must follow regimes of self-discipline, such as the ones offered by Stoicism, Christianity, or the discourse of patriotism and service to the king, the upper classes are especially bound to do so. If they cannot control their passions, they fail to fulfil their leading role in society. Furthermore, one passion is especially dangerous for them: ambition for absolute power. As with Lucifer or the Titans of antiquity, they may be tempted to become godlike and usurp the place of the king, a position to which they are never entitled. For the rest of society, especially for its lowest members, an autonomy based on the dictates of their embodied individuality would result in surrendering to the capriciousness of the mechanical forces inside them. This would imply a dangerous attack on the order that keeps society together. Since for these groups internal self-discipline is not possible, coerced submission may be necessary.

# 4

# Cervantes's Mechanical Interiors and
# Zayas's Female Anatomies

The texts studied in this chapter lack direct allusions to anatomical dissection but are, nonetheless, true dissective narratives dealing with personal privacy and its exposure. As was the case in previous texts, they describe the punitive inspection of interiorities and reactions to the inspection ranging from resistance to compliance in highly embodied terms. They also conclude with the inquisitive project's failure to establish the subjects' innocence or guilt against the intrinsic complexity and resilient opacity of the interiors. To represent these kinds of texts I chose Cervantes's and Zayas's *novelas* because they are emblematic instances of a newly born genre characterized by the free use of fantasy and a preference for contemporary themes and scenarios. This results in a free treatment of pressing issues that is ideal for a more or less conscious resurfacing of the anxiety of interiority. The two most widely studied Cervantine *Exemplary Novels*, namely, *El coloquio de los perros* and *El licenciado Vidriera*, are excellent illustrations of how the liberty of the *novela* to rework old themes and motifs permitted Cervantes to express the contemporary anxiety of interiority through the culture of dissection. The two stories deal with the risks of a misguided cultivation of an autonomous interiority. In order to do this, *El coloquio de los perros* resorts to the legendary properties attributed to witches' bodies since antiquity. *El licenciado Vidriera* elaborates on the similarity between the body and machines, which was starting to emerge as a new paradigm to accommodate the discoveries of contemporary anatomical science. For the second part of the chapter, I chose to analyse Zayas's *Desengaños* (1647) because they offer a female perspective rare in the literature of the time. She gives a peculiar turn to the violence against women that informed other contemporary genres, such as honour plays and martyrology, in four stories: *La inocencia castigada, El verdugo de su esposa, Tarde llega el desengaño,* and *Mal presagio casar lejos.* In them, the violence is directed against a gender- and class-specific form of interiority constructed around the sexual/reproductive anatomy of upper-class women. The anxiety corresponding to this type of interiority is expressed in Zayas's gory tableaux of tortured and executed wives, which bear a disturbing resemblance to the imagery illustrating female anatomy in the contemporary medical books.

Cervantes's *El coloquio de los perros* and *El licenciado Vidriera* display characters that pursue autonomy to the point of altering their human nature and detaching themselves from those surrounding them. Published in 1613, the novels predate Descartes's philosophy by more than ten years but show signs of the rising tide of mechanism starting to be used to explain the functioning of the human being and the cosmos. As I will try to show, these two stories rely on the implicit assumption that the human fabric has so many points in common with machines that the body risks succumbing to mechanical behaviours. Both Cañizares and the Glass Licentiate, by dangerously manipulating their inner realm, alter their human nature to the point of resembling two of the most advanced machines of the period: clocks and automata. The first story, *El coloquio de los perros,* presents the witch Cañizares as an example of how tinkering with one's inner realm can seclude the individual from meaningful contact not only with other human beings but also with oneself. After years of solitary, misguided lucubration about the nature of good and evil, she becomes autonomous in the negative sense of a malfunctioning clock that is ticking out of time with the rest of the worldly and heavenly orders. In the latter story, *El licenciado Vidriera,* the young scholar Tomás Rodaja, because of his life of pure bookish learning and the eventual ingestion of a poison, becomes an automaton – the Glass Licentiate – that displays its mechanized interior in hackneyed answers to whoever may challenge him.

### Cañizares: The Mechanical Clock Out of Sync

Although none of Cervantes's known writings contain extended references to anatomy or dissection, he must have been well acquainted with the subject. His father, Rodrigo de Cervantes, was a barber-surgeon, an occupation that, as mentioned, was one of the lowest echelons of the medical profession.[1] Physicians, who held university degrees, tended to concentrate on scholastic knowledge and relegate the hands-on practice to barber-surgeons, midwives, and other lower members of the profession. These humble practitioners had to know anatomy in order to carry out bloodlettings in the main and secondary veins, as well as to perform other basic medical procedures, without endangering the lives of their patients. That barber-surgeons were well acquainted with anatomy is reflected in the fact that many anatomy books were purposely printed and made available at moderate prices for their education. Especially intended for barber-surgeons were sheets that contained detailed illustrations of human bodies.[2] Also, barber-surgeons were customarily in charge of the mechanical aspects of dissections because the doctors often limited their role to identifying the names of the organs revealed and to repeating the statements of medical authorities.

Another aspect of Cervantes's biography that allows us to presume first-hand acquaintance with anatomy is the years he served as a soldier. Armies were accompanied by battlefield doctors who specialized in aggressive methods to heal the horrific wounds that the contemporary warfare caused. Some doctors achieved such expertise in anatomy that they eventually wrote innovative medical books. Especially famous is the French battlefield doctor Ambroise Paré (1510–90), whose complete works, initially published in 1575, were reprinted many times. In Spain, Dionisio Daza Chacón, before becoming Charles V's personal physician, served as a battlefield doctor. This experience is detectable in his *Práctica y teórica de cirugía en romance y latín* (Valladolid, 1582). One can assume that Cervantes witnessed many of these wounds and their subsequent treatment in his days as a soldier. In the battle of Lepanto he received three gunshot wounds – two in the chest and one in his left hand – that must have required extended interventions by similar physicians. Not surprisingly, *Don Quixote* contains detailed descriptions of all kinds of traumatisms inflicted upon the eponymous hero and other characters, as well as of the subsequent cures.[3]

In spite of Cervantes's exposure to anatomy and the widespread contemporary interest in the subject, extended references to anatomy are not present in his texts, unlike those of Fray Luis de Granada and Quevedo. The word "anatomy" appears several times in Cervantes's works but only to refer metaphorically to an extremely skinny person or animal, which was a common use at the time. This is the case, for instance, in the episode of the Cart of Death in *Don Quixote* part 2, chapter 11, in which Cervantes writes that a scared Rocinante "started to gallop across the field with more speed than the bones of his *anatomy* promised" (535, 1308; dio a correr por el campo con más ligereza que jamás prometerieron los huesos de su *notomía*; emphasis added). In the exemplary novel *Rinconete and Cortadillo*, the prostitute Cariharta, upset with her pimp Repolido, insults his looks by calling him "an anatomy of death" (sotomía de muerte), but she mispronounces the word *anatomía* as *sotomía* (847, 95).[4] Significantly, one of the few instances in which Cervantes uses the word anatomy in a non-humorous context is in *El coloquio de los perros*, when the dog Berganza witnesses the witch Cañizares spreading an ointment all over her naked body and falling into a death-like trance. Berganza describes the frightening vision of her body as "an anatomy of bones covered with a dark, hairy, leathery skin" (289, 1018; notomía de huesos, cubiertos con una piel negra, vellosa y curtida).[5] As will be seen, this use of the word "anatomy" to refer to the corpse-like body of the witch Cañizares is not a gratuitous trope but the surfacing of the dissective undercurrent that permeates the whole story.

Several critics have pointed out that the episode of Cañizares is the centre – or more appropriately, the bottom – of the complex narrative of lies, deception, and decay that characterizes *El casamiento engañoso* and *El coloquio de los perros*.[6] These two exemplary novels dovetail: the end of the first story becomes the beginning of the dialogue of two dogs that the ensign Campuzano claims to have overheard while he was sweating out a bout of a venereal disease in the Hospital de la Resurrección of Valladolid. Many critics point out that *El casamiento engañoso* not only acts as a frame for *El coloquio de los perros*, but also anticipates some of the latter's central themes of deception, conversion, and the role of art and literature.[7] In addition, it forestalls dissective elements that are fully developed in *El coloquio*. *El casamiento* begins with the emaciated body of the ensign Campuzano as he comes out of the hospital and meets the licentiate Peralta, who is shocked at the sight of him. As Forcione remarks, Campuzano is so consumed that he resembles a resuscitated Lazarus, which anticipates the dog Berganza's sight of Cañizares's decrepit naked body during a trance so deep that he takes her for dead.[8] Had Campuzano not recovered in the symbolically named Hospital de la Resurrección, he would have become one of the corpses that supplied the anatomy theatres – the destitute who died at these hospitals being a common source of corpses. Furthermore, the first manifestations of his disease, the buboes that covered his entire body, bring to mind the corpses of those affected by the plague of Zaragoza that, as we saw, were dissected by Dr Joan Tomás Porcell. The instinctive reaction of his friend, the licentiate Peralta, upon seeing him is the same surprise, even repulsion, that the vision of a corpse would elicit. Also, as a dissected corpse teaches a lesson to those alive, the story of Campuzano, corroborated by his emaciated body, functions as an admonition for Peralta.

The idea that truth lies inside or at the bottom is present both at the structural and at the anecdotal level in *El casamiento* and *El coloquio*. As said, the *desengaño* of Berganza culminates with the contemplation of Cañizares's corpse, an episode that lies at the centre of the two stories. Equally embedded at the heart of the two stories is the idea that art – in the form of the narrations of Campuzano and Berganza – can recreate reality and become the last bastion of truth, as El Saffar puts it.[9] At the level of the plot, the opposition between the outside and the inside is omnipresent in *El casamiento*. Deception plays an important role in the story, to the point that the truth that it is supposed to contain is also false. In the first appearance, Doña Estefanía is covered by a veil except for her white hand, which seems to promise a purity in the rest of her person that she does not possess. Although later she confesses to Campuzano that her previous life had not been chaste but that she intends to reform, what Campuzano finally gets from her is deception and venereal disease. He is equally false in his dealings with her since his external appearance of wealth is also fabricated. None of the pieces of jewellery that he dons, especially an eye-catching chain, are solid gold, but they are all so well crafted that "only close examination or the heat of fire could reveal the deception" (245, 995; que sólo el toque o el fuego podía descubrir su malicia). Any hopes of finding the truth lying deep inside the story vanish because even its deepest layers are false. Doña Estefanía's secret plans of duping a wealthy soldier are thwarted when it turns out Campuzano is a *pícaro* trying to take advantage of her. Such an impossibility of finding truth in the innermost layers is mirrored in the structure of the stories. Thus, *El casamiento* concludes with the conversation that a feverish Campuzano thinks to have heard between two dogs one night while he was in the Hospital de la Resurrección. As if to prove the genuineness of the story he is about to narrate, he "drew a notebook from *his breast*" (249, 997; sacó *del pecho* un cartapacio; emphasis added). But nobody, not even himself, can be sure of the veracity of such a story, which may have been a dream. Equally, the core of *El coloquio* is Cañizares's relation of events that she is supposed to have experienced during her trances. But she is not sure if these experiences really occurred or were mere hallucinations.

The exposure of deception plays a central role in helping literature fulfil an edifying role in *El casamiento* and in *El coloquio*, as well as in the story of the Glass Licentiate and in the episodes of the Enchanted Head and of Maese Pedro's puppets in *Don Quixote*. These stories coincide in presenting artifices that are eventually unveiled for the moral benefit of the readers. In every story, dissection acts as a heuristic method that facilitates the discovery of the reality hidden behind a misleading facade of magic. Cervantes is instrumentalizing dissection in the service of his well-known fondness for writing *tropelías*, namely, elaborate stories that include, as one of their main ingredients, a deception that is eventually revealed for the enlightenment of the reader. Specifically, these stories match Wardropper's remark that Cervantes fully embraced the spirit of the *tropelía* in his construction of characters who, willingly or unwillingly, give up their true identities to unavoidably return to them at the end. As we will see, artifice in the form of witchcraft, bookish learning, and mechanical contrivances contributes to create apparently portentous characters whose true nature is revealed with the help of dissection. The *lusus scientiae* (the joke of knowledge), in the meaning of artifice, is thus uncovered by another form of *scientia*, a new medical technology, and all done for the enlightenment of the reader.[10]

The deepest layer of the embedded narratives in these two novels, the heart of the *tropelía*, is the episode in which Cañizares tells the story of her life to the dog Berganza. He will repeat her words to the dog Cipión literally, as if Cañizares were speaking in the first person. As the narrative spiral of the two novels progresses, the presence of dismemberment becomes stronger, as Forcione noted.[11] Thus, significantly, Berganza's birth takes place in a slaughterhouse. His narration of the years he spent there abounds with references to the slaughtering and taking apart of animals, and to the rapacious activities of the slaughterhouse employees, who systematically pilfered cows' tongues, bulls' testicles, and other parts to present to their lovers. Berganza participated in this process by soon learning to bite off the ears of the bulls and to carry the pilfered spoils in a basket to his owner's lover. In this description of Berganza's early years, the animals and the men who work in the slaughterhouse are subject to being torn apart: "At the slightest provocation and without a moment's hesitation they plunge their horn-handled knives into the belly of a man as if they were slaying a bull" (253, 990; estos jiferos con la misma facilidad matan a un hombre que a una vaca; por quítame allá esa paja, a dos por tres, meten un cuchillo de cachas amarillas por la barriga de una persona, como si acocotasen un toro).

Similarly rich in dismemberment is Berganza's stay with the shepherds. As in several other instances of Cervantes's writing, the shepherds' world does not match the bucolic literary conventions. The realistic shepherds of the story surreptitiously kill and eat the sheep they are supposed to care for, and then blame it on the wolves. When instructed to do so, the naive Berganza runs after the imaginary wolves until he is "weary, exhausted, with my feet torn to shreds by fallen branches" (258, 1002; hecho pedazos y los pies abiertos de los garranchos). Other dismembering attacks on bodies are scattered throughout Berganza's story, as when, during his stay with a rich merchant in Seville, he ferociously scratches and bites a black slave woman every time she goes to meet her lover surreptitiously at night. Similarly, during his sojourn with the corrupted justice officer, Berganza, when ordered to chase a thief, attacks and severely bites his owner instead of the alleged thief.

Next to these literal cases of bodily harm, the metaphor of dismemberment appears throughout the text, as when Berganza talks of those who boast of knowing Latin without really knowing it: "I'd like such people to be put in a press and the juice of what they know squeezed out of them until the pips run dry, so that they don't go round deceiving everyone by flashing their tatty Greek and phoney Latin" (268, 1007; quisiera que a estos tales los pusieran en una prensa, y a fuerza de vueltas les sacaran el jugo de lo que saben, porque no anduviesen engañando el mundo con el oropel de sus gregüescos rotos y sus latines falsos). Indirect references to dismemberment are implied in the satirical tone that pervades the dialogue. On several occasions, the two dogs deviate from their main topic to indulge in gossip. As was pointed out in the discussion of Quevedo, satire is often associated with dismantled or shapeless bodies because of its scathing content and polymorphous structure. This association shows in the moderating expressions that the two dogs use to control their conversation. When Cipión advises Berganza to stick to the agreed-upon theme, he tells him not to let his narration grow in the amorphous way of "octopuses' tentacles" (267, 1006; colas [de pulpo]). Similarly, when Berganza refers to his intention to refrain from gossiping, he uses in several instances variants of the common expression "to bite one's tongue" (263, 268; 1004, 1007; morder la lengua).[12]

Cañizares's appearance on the scene increases the already abundant presence of dismemberment.[13] Disguised as a saintly woman who tends the sick and dying, she is actually wicked and duplicitous: "I take care of the poor, and some die who leave me the wherewithal to live on in what they bequeath me or what they leave me among their rags, which I painstakingly pick clean" (286, 1016; Curo a los pobres; algunos se mueren que me dan a mí la vida con lo que me mandan o con lo que se les queda entre los remiendos, por el cuidado que yo tengo de espulgarles los vestidos). To rip apart the clothes of the dead and scrutinize their bodies evokes a vulture feeding on corpses. Furthermore, Cañizares can be seen as the first link in the process of dismantlement to which many of the bodies of the destitute were destined, since it was common for the bodies of those who died in charity hospitals and asylums to be bought or snatched for anatomical practices in the universities. Also, the potions and ointments in which she specializes conjure up the use of body parts and nocturnal visits to cemeteries and gallows to acquire them, as was the case with Don Pablos's mother in *El Buscón*.[14]

The climax of dissective overtones is reached towards the end of Cañizares's story, when the tables turn and she becomes a corpse-like body submitted to an intrusive exploration resembling an autopsy. Under the eyes of Berganza, in the privacy of her small cubicle, she applies an ointment to her naked body and falls into such a deep state of unconsciousness that the dog is afraid that she may have died. This is the passage in which Berganza calls her body an "anatomy." Like a corpse, she has stopped breathing, and her body is so emaciated, so consumed by age that it seems to have entered the initial stages of decomposition in her tomb-like room. Terrified by Cañizares's body, Berganza drags it into the yard of the hospice. As the sun comes out, several people surround the naked, motionless body. Intrigued to know whether she is dead, in a mystical trance, or passed out after having anointed herself in witch-like fashion, some curious bystanders start to prick her flesh with pins. This was a common practice to detect a witch or a sorcerer since the points that had been touched by the devil in their secret encounters were supposed to be insensitive to pain. Initially, Cañizares does not react to the painful procedure. Finally, she wakes up to find herself the subject of an improvised autopsy or inquisitorial interrogatory: "she found herself riddled with pinpricks, bitten on her ankles, [and] bruised as a result from being dragged outside from her room" (290, 1018; se sintió acribada de los alfileres y mordida de los calcañares, y magullada del arrastramiento fuera de su aposento). The story ends with Cañizares's body being pulled around the yard by Berganza, who has bitten into and held on to the skin hanging from her belly when, enraged, she blames him for the public revelation of her duplicitous life.

The mistreatment that Cañizares undergoes in the yard bears a resemblance to the flaying of Marsyas by Apollo, even if the vexations to which she is submitted never reach the cruelty of the myth narrated by Ovid in his *Metamorphoses* (book 6, lines 382–400). The satyr Marsyas was a gifted flautist who challenged Apollo to a musical contest. The conditions of the contest stipulated that the winner could do whatever he wanted with the body of the opponent. When Apollo was declared victor, he flayed Marsyas alive and nailed his hide to a tree. This myth, popular among early modern painters, was often represented in the engravings of medical books to symbolize the importance of dissection for anatomy.[15] The story of Marsyas is also often used as an allegory of human hubris, of daring to challenge the gods, and the consequent punishment. Cañizares, like the satyr Marsyas, is associated with a pre-Christian world of pagan rites in the wilderness and suffers cruel bodily punishment for her hubris. She attends Sabbaths in forests and fields where orgiastic rites are celebrated in honour of the devil. In these events, the devil takes the form of a male goat, which is the Christian version of the same tradition that attributes animal features to Pan and the satyrs.

Similarly to Marsyas, Cañizares possesses exceptional abilities, in her case not in playing musical instruments but in mixing ointments that induce trances. Precisely during one of her trances, Berganza punishes her for the hubris of taking part in ceremonies that defile God. The dog symbolically flays her when he reveals her secrets to the whole community by exposing her naked, ointment-covered, and in a trance. Although her skin is never literally removed, it is repeatedly mentioned in the story because of its sagginess, which will offer Berganza's teeth a holding point with which to drag her around the yard. Previously, he had removed her senseless body from the cubicle by grabbing it by the heel. The choice of this body part coincides with some paintings – such as Ribera's *Apollo Flaying Marsyas* (1637) – that represent Apollo starting to remove the satyr's skin at the ankle, where his hooves end and his human body begins (see Figure 8).[16] Meaningfully, Berganza chooses to bite the point at which her human and her demonic natures meet – witches being reputed to have hooves instead of feet. Achilles's heel, the only point on the hero's body that was not bathed in the Styx and thus remained mortal, also resonates in this attack. Cañizares's body, in spite of her forays into the supernatural, is still that of a common human being and therefore mortal and subject to all kinds of accidents.

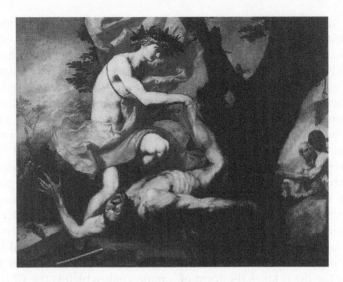

8  *Apollo Flaying Marsyas*, by José de Ribera, 1637. Royal Museum of Fine Arts
of Belgium, Brussels. (By permission of Wikipedia Commons)

Cañizares's story is a failed attempt at creating an inner realm that is
independent from the prevailing norms of society. Her self-fashioning
effort was doomed from its inception because it relied on the wickedness acquired through years of study with an evil master, exchanges
with equally evil colleagues, and encounters with the devil. The effect of
her training in wickedness was that she was forced to isolate herself
from the rest of society and to live in a narrow and distorted inner world.
In her secluded world, a perverted creed combined orthodox Christian
dogma with witchcraft. The convoluted logic of this makeshift theology
justified her practice of witchcraft under the disguise of a saintly woman,
as well as her incongruous decision to practise evil while simultaneously accepting God's omnipotence. Furthermore, her religion went so
far as to place her out of the reach of God's redemptive grace. The horror
of the travestied order this woman created for herself is expressed by
Berganza when he contemplates her entranced body in her room:

I asked myself, who made that wicked woman so wise and yet so evil?
How does she know the difference between harmful and culpable evil?
How does she understand and speak so much about God and yet do so

much of the devil's work? How does she sin so deliberately without the excuse of ignorance? (290, 1018; [M]e preguntaba yo a mí mismo: ¿quién hizo a esta mala vieja tan discreta y tan mala? ¿de dónde sabe ella cuáles son males de daño, y cuáles de culpa? ¿cómo entiende y habla tanto de Dios y obra tanto del diablo? ¿cómo peca tan de malicia no excusándose con ignorancia?)

Cañizares is presented as having reached autonomy at the price of falling into a near-solipsistic universe in which she cannot establish the reality of her own experience. In her confession to Berganza, she acknowledges that she cannot ascertain if her conferences with the devil and other witches were real or figments of her imagination. Similar doubts extend to the predictions the devil reveals to her, which she suspects to be mere lies and conjectures. Isolation and the impossibility of ascertaining the reality of the inner world that Cañizares crafted for herself resemble some of the negative features of how the functioning of the machine was envisioned at the time. In the story of Cañizares – as well as in that of the Glass Licentiate, as will be seen later – the dangers of modifying human nature are connected to the growing awareness that human beings are not that different from machines, the boundaries between autonomy and automatism being imprecise and dangerously slippery. In fact, Cañizares and the Glass Licentiate both accidentally become mechanized in their ill-fated quest for autonomy. Their mechanization implies acquiring negative characteristics associated with the machine, especially repetitiveness and the inability to change, to relate, and to adapt to the surrounding world.

The subtle yet important role that the machine plays in these two stories can be understood only by properly reconstructing the specific scenario of early modern machines and, especially, their peculiar impact on the collective imagination. The important role that machines would come to play in industrial production, as well as its effects, such as workers' alienation or the creation of new social identities, was barely developed at the time. Only with the Industrial Revolution would machines become ubiquitous in the production processes, although in the early modern period a few industries deployed some machinery – think of Don Quixote's famous episode with the windmills or the water-driven fulling mill.[17] In early modernity, the most technically complex machines and the ones that left the deepest imprint in the collective imagination were mechanical clocks and the automata closely associated with them. As clocks became common, tropes in which they were compared to human beings invaded everyday language.[18] The invasion of discourse by clocks was due not only to their widespread use but also to their peculiar status as novelties that inhabited a borderland between the realms of reality and imagination. The fact that clocks were considered marvellous playthings as well as useful machines can be seen, for instance, in their often unnecessarily intricate machinery. Unlike today's custom of designing all machines as simply and straightforwardly as possible, wheels and contraptions were added to many early modern clocks for functions that could have been more efficiently and simply achieved. The results were that many clocks were a labyrinthine entity of pulleys and wheels meant to astound the viewer. As Sawday succinctly states, "Renaissance interest in the machine [was] not just for what it does, but, rather, for what it might do. Renaissance machinery had come to inhabit fantasy as much as reality."[19] This spectacularity was enhanced by the addition of moving automata in the shape of miniature animals and human figures. Not surprisingly, these intricate machines were perceived as somehow living entities belonging somewhere between science and magic. This liminality was possible because science and magic were not distinctly separated, as the alchemists exemplified in their pursuit of such chimerical enterprises as the philosopher's stone or the elixir of eternal youth. In this sense, clocks were the successful inheritors of the medieval obsession with building perpetual motion machines and, as such, shared an aura of magic. Furthermore, clocks, automata, and other machines fell in the category of the living because the distinction between live and inert matter relied on the capacity for independent movement generated from an internal source. Not surprisingly, the concept of "mathematical or artificial magic" was used by Athanasius Kircher and other protoscientists of the seventeenth century to describe the functioning of the many hydraulic machines and similar devices that populated the gardens of Rome and some European courts.[20]

Another reason why clocks came to play such an important role in the early modern imagination is that they served as a convenient image for the increasingly prevalent mechanistic view of the human being, to which anatomical discoveries contributed. Through the opposite processes of assembling and disassembling, mechanics and anatomical dissection showed that machines and human beings were not indivisible ontological units but the results of an accumulation of parts. Descriptions of the functioning of the human body that used mechanical terms were common in the anatomical treatises published from the beginning of the sixteenth century on. The texts regularly compared the role of bones and muscles to that of levers, pulleys, and other contraptions described in the engineering books circulating since antiquity. Anatomical books highlighted the similar functioning of the human body and the machine not only in their written descriptions but also in the representational conventions of their numerous engravings. For instance, images that illustrated anatomy and those that illustrated the construction of machines shared the implicit removal of the external layers to graphically project organs and devices, or to expose them in vignettes within the main image. The results of these graphic practices were images of human bodies that closely resembled the representation of machines, and vice versa. These concomitances may explain why, in the eighteenth century, the famous French inventor Jacques de Vaucanson, the author of a mechanical flute player and a digesting duck, called his creations "moving anatomies."[21]

The comparison between the human body and machines became a de facto standard in the course of the seventeenth century. The image of the machine was applied to the human body and all its functions and was also extended to metaphorical bodies. Thus, in many contemporary political treatises the traditional image of society as a body politic was gradually displaced by the image of a machine. Even before Hobbes famously formulated that society works as a machine, many other texts included comparisons of the state to a clock. For instance, Pedro de Rivadeneira's *Tratado de la religión y virtudes que debe tener el príncipe cristiano para para gobernar sus estados* (1595) speaks of the "clock of the republic" (el reloj de la república) and elaborates on this image by comparing the attention needed to keep society properly running to the care needed to keep a clock in working order.[22] But the trope of society as a clock is not limited to political treatises: it also appears in the fictional literature of contemporary Spain. In Lope de Vega's play *Servir a buenos*, one of the characters proclaims, "I understand that republics are like clocks because the two of them are made from the same wheels and run the same way, as the clocks of our breasts and the clocks on the towers" (Las repúblicas entiendo / que son como los relojes / que el mismo gobierno corre / de las mismas ruedas hecho / para el que se trae al pecho / que para el que está en la torre).[23]

The many comparisons between human beings and clocks in the contemporary discourse are a clear sign of the triumph of the clockwork paradigm. Tropes abound in which the clock is subject to anthropomorphism and, vice versa, in which human beings are described as clocks.

How this assimilation affected the description of clocks is still detectable in several modern languages. For instance, in today's Spanish and English, the pointing metal pieces that indicate the hours and the minutes in a clock are referred to as the "hands" of the clock – *manillas* in Spanish. These denominations were so well established by the early modern period that they could be used as the departure point for more elaborate tropes. In Cervantes's comedy *Pedro de Urdemalas*, John the Baptist's emblematic act of pointing his finger to Christ to indicate that he is the true Messiah is described by alluding to the hand of a clock: "Saint John's night, the night of the great Forerunner, whose hand was better than the hand of a clock since his holy finger pointed the day that had no night" (*Obras completas*, 511; Noche de San Juan, / el gran Precursor, / que tuvo la mano / más que de reloj, / pues su dedo santo tan bien señaló, / que nos mostró el día / que no anocheció). To refer to other components of clocks by the name of body parts was also common, as calling the dial the *cara* (face), or equating the weights of a clock with the testicles of a man, as in the following witticism in Timoneda's *Buen aviso y portacuentos* (1564): "When a woman asked the time of a castrated man, a nearby suitor replied that it is not a question to be asked of a clock with no weights" (Pidiendo qué hora era a un capado cierta señora, respondió un galán, y dijo: Mala cuenta le puede dar de eso el reloj sin pesas).[24]

The comparison between human beings and clocks extends also to the internal organs and the deepest functions of the human being, as in Tirso de Molina's *Cigarrales de Toledo*: "She had her right hand on her breast, pointing to the clock of her heart" (Tenía sobre ellos [sus pechos] la diestra mano apuntando en el reloj del corazón).[25] Other inner organs are also subject to the analogy, as in Arce de Otálora's *Coloquios de Palatino y Pinciano* (c. 1550): "My stomach's clock tells me that it is not late because I am not hungry" (En el reloj de mi estómago veo yo que no es tarde, porque no he gana de comer).[26] "Horologization" is not only applied to the physical functions of the stomach or the heart, but also extended to more subtle ones. In Cervantes's *Los trabajos de Persiles y Sigismunda*, King Policarpo complains of the disturbing visit of Persiles and his companions: "their arrival disturbed the clock of my mind" (*Obras completas*, 1585; después que han venido estos nuevos huéspedes a nuestra ciudad, se ha desconcertado el reloj de mi entendimiento). Frequent also is the analogy between a clock and memory, which is based on the fact that clocks, in their functions as alarms, serve as reminders or awakeners. Not only can discrete organs and functions be compared to a clock, but so can human manners and countenance. The comparison is especially fruitful in giving advice about how to conduct one's business. Juan Rufo's *Seiscientas apotegmas* (1596) encourages clockwork behaviour in certain delicate matters: "[T]he thoughtfulness required in matters of discretion should be like the hand of a clock, which, while dissimulating its continuous movement, strikes when it reaches its destination" ([E]l artificio y primor que se requiere en todas las cosas de gala y discreción, había de ser como la mano del reloj, que, disimulando el movimiento, señala los lugares donde llega).[27]

The propensity of clocks to malfunction is especially fruitful for establishing analogies with human behaviour. In early modern Spanish the expression most commonly used for a malfunctioning clock is *reloj desconcertado*.[28] This turn of phrase, which has not survived into present-day Spanish, can be best translated into English as "clock out of sync." The Spanish original implies that the clock is not necessary inoperative, since it could still be ticking, but lacking *concierto* (agreement) with the true time accurately indicated by the position of the sun or the stars. Such a shortcoming is especially meaningful in a period in which the concept of cosmic harmony had serious implications. Not to agree with the rhythm of the planets and the celestial spheres meant not to follow God's plans for His creation.[29] Behind the popularity of literary allusions to clocks out of sync is the undeniable reality of the imprecise working of contemporary clocks as well as the assiduous maintenance they required. Clocks were not accurate until late in the seventeenth century, when the Dutch astronomer Huygens introduced the pendulum to fine-tune the crown wheel, or verge, and the foliot that regulated the speed of the mechanism. Before this modification, losing or gaining fifteen minutes in a twenty-four-hour period was common and often made the public clocks in the same city strike the hours in disagreement with each other.[30] This propensity of early modern clocks to malfunction is reflected in many comparisons between humans and clocks. For instance, López de Úbeda's novel *La pícara Justina* (1605) establishes the following witty analogy between a woman and a clock, emphasizing how easily the machinery may malfunction:

> My mother used to tell me that the woman in charge of an inn is like a clock, and she was right. The clock, when it moves gradually from notch to notch, makes a pleasant, soft noise. Similarly, the woman who owns an inn shakes the purse in which the money paid by the guests that come and go rattles pleasantly at the same rhythm that the keys she carries, and

doing so she livens up the ambience of the inn, which is her dial. But if a guest leaves the inn without paying, she makes a racket, like an out-of-order clock when it misses a notch. (Decíame a mí mi madre que una mesonera es como un reloj. Decía bien. El reloj, cuando va de lance en lance y de muesca en muesca, ruido hace, pero es pequeño y gustoso; mas si da un golpe en vago, todas las ruedas se descomponen y hace gran ruido. Así, una mesonera, que de momento en momento va golpeando la bolsa con dinero fresco de huéspedes que van y vienen, hace un ruidito suave, y al son de las llaves del llavero alegra el hemisferio de su mesón; mas si un huésped se le escapa sin pagar, da el golpe en vago, desconciértase el reloj y arma un ruido del diablo.)[31]

In the analogies between clocks and human beings, the propensity of clocks to be uncoordinated or quit working altogether is often accompanied by references to their need for regular maintenance and resetting.[32] In Cervantes's short theatrical piece *El juez de los divorcios*, the insoluble dissensions of a married couple who come to the judge for a divorce make one of the court officers exclaim, "Who the hell will be able to reset these two clocks whose wheels are so unbalanced?" (¿Quién diablos acertará a concertar estos relojes, estando las ruedas desconcertadas?).[33] In his *Libro de la oración y la meditación*, Granada compares the practice of praying several times a day to the resetting and maintenance of a clock:

As those in charge of a clock raise the weights that slowly go down on their own two times a day, the same way those who want to keep their souls in harmony and concert need to raise their weights at least twice a day because our miserable nature pushes them down to the lowest ground. (Así como los que rigen un reloj suelen comúnmente dos veces al día subir las pesas a lo alto, porque ellas mismas poco a poco van siempre caminando para abajo, así los que quieren traer sus ánimas bien regidas y concertadas han menester a lo menos estas dos veces al día subir las pesas a lo alto, pues la naturaleza miserable tanto cuidado tiene de inclinarlas a lo bajo.)[34]

This passage by Granada bears witness to how often religious writings resort to the analogy of clocks in need of tuning and resetting to express human beings' need for assiduous religious instruction and practice. This need for continuous spiritual care is connected to the image of God as a conscientious clockmaker in the following comparison in *Algunas penas en el justo camino de la perfección* by the Trinitarian San Juan Bautista de la Concepción (1561–1613):

> A clock keeps time because a clockmaker takes good care of it and keeps it clean and high up in a tower, but if a clock is not properly maintained and guarded in a safe place, it does not keep time; the same applies to the human being, which God, the universal clockmaker, made, and grace was its protection. (Así como cuando un reloj está bien concertado, está en alto y subido en una torre y hay relojero que lo limpie y aderece, sacuda el polvo y lo guarde [está concertado], pero, desconcertado, anda rodando por los suelos, [s]alió el hombre de las manos de Dios, el mismo Dios era su relojero, la gracia el guardapolvo, etc.)[35]

The image becomes such a commonplace that it can be used in abbreviated form, as in the prologue to the *Aucto de la prevaricación de nuestro padre Adán* (c. 1570–8), where the customary *captatio benevolentiae* by the anonymous author includes the confession of having written the play "so that everybody could correct my mistakes, as if I were a clock" (hacerme reloj para ser de todos corregido).[36]

The story of Cañizares presents many points in common with the analogies between human being and machine that flooded contemporary discourse. Although she is never compared to a clock or machine directly, the whole narrative develops the theme of how close human beings are to machines and the subsequent risk of malfunctioning. Cañizares's story exemplifies the dangers of altering one's own inner functions in a quest for autonomy that may easily end up in mechanized automatism. The self-imposed intensive regime of vilification that Cañizares followed for years severely altered her inner operations while, at the same time, it placed her in a completely isolated world comparable to that of a *reloj desconcertado* that cannot be reset and brought into agreement with the universal order. She disconnected herself completely from those who surround her until she was cornered into a near-solipsistic form of existence. In her isolation, she cannot even establish if her most meaningful experiences, her nocturnal flights to attend ceremonies in which she converses with the devil, are real or imaginary. She is in severe need of correction because her self-fashioning regime of witchcraft makes her run *desconcertada* under an impenetrable cloak of hypocrisy. Unfortunately for her, she is too far removed from those who surround her to be helped and brought into synchrony with God's world. Furthermore, through her own reasoning, she has excluded herself from the possibility of being reached by God's grace. She is comparable to a mystic who, in the isolated cultivation of interiority, has gone astray. Cañizares's case seems to justify the vigilance that the Inquisition exerted upon those who followed the inner route. The suspicion that mystics, even those who would later be canonized, such as Saint Teresa and Saint Ignatius, inspired among the official ranks of the church was mentioned in previous chapters. In their autonomy, guided only by their reason, they could easily fall out of tune with the God-inspired universal harmony. The punishment, even the destruction that is expected to follow Berganza's public exposure of her, is presented as the only possible way out of the unreachable malfunctioning autonomy she constructed for herself.

## The Glass Licentiate: The Accidental Automaton

The story of the Glass Licentiate, like the story of Cañizares, is of a self-fashioning process that goes awry. The central character of the exemplary novel *El licenciado Vidriera* is Tomás, a young man who follows a strict program of personal development that dangerously emphasizes detachment and autonomy. The disastrous results of his quest, as in the case of Cañizares, resemble the shortcomings of contemporary machines. Tomás's excessive acquisition of knowledge comes to a head when he ingests a love potion. This is the catalyst that accidently brings his unwise enterprise to its fatal results: Tomás becomes the Glass Licentiate, a man whose behaviour is characterized by the automatism of a self-moving machine. Tomás is an anti-Pinocchio, a man who embarks upon a personal quest but who, by missing the importance of having feelings, ends up becoming a walking and talking automaton that is eventually destroyed.

As with *El coloquio de los perros*, *El licenciado Vidriera* is a complex narrative of accumulated elements; therefore, I am not aiming at a totalizing interpretation of the story but only of an episode within the story: the period of insanity when Tomás becomes the Glass Licentiate. But because this part of the story occupies most of the text – and, appropriately, gives the novel its title – my interpretation affects the whole text to a greater extent than was the case with Cañizares in *El coloquio de los perros*.[37] Other important differences separate the stories of Cañizares and Tomás Rodaja. Notable is the absence in Tomás's tale of the religious overtones that are so important in Cañizares's self-fashioning. For Tomás, the dangers of self-fashioning are expressed in terms of expanding the intellect to occupy the totality of one's inner realm. In his excessive quest for knowledge, Tomás is the successor of a long line of male figures who are in search of power and knowledge, such as Prometheus or Adam, as well as being the predecessor of the mad scientists of later centuries.[38]

Another difference between the two cases is that mechanical overtones are more notable in the story of the Glass Licentiate than in that of Cañizares. Contrarily, the presence of dissection is less notable in the biography of Tomás, which is missing the dismembering overtones of *El coloquio de los perros*. The culture of dissection is, however, present in a subtle way. The noted Spanish Enlightenment writer José Cadalso (1741–82) astutely detected this ingredient in *El licenciado Vidriera* in his posthumously published epistolary novel *Cartas marruecas* (1789). Letter XXXII is the reply that the fictional Moroccan character Ben-Beley writes to his friend Gazel, who is travelling through Spain. In the letter, the well-read Ben-Beley thanks Gazel for the books Gazel has sent him. Among the books received, he mentions "one about anatomy, the kind of books whose reading clearly inspired Cervantes to write his story of the insane man who thought he was as fragile as if he were made of glass" (otro de anatomía, cuya lectura fue sin duda la que dio motivo al cuento del loco que se figuraba ser tan quebradizo como el vidrio).[39]

Cadalso's insight is interesting because, as said, no overt references to anatomy or dissection appear in Cervantes's narrative. Although Cadalso does not explain how he established this connection between *El licenciado Vidriera* and anatomical books, it can be surmised that he was thinking of the many anatomical illustrations in medical texts in which human beings have their skin, muscles, and other tissues removed so that the reader can see directly inside their bodies, as if they were made from glass. A contributing factor may have been the strong dissective overtones of the Glass Licentiate's first name, Tomás, which is related to the same Greek etymon *tomos* (a cut) of "ana-tomy." Equally dissective is the family name he adopts during his period of insanity, "Rodaja," which has, among other meanings, that of a slice or crosscut. As will be seen, the culture of dissection underlies the story in the form of the silent assumption that human beings are aggregates of parts functioning together in a delicate balance, an idea that originates in the anatomical research of the period. This assumption implies that human beings are so close to machines that tampering with their natural fabric – as can happen in a misguided search for autonomy through an excessive diet of knowledge – may alter their functioning and raise the mechanical aspects that are dormant in their nature.

Tomás is presented as somebody who has decided to take destiny into his own hands through the acquisition of knowledge. He believes that he can change himself through the application of will and intellect. When the two gentlemen who find him by the river question him about his origins and family, his answer that he does not want to remember his native land and social origin shows this will to reshape his life by taking his future into his own hands. The same will is apparent in how relentlessly he applies himself to his studies at the University of Salamanca and in his travels through Italy. The ingestion of the quince is the catalyst that causes his excessive regime of knowledge acquisition to reach its fatal results. He gets so sick that he ends up looking like a living anatomy of "just skin and bones" (113, 880; se secó y se puso, como suele decirse, en los huesos). When he recovers enough to walk, he becomes the Glass Licentiate. The delusion of being made out of glass is not Cervantes's original creation but a reference to a mental disorder that appears documented as early as the classical medical treatises of Rufus of Ephesus or Galen, who report cases of people who believed that they were made from fragile earthenware. This peculiar delusion caught the attention of writers in the early modern period. Similar cases are reported in contemporary medical treatises as well as in such other writings as Robert Burton's *The Anatomy of Melancholy* (1621) and Descartes's *First Meditations* (1641), which includes a reference to people who believed themselves to be *vitro conflatos* (made from blown glass).[40]

The story of Tomás masterfully expands on some qualities of glass and their symbolic meanings. Its fragility is turned into the Glass Licentiate's fear of being shattered to pieces, while its transparency helps him believe that his reason, unimpeded by his crystalline body, has become subtler.[41] To be made of glass instead of flesh and bone entails also a loss of humanity. When he turns into the Glass Licentiate, Tomás becomes a delicate object that has to be wrapped in straw for protection, as when he is carried to the capital in a cart. Objectification is also reflected in the names that he uses during his period of insanity. "Vidrio" (glass) was used to refer metonymically to objects made of this material, such as cups or mirrors, and even clocks.[42] Mechanical overtones are also implied in the family name he adopts, Rodaja. According to the *Diccionario de autoridades* of 1737, "rodaja" is a "small or little wheel ... carved without spokes that is used as a pulley in some machines" (rueda pequeña ... ruedecilla sin rayo y cavada en la circunferencia que se usa en algunas máquinas, moviéndose al impulso de una cuerda que pasa por ella).[43] Finally, the name Tomás evokes Thomas Aquinas – Santo Tomás in Spanish – whose tutor, Albert the Great, made a brass automaton that continually chattered and annoyed Aquinas, driving him to smash it to pieces.[44]

The importance of dehumanization in *El licenciado Vidriera* has been pointed out by several critics who consider that Tomás fails to become human in the true sense of the word. For Alban Forcione, Tomás is a fanatical student, obsessive, antisocial, egocentric, and hubristic; for Ruth El Saffar, a fear of the Other is Tomás's main characteristic; he is a "Salamanca educated fool," according to George Shipley.[45] Part of his failure to become fully human is evident not only in the time he spends obsessively studying in Salamanca but also in his travels through Europe with the Spanish army, as a curious bystander rather than an enlisted soldier. His lack of engagement continues when he returns to Salamanca to further his dry intellectual training while ignoring women. Significantly, the love potion that he ingests with the quince is the catalyst that turns him into the Glass Licentiate.

Critics have also noted Tomás's mechanization in his state as the Glass Licentiate. Forcione speaks of a "ridiculous satirical descent ... into the world of the thing and the mechanism."[46] Shipley points out that the Glass Licentiate lacks a self. Surrounded by an audience that expects to be entertained, he repeats worn-out sayings like a parrot. His words, continues Shipley, are not really threatening to the social order, just pure gossip, since "Vidriera is confined to refashioning scraps of wit that lie in language and memory, his and his community's, awaiting reformulation." He regurgitates calcified language to entertain the crowds with a combination of what he has learnt in Salamanca and prejudices distilled from the dominant discourse. Many critics have pointed out that Tomás becomes a Cynical philosopher who shuns society, assumes a life of poverty, and scorns the banality of the people who come to see him. There is, however, no true social criticism in his many trite sayings, and in no way should one try to find the true opinions of Cervantes behind what he says.[47] More than recalling the itinerancy of a Cynical philosopher, the way the Glass Licentiate moves around the city surrounded by a group of children and curious bystanders evokes the legendary automaton known as the Hombre de Palo (Wooden Man), which was said to walk through the streets of Toledo collecting alms among crowds of curious onlookers.[48] Similarly, the way the Glass Licentiate answers the questions people put to him brings to mind another (pseudo)automaton, the Enchanted Head encountered by Don Quixote. This was a bronze head on a jasper table with legs that imitated the talons of an eagle, as if it were a sphinx. The supposedly mechanical head was kept in a private room that only a few friends were allowed to enter to ask questions, which the Head promptly answered. At the end of the tale, the narrator acts as a dissector for the enlightenment of the readers, revealing what is inside this contraption. We learn that the Head and the table were not made of the materials they seemed to be, but rather were constructed of painted wood and cardboard.[49] Furthermore, we are told that the whole apparatus was empty on the inside. A tin pipe ran through it all the way to the room underneath, where the owner's nephew, a learned, witty student, like Tomás, listened to and answered the questions with worn-out truisms. When asked questions that would require truly extraordinary insights, the Head avoided giving a real answer by replying, "I have no knowledge of thoughts" (873, 1488; yo no juzgo de pensamientos).[50]

The Enchanted Head is a fraudulent object, made not of precious but of vulgar materials, that delivers formulaic answers. Similarly, the Glass Licentiate, made from flesh and not from glass, delivers equally empty answers from the arsenal of bookish knowledge that Tomás accumulated as a student in Salamanca. The answers given by the Enchanted Head and the Glass Licentiate are hackneyed truisms of general application or, in some cases, puns, proverbs, and sayings that play with the meaning of words but actually do not say anything pertinent in response to the question. When the Enchanted Head was asked by a woman what she could do to be beautiful, it answered, "Be very chaste" (873, 1488; Ser muy honesta), and when another woman asked how she could know if her husband truly loved her, it answered, "Think what he does for you, and you will know" (873, 1488; Mira a las obras que te hace y echarlo has de ver). Furthermore, the answers given by the Enchanted Head and the Glass Licentiate reveal their pessimism and their low opinion of human nature. When asked by a wealthy man what his oldest son's thoughts were, the Enchanted Head answered that his son just wanted him to die so he could collect his inheritance. These and the Enchanted Head's other similarly trite witticisms are of the same ilk as the Glass Licentiate's answers during his walks through the city. The Glass Licentiate and the Enchanted Head, in spite of being human beings, act as automata that limit themselves to repeating canned knowledge applicable to many situations and not requiring a true understanding of events. The Glass Licentiate and the Enchanted

Head are not wise but spectacular, and it is only thus that they attract an audience. They function as toys or novelties and represent the kind of appeal that, as we will see, was associated with contemporary automata and other mechanical contraptions. Also like the Enchanted Head, which was an object zealously kept and proudly displayed in a room by its owner, the Glass Licentiate becomes the precious property of a prince. He brings fragile Vidriera from Salamanca to the court in a cart loaded with straw to let his human toy display itself around the city, but always escorted by a guard who keeps the onlookers at a distance.[51]

Dehumanized mechanization, spectacularity, and deception are also central ingredients in the episode of Maese Pedro (*Don Quixote* 2:25–7).[52] In the story, the convict Ginés de Pasamonte, who was released by Don Quixote in a previous adventure, poses as the impresario of an itinerant show that includes a *retablo*, or puppet show, and a monkey who supposedly gives prophetic answers. The animal climbs on his owner's shoulder and seems to speak in his ear, while Maese Pedro appears to listen to the monkey and then answers the audience's questions. In reality, he and the monkey are like the moving figurines of a music box that replays pre-recorded songs for a coin. The monkey has been trained to jump onto his owner upon request and chatter nonsense in his ear, which Maese Pedro pretends to translate. Cunningly, he chooses to answer only questions about the present, replying with conjectures based on information that he secretly gathered before the show. His replies are as empty and trite as the truisms pronounced by the Glass Licentiate and the Enchanted Head. When Sancho asks what his wife Teresa is doing at home, Maese Pedro, after seemingly listening to the monkey, rehashes what he knows about Sancho and describes her in the verisimilar scenario of working in a field, with a generous portion of wine at hand. On other occasions, his answers are uncompromisingly vague. When questioned about the reality of Don Quixote's experiences in the cave of Montesinos, Maese Pedro astutely replies that some were true, some false.

Dehumanized mechanization is also a central ingredient of the puppet act. Although puppets are not machines in the modern sense of the term, in the early modern period they were considered close to automata. Both were anthropomorphic contraptions operated by strings pulled by human hands or by the torque of a coiled spring, as if they were capable of autonomous movement. Puppets and automata were used in dramatic representations and even shared the stage.[53] The conceptual proximity in which both types of moving figurines were held is reflected in the definition of the word "títeres" in Covarrubias's 1611 dictionary. After describing them as figurines animated by hand, Covarrubias adds,

> There is another type of *títeres*, which have wheels, such as the ones in clocks, that, when pulled by strings, move on a table as if they were people who are alive. The master keeps them so finely tuned that they turn around when they reach the edge of a table and return to the point where they started. Some play a lute while moving their heads and the pupils of their eyes; and all that is done through wheels and strings. In our days we have seen some, invented by Juanelo [Turriano]. (Hay otra manera de títeres, que con ciertas ruedas como reloj, tirándole las cuerdas, van haciendo sobre una mesa ciertos movimientos, que parecen personas animadas, y el maestro los trae tan ajustados que en llegando al borde de la mesa dan la vuelta, caminando al lugar de donde salieron. Algunas van tañendo un laúd, moviendo la cabeza y meneando la niña de los ojos; y todo esto se hace con las ruedas y las cuerdas. En nuestro tiempo lo hemos visto, y fue invención de Juanelo [Turriano].)

From the description in the text, Varey infers that Maese Pedro's puppets cannot be automata but figurines moved by a person hidden behind the stage.[54] Guillermo Díaz-Plaja is more precise in claiming that they have to be string and not hand puppets because only these are capable of vertical movements, such as in the comical mishap when the skirt of the puppet of Melisendra is caught in the railing as the figurine descends from a balcony. The strings that move these puppets are dexterously pulled by Maese Pedro, hidden behind the stage. Meanwhile, in front of the audience, a boy acts as the interpreter of the acts that the voiceless puppets recreate. The boy's role of intermediary between the spectators and the puppets, which seem to magically come to life on stage, resembles that of Maese Pedro as translator of the monkey's supposedly supernatural insights. As was also the case with Maese Pedro, the boy's discourse lacks the spontaneity and meaningfulness characteristic of human communication because he must stick to the memorized description of the events on stage. Whenever he deviates from or tries to elaborate on the narration, he is rebuked by Don Quixote and by Maese Pedro from backstage.

Maese Pedro's dexterity and the boy's recitation are not the only ingredients in creating the illusion of dead matter coming to life on stage. The *mise en scène* of the show is also carefully arranged to foster an aura of magic. The boy points to the specific actions of the puppets with a stick that resembles a sorcerer's wand, while the candles that illuminate the stage make it look like a liminal zone between two realms of existence.[55] In addition, Maese Pedro's decision to change the customary order of the show and first perform the trick of the divinatory monkey helps to create an ambience of wonder among an audience that was predisposed to expect extraordinary events in these shows. Contributory factors to such expectancy were the religious connotations of the term "retablo" (decorated altarpiece), used to refer to the shows because many represented scenes of the lives of saints, especially their miracles.[56] The illusion of pasteboard figurines becoming human on an altar-like *retablo* was reminiscent of the transubstantiation: bread and wine turning into the flesh and blood of Christ on an altar during mass. The susceptibility of contemporary audiences plays a central role in Cervantes's short dramatic piece *El retablo de las maravillas*. Based on the traditional tale of the emperor's new clothes, the word "maravillas" (marvels or wonders) refers to the allegedly supernatural show that only those of *cristiano viejo* descent are supposed to see. The act is but a practical joke played on the self-satisfied and gullible inhabitants of a small town, who easily convince themselves that they can see the nonexistent spectacle.[57]

Because deception and self-deception run as leitmotifs through the episode of Maese Pedro, critics have interpreted the passage as an allegory of authorial control over story and readers. As Haley has stated,

> Maese Pedro's puppet show is, then, an analogue to the novel as a whole, not merely because the burlesque legend that Maese Pedro recreates with puppets is a *reductio ad absurdum* of the same chivalric material that Cervantes burlesques through his characters, but also because it reproduces on a miniature scale the same basic relationships among storyteller, story, and audience that are discernible in the novel's overall scheme.[58]

Haley also points out that the author's control of the audience through the careful disposition of the materials is reflected in Cervantes's masterfully placing the episode of Maese Pedro after two adventures dealing with the confusion between reality and its representation. Indeed, the episode of Maese Pedro follows the descent of Don Quixote into the cave of Montesinos, in which he cannot tell reality from dream (2:22), and the story of the two braying aldermen, whose superb imitation of a donkey makes them take each other for the lost animal they are trying to recover (2:25). When the readers proceed from these two chapters to the episode of Maese Pedro, they are, like the audiences of the puppet show, predisposed to question any sharp separation between reality and its recreation.

The capacity to artistically create convincing imitations of reality is also central in Maese Pedro's show, in which an animal appears to be able to prophesy and figurines made from inanimate matter seem to come to life on stage. The two are in reality fictions that rely on the illusion that the monkey's and the puppets' movements are not senseless and mechanical but spring from their autonomous interiors. The monkey and the puppets seem not only to have human shape but also to act like, even surpass, human beings. While the monkey appears to understand language and to prophesy, the puppets act as if they have the capacity to bring old stories back to life. However, the turn of events proves that the monkey and the puppets are only mechanisms unconscious of their acts. The monkey's irrational nature eventually manifests itself when, succumbing to its instincts, it escapes over the roofs, frightened by Don Quixote's charge against the puppets.

The events that lead to the revelation that the puppets are mechanical agents without consciousness are paradoxically triggered by their uncanny impersonation of life. Their disturbing verisimilitude provokes Don Quixote's attack, which will reveal that they are, in fact, stuffed figurines. Convinced that Melisendra and Don Gaiferos are about to be captured by their pursuers, Don Quixote charges the stage with his sword, raining blows over the figurines. His sword acts as a dissecting knife that accidentally uncovers the imposture to which he had succumbed. The damage inflicted upon the puppets is ironically described in near-dissective terms: Charlemagne's "head cut in two" (642, 1365; la cabeza en dos partes); his body has a "gash from top to bottom" (644, 1366; abertura de arriba abajo); the other puppets are "hacked ... to bits" (642, 1365; hechos pedazos).[59] The horrific wounds and dismemberment reveal that the puppets' interiors contain only pasteboard and not the organs necessary for the autonomous life that they were impersonating on stage. Their sudden return to the realm of objects is comically exploited when Maese Pedro, as if he were the coroner in a forensic inquiry, examines each figure. The puppets return to being commodified wares and, as such, they are assigned a monetary value that Don Quixote is expected to reimburse.

Similarly to previously cited dissective texts, the puppets serve as sacrificial victims whose insides are scrutinized through more or less punitive dissective methods for the enlightenment of an audience. In this case, Don Quixote's *desengaño* is achieved through the contemplation of the puppet's empty entrails. Although at first sight puppets may not seem the ideal candidates for dissection, they are strangely prone to suffer this treatment in contemporary texts. As seen in the previous chapter, Quevedo did not hesitate to discursively eviscerate puppets when he compared the "old rags and sticks" (andrajos y palillos) hiding inside puppets to the fabricated merits adduced by some people to extol their honour (*El sueño de la muerte*, 1:184). To make a moralizing remark about the deceiving ways of the world of power and politics, Covarrubias also exposes puppets and automata. His emblem 50 (*Emblemas morales*, vol. 2) shows a man playing a lute and two puppets dancing, to which the following explanation is given:

> Many of those who command are actually under somebody else's command, they are puppets moved by wheels ... Such people and authorities resemble the figurines that a minstrel puts on a table and, by having their strings pulled as if they were clocks, move following the strings' movements, dancing at the tone that the showman plays. (Muchos de los que mandan son mandados, son títeres por ruedas gobernados ... son semejantes los tales señores y potestades a las figuras que el juglar pone sobre una mesa y alzándoles las cuerdas como a relojes, se mueven al movimiento de las cuerdas y danzan al movimiento que el charlatán les hace.)

In its characteristic brevity, the motto of the emblem also points to an empty (wooden) interior as a symbol of lack of autonomy: "Like a wooden puppet drawn by wires pulled by others" (Nervis alienis mobile lignum).[60] Although *nervis* is used here in the generic meaning of "wire" or "string," its dissective connotations are inescapable given that this term – and its Spanish equivalent "nervio" – was commonly used to refer to tendons and muscles.

In spite of clear dissective ingredients, this episode of Don Quixote's adventures ends without allowing us to peer inside Ginés de Pasamonte. Not only is he a convict and therefore the ideal candidate for a punitive dissective procedure, but he also dons a presumably complex and therefore interesting interior that allows him to transform his external appearance and escape his pursuers.[61] He uses this ability to remove his body from a scene that could have led to his dissection. Nimbly ducking behind the stage, he dodges one of Don Quixote's blows that "would have sliced off Master Peter's head as easily as if it had been made of [paste of] marzipan" (642, 1365; le cercenara la cabeza con más facilidad que si fuera hecha de masa de mazapán).[62] He would have then shared the destiny of the puppet of King Marsilio of Zaragoza, whose head is cut off by one of Don Quixote's blows, and of the other mangled puppets, whose dismembered bodies Haley perceptively refers to as "Maese Pedro's bodies, other selves" (159). Because Maese Pedro escapes Don Quixote's sword, we never come to see what is inside him, whether he is made from flesh or merely from paste, as the reference to marzipan seems to suggest. Cunningly, he manages to offer his figurines as sacrificial victims in lieu of himself.

As in the episodes of the Enchanted Head and Maese Pedro in *Don Quixote*, and in the story of Cañizares, some of Tomás's behaviours in *El licenciado Vidriera* recall the mechanical operation of clocks and automata, which were closely associated at the time given that the most widespread automata were figurines that struck the hours or moved their mechanical limbs in synchrony with the main train of a clock. The few automata not connected to clocks were created by the same artisans who made clocks, who used similar turning wheels and springs to make their automata imitate the movements of human beings. Also as in the case of clocks, automata played an important role in the imagination of the period. It was not their ubiquity that made them play such a role, but their blatant anthropomorphism, which made them ideal for expressing the prevalent interest in similarities between human beings and machines. This may help to explain why the sixteenth and the seventeenth centuries are considered the golden age of automata in spite of the fact that they were not abundant nor had they reached a significant breakthrough point in their construction, unlike the clock.

Many testimonies reflect the admiration that automata elicited. This is the case in the following passage in Cristóbal de Villalón's *Ingeniosa comparación entre lo antiguo y lo presente* (1539), which also shows that automata were closely associated with clocks:

> What can be more marvellous than how men have devised figurines and wooden statues that, thanks to clockwork mechanisms inside, walk by themselves on a table while holding and playing a kettledrum, a guitar or another instrument, and wave a flag even better than a real human being? (¿Qué cosa puede haber de más admiración que haber hallado los hombres industria como por vía unos relojes que unas imágenes y estatuas de madera anden por una mesa sin que ninguno los mueva, y juntamente,

andando, tañan con las manos una vihuela o atabal y otro instrumento, y vuelva una bandera con tanto orden y compás que un hombre vivo no lo pueda hacer con más perfección?)[63]

Their lifelike movement inspired in those who saw them a near-hypnotic impression, as is stated in *Coloquios de Palatino y Pinciano*:

PALATINO: I swear that I would never leave this shop after seeing such magical wonders, which astonish me as if I were a peasant in a palace. If you do not mind, I would like to see every trinket, especially the miniature fountains and dolls, which are so ingeniously and realistically made that they seem as if they were about to walk and talk. (Por mi fe que no tengo pies para salir de esta tienda, mirando estas brujerías, que me hacen estar embelesado, como labrador en palacio. Si no fuera pesadumbre, no dejara de ver particularmente cuantos dijes y menudencias hay aquí, y estas fuentecillas y muñecas que están tan ingeniosas y vivas que parece que quieren andar y hablar.)[64]

The tendency to equate machines and humans that is at work with clocks is stronger in the case of automata because of their anthropomorphism. As with clocks, the perceived similarity between human beings and automata serves humorous purposes in the literature of the time. In Quiñones de Benavente's "Entremés de los ladrones y el reloj," to surprise some thieves, two characters hide themselves by pretending to be automata and strike the time: "take this bucket and I will strike it with this mallet as if we were a clock" (tú con este caldero y yo con el mazo dando que parezcamos reloj).[65] In López de Úbeda's *La pícara Justina*, the behaviour of stingy lovers is compared to the actions of the automata that strike the hours in some clocks:

Do you know to what I like to compare these bragging lovers, who pretend to be very generous but who never give you anything? They are like bells, like organ tuners who tune the instrument but do not play it, they are like the automata in clocks, which seem as if they were to smash the bell to pieces with their hammers but they only make some noise. (¿Saben a qué los comparo yo estos amantes campanudos que hacen apariencias y no ofrecen? Símiles de los amantes campanudos. Parécenme que son como afinadores de órgano, que le templan y no le tocan; son como hombres de reloj, que amagan a quebrar la campana y sólo la hacen sonar; son como truenos, que hacen ruido y nunca daño.)[66]

As has been said, the role that automata played in the contemporary imagination was disproportionate to their actual numbers and mechanical capabilities. The automata of the period – stand-alone toys in the hands of a few rich collectors or attached to clocks – were actually basic machines of limited movements. In Spain, documentation of public clocks with simple automata goes as far back as the fourteenth century. The best known of this type is the famous Papamoscas (Fly-eater) in the Cathedral of Burgos, first installed in 1385. The version that can be seen today is a male human figure that strikes the hours while opening its mouth, as if it were a singer. Equally limited in their movements are the surviving automata attached to public clocks in Astorga and Medina del Campo.[67] As well as the automata attached to clocks, a few stand-alone ones were made for wealthy patrons. The most famous and illustrative are the automata attributed to the aforementioned Juanelo Turriano. He was the royal clockmaker and spent a considerable part of his time making mechanical toys for the emperor Charles V, who is said to have enjoyed assembling and disassembling them during his retreat in Yuste. Only a few of Turriano's creations have survived, such as the automaton of a 39-centimetre-tall mechanical monk, currently in the Smithsonian Institute, that walks back and forth with a cross in his hand while hitting his chest with the other hand. Several exaggerated reports have survived describing automata that could play musical instruments or wonderful birds that flew. Some of them, as the Hombre de Palo that walked the streets of Toledo, have been proven to be just myths but confirm the powerful grip that self-moving anthropomorphic machines had on the collective imagination.[68]

The toys that Turriano made for Charles V are not the only known automata in the Spain of the period. Charles V's son, Philip II, was also interested in clocks. In his will, over 100 clocks are mentioned, some of them with added figurines, of which several were possibly automata. Turriano also made animated self-moving toys for Philip II, who collected and displayed them together with other curious objects in El Escorial. Other collections that contained automata and similar curiosities are known to have existed in Spain and the rest of Europe during the late sixteenth century and the seventeenth century. Juan de Espina Velasco, a wealthy and cultivated man praised by Quevedo, was also a known collector in Madrid, as were the Duke of Monterrey and the Marquis of Leganés. In Huesca, Vincencio Juan de Lastanosa (1607–81) had a collection that Baltasar Gracián and others praised, which included automata.[69] A common feature of these men was a clear will to enhance the effect objects had on the onlookers by controlling their presentation. They were displayed in the so-called *Wunderkammern*, *studioli*, and *gabinetes de curiosides*, which ranged from cupboards or small rooms to buildings with annexed gardens to which elaborate mechanical fountains and grottoes had been added.[70]

The same economy of spectacularity that informed the theatrical display of these private collections is detectable in the stories of Cañizares, the Enchanted Head, and the Glass Licentiate, in which theatricality is artfully enlisted to provoke a calculated effect of astonishment on the audience.[71] Cervantes carefully devises complex deceptions and stages the discovery of the truths underlying these *tropelías*. Likewise, Cañizares is well aware that the display of her demonic creed and practices will shock the onlookers and, therefore, she zealously keeps her inner world hidden behind a facade of charities and prayers. When she decides to reveal her real self to Berganza, she carefully arranges the theatrics of the display for maximum effect. Before she makes him accompany her into her private cubicle – which serves as *studiolo* (a cabinet room used for meditation and study) for her witchcraft – Cañizares warns Berganza of the portentous nature of what he is about to see, as if he were about to enter a cabinet of curiosities or a small tent sideshow in a carnival. She instructs him to keep his composure, no matter how astonishing the events he may witness. Inside, she offers a private performance for him: she takes her clothes off, covers her naked body with hallucinogenic ointment, and enters into a trance. The purpose of the trance is to enable her to access the supernatural realm and answer the question of how to fulfil the prophecy of Berganza's return to his original human shape. The realm she is trying to access resembles the ones that the Glass Licentiate and the Enchanted Head allegedly contact when they answer their audiences. In the end, as in the cases of the Enchanted Head and the Glass Licentiate, Cañizares's supernatural access is proven to be nothing but (self-)deception and delusion.

Mechanical objectification in *El licenciado Vidriera* extends past the period of Tomás's insanity and reaches to the end of the story. After being cured by a monk who, meaningfully, specializes in the deaf and the mute, the story hurriedly comes to an end: Tomás Rueda – his new name – goes to the capital of the kingdom to work as a lawyer, but his previous reputation as an amusingly insane man does not allow him to succeed because people still follow him around expecting to be entertained by his witticisms. He then joins the Spanish army, this time in earnest, and dies as a brave fighter in Flanders. It is not clear if his courage redeems him and implies that he has finally become human. One cannot but think that his death in Flanders makes him just a small part in the big machinery that is the army in a period when war was becoming a communal enterprise of organized squadrons moving in disciplined coordination. Tomás's death would then exemplify one of the most common uses of the word "machine" during the time, namely, to signify a war device.[72] If this is the case, self-destruction is the only alternative left for the man who transformed himself into a machine, the same destiny of self-destruction that Cañizares, and the anthropomorphic monsters and their hubristic creators, have deserved in later literature.

### Self-fashioning Gone Awry: Autonomy vs. Automatism

The stories of Cañizares and the Glass Licentiate are dissective narratives in which a complex form of interiority is recreated to be later disassembled. Instead of containing literal dissections or anatomical passages, these narratives rely on the awareness that human beings are a mere assembly of parts working together, not so different from machines. Associated with this awareness is the fear that the human being relies on a delicate balance that can be easily altered. Such alteration, be it by wilful intervention or by accident, may affect the deepest core of the human being, its personality and selfhood. The specific anxiety of interiority at play in these narratives is the realization that people can neither understand nor control their innermost fabric, which can be altered in unpredictable directions. Cervantes shows a deep awareness that every person has a complex, highly malleable interior which can – even must – be transformed. At the same time, he recognizes that many pitfalls lie waiting in this process. The threat that the transformation may bring unintended consequences – automatism in this case – can be framed within the larger theme of the unpredictable effects of manipulation of the natural order. The risks implicit in the acquisition of knowledge and its application to change nature is a well-established theme that can be traced as far back as Prometheus's appropriation of fire or the Tree of Knowledge in Genesis.[73]

Tomás and Cañizares are the initiators of ill-advised self-fashioning processes in which they tinker with their inner functioning with disastrous results. Instead of helping them reach the enhanced personal autonomy they strived for, their self-imposed regimes turn them into entities that behave with the out-of-control self-sufficiency and the mindless automatism seen as the trait of contemporary machines. Cañizares's misguided spiritual quest alters her nature to the point of isolating her in a perverted inner world of her own manufacture. In her seclusion, she acts like a faulty clock that keeps ticking away on its own, badly in need of being brought into harmony with God's creation. Such tuning is, however, impossible because she is so withdrawn that she cannot communicate with the rest of the created world, even so far, she thinks, as to be out of the reach of God's grace. Such a deadlock comes to an unintended end when, as a consequence of having confided her secrets to Berganza, her motionless, naked body is publicly exposed and repeatedly pierced and her secrets revealed as if in a public autopsy or auto-da-fé. Unlike the clear punishment that Cañizares receives, Tomás's end is ambiguous: after being cured of his insanity by the intervention of a friar, he fails in his attempt to become a useful member of society by practising law because he cannot let go of his past. In the end, his only way out is to die in war, like a hero. This can be seen as a meaningful fulfilment of his life or simply as the expected destruction of a war machine in battle, thus foreshadowing the often-suicidal demise of later half-human half-mechanical monsters.

If Cañizares is comparable to a mystic who has isolated herself from the rest of creation in her pursuit of the inner path, Tomás resembles an ascetic who has gone too far in his quest for spiritual mastery. Whereas true Christian ascetics suppress their bodily appetites but remain connected to their fellow human beings by charity and piety, Tomás's foolish discipline of selfish learning and detachment has resulted in the laughable replacement of flesh with glass and placed him in complete alienation. Truly, he has disposed not only of his flesh but also of his humanity. He has isolated himself from his true nature and from those who surround him. In this state, he is the travesty of a holy man. Like prophets and saints, he is an emaciated figure, a homeless wanderer who finds occasional shelter in barns and inns. But while those who have reached true wisdom are surrounded by disciples who reverently listen to their sage words, Tomás acts as an automaton that regurgitates canned witticisms for the entertainment of improvised audiences. His insane belief that he is made of glass is a punishment comparable to the one Apollo inflicted upon Marsyas for his hubris in competing with a god. In the case of the Glass Licentiate, he punishes himself with his insanity. He deprives himself of his flesh and humanity, and he could cry out, as Marsyas did to Apollo, who was flaying him, "Why do you tear me from myself?" (Quid me mihi detrahis?).[74]

Discussing Don Quixote, Greene says that "Cervantes wrote the most powerful of all attacks upon the transforming imagination ... The knight of La Mancha is so lovable because he is so inflexible ... The blurring of man's upper limits had gradually yielded to humbling lucidity."[75] Don Quixote (immobilized on his horse by the rigidity of his makeshift armour and his mental constructions), the robotic Glass Licentiate, and Cañizares (the clock out of sync), started self-transformations that went awry. They ignored or disturbed key aspects of their human nature with disastrous results.[76] But in spite of their calamitous endings, their stories cannot be flatly understood as exemplifications of Saint Augustine's dictum "hands off yourself, try to build up yourself and you build a ruin." These words are famously quoted by Greenblatt to encapsulate the negative attitude towards self-fashioning before the Renaissance. Saint Augustine's words are, however, taken out of a meaningful context since he wrote them as a commentary on Psalm 127:1: "Except the Lord build the house, they labour in vain that build it" (Nisi Dominus aedificaverit domum, in vanum laboraverunt qui aedificant eam).[77] Saint Augustine's whole commentary is really meant not so much as a call to inaction but as a call to attention to the central role of God's grace in all human enterprises. Cervantes's attitude towards self-transformation must be understood not exclusively in this religious sense but also as a reminder of the limitations and risks of such an enterprise. His stories show that the process of self-construction is not entirely in a person's hands. Pico della Mirandola's *On the Dignity of Man* claims that "thou mayest fashion thyself in whatever shape thou shalt prefer."[78] But next to the opportunity of growing into angels, Pico also mentions the risk of degenerating into lower forms of life. Cañizares and Tomás Rodaja, by proceeding without the required skilfulness, go even lower and become machines.

## The Anatomizer of His Honour in Zayas's Stories

María de Zayas, famous in her day for her novellas, is recognized by critics today as one of the rare female voices of the period. Little is known of her life, except that she lived in Madrid in the mid-seventeenth century, belonged to a wealthy family, and was a celebrated writer well known in literary circles. Her writing is concerned with the contemporary situation of women.[79] Her novellas deal with one of the main concerns of high-class women of the time: navigating the intricacies of the honour code. As Goytisolo and other critics have remarked, her narratives express a continuous, irresolvable fight between honour and passion, between duty and desire.[80] The heroines of Zayas's stories are Spanish noblewomen who, proudly aware of the privileges and obligations that their social status implies, incarnate the "soy quien soy" formula. Her *Novelas amorosas y ejemplares* (*Exemplary Tales of Love*, 1637) and *Desengaños amorosos* (*The Disenchantments of Love*, 1647) include twenty stories that share a common Boccaccian frame. Each story is related by one of the distinguished young women and men who meet to entertain the equally noble young Lysis during her convalescence from quartan fever in contemporary Madrid. She is enamoured of a young man who does not return her affection. Befitting her sentimental situation, the exemplary and entertaining stories told contain turbulent relationships between women and men. At the end of the second volume, Lysis turns down a new suitor and decides to enter a convent. Such an ending is the logical conclusion to the pessimistic tone of this second collection of stories, in which women are systematically the victims of men's deceptions and abuses.

Although the first volume contains some violence, it reaches its climax in the second, whose stories are narrated exclusively by women and appropriately labelled *desengaños* instead of *novelas*.[81] Violence takes different shapes throughout the book, but several stories coincide in presenting jealous husbands who cruelly kill their innocent wives. Different reasons have been adduced for Zayas's choice to include so much violence in the second volume. The hypothesis that Zayas may have suffered a sentimental disappointment between the first and second collection of stories is too simplistic. Her choice to portray this issue may well have been a literary choice dictated by aesthetic or commercial motives. As a matter of fact, similar violence was common in many *novelas* of the period, as well as in the literary models of the genre. Furthermore, many plots of contemporary *comedias* included wives killed by their husbands, such as Calderón's *El médico de su honra*, *El pintor de su deshonra*, and *A secreto agravio, secreta venganza*. Also, as Levisi pointed out, violence against women is present in martyrology, a genre whose influence is easily detectable in Zayas's stories. Finally, it must not be forgotten that violence and its representation was so prevalent in the period that Maravall considers it part of the pessimistic outlook on life of the Baroque culture.[82]

What makes Zayas's *Desengaños* peculiar is not that they contain violence against women but rather the amount and the quality of that violence. Although women are not the only victims of violence in the stories (some women perform violent acts against men and other women), the body count shows a prevailing pattern of men killing women. Talking about the extent of the violence, Greer writes, "Zayas in this volume carries to such extremes her depiction of the violence of the patriarchal order against women that it seems to threaten the very survival of that order, if not of the human species itself."[83] Next to this quantity, the elaborate preparations and cruel executions are described in such detail that they have been qualified as pornographic and grotesque.[84] The conspicuous violence in Zayas's stories was noticed already by early twentieth-century critics, who considered it part of her realistic style.[85] Later critics disagreed with this assessment, which they deemed a biased vision resulting from the prestige of realism in the novel of the nineteenth century. Furthermore, to qualify Zayas's presentation of violence against women as realistic failed to take into account that her stories did not portray the daily life of the period. Legal and historical records indicate that husbands who killed their wives for supposed adulteries were the exception rather than the norm. In most cases, financial settlements and other discreet arrangements were reached.[86] For many critics, such as Vollendorf, Zayas's decision to include so much detailed violence is a didactic resource that is part of her feminist agenda of denouncing the contemporary situation of women. Thus, O'Brien writes that these stories deal with "the accumulating perils that secular Spanish society poses for the highly born woman who is the focal point of Zayas' *novelas*." Some critics, such as Clamurro, see the violence in Zayas also as a transcoder of a generalized ambience of social tensions. Boyer connects it with the militarism that ravaged Spain. For Greer, many instances of violence in Zayas are to be understood also as manifestations of subconscious drives.[87]

Without discarding these explanations, I contend that the conspicuous presence of violence against women in some of Zayas's *Desengaños* reveals dissective narratives that reflect an anxiety comparable to that seen in texts studied in previous chapters. Her stories are unique, however, because they deal with a gendered form of embodied interiority that is specific to upper-class women. Whereas the previously studied forms claimed the head, the heart, or the intestines as loci for their functions and contents, the interiority at work in the *desengaños* claims the sexual/reproductive female anatomy. As in previous cases, these organs are credited with roles and values that go beyond their physiological functions. In this case, female anatomy becomes the seat for the chastity and fidelity that the honour system demanded from noble women of that period in Spain. The stories present men's assaults on these organs and on the values they embody and, especially, women's reactions.[88] One caveat that needs to be made clear is that Zayas's positing of this female interiority does not mean that she denies women brainpower. Quite to the contrary, she attributes to women the same psychological capacities as men. In the introductory materials to her *Novelas amorosas y ejemplares*, she states that "if our blood is the same thing, our senses, faculties, and organs through which their effects are wrought are all the same, the soul the same as theirs – since souls are neither male nor female – what reason is there that they would be wise and presume we cannot be so?" (47, 159; si es una misma la sangre; los sentidos, las potencias y los órganos por donde se obran sus efectos son unos mismos; la misma alma que ellos, porque las almas no son ni hombre ni mujeres: ¿qué razón hay para que ellos sean sabios y presuman que nosotros no podemos serlo?).[89] Accordingly, her heroines' actions repeatedly prove their courage and intelligence. In *El juez de su causa* (*Judge Thyself*), the female protagonist dresses as a man and excels in war and politics, which were traditionally men's turf.[90] Furthermore, most women show perseverance and other virtues that their fickle male counterparts fail to match.

Up to which point Zayas was familiar with the culture of dissection is difficult to ascertain given how little we know of her life. Although dissection was a male enterprise, given that she was a cultivated woman who frequented literary circles, she must have had access to the same texts as her male counterparts. Even if she had not had access to the medical texts themselves, she would have been exposed to them second-hand. Certainly she would have read Granada's pious books, which were especially widespread among female readers and, as we saw, contained extended passages on anatomy. In her stories, however, no direct references to anatomy and dissection are to be found, although some scenes contain echoes. For instance, in *La fuerza del amor* (*The Power of Love*), the protagonist wants to concoct a love philtre that calls for body parts as ingredients. To obtain them, she pays a nocturnal visit to a chapel whose churchyard is used to exhibit the corpses of executed men (365). Such excursions, although belonging to the practices traditionally associated with witches, recall similarly gloomy expeditions of Vesalius and other anatomists to procure specimens for their dissections. Also, some anatomical echoes are evoked by the fact that the *desengaños* are narrated during the celebrations surrounding Carnival. Public dissections took place during this season because they were

festive events that contained *memento mori* imagery to prepare the audiences for Lent. By providing a salutary moral lesson for the audience,
the heroines sacrificed in the *desengaños* serve the same function as the
corpses on the dissection table.[91]

Unlike the previously analysed texts, Zayas's stories do not contain
direct references to the organs upon which interiority is posited. The
reason for this absence is that conventional modesty did not permit
written references to female organs. The *secreta mulierum*, as gynaeco-
logical issues were euphemistically called, were only whispered in the
most private conversations among women, never as part of public discourse.[92] Thus, gendered interiority has to be found not in allusions to
female anatomy in the text, but in the heroines' near-obsessive awareness of the standing of their reproductive organs within the parameters
imposed by the honour code. Acutely attuned to the social implications
of transgression, the female protagonists struggle to hide their sullied
sexual/reproductive status, keeping secret their lost virginity, seduc-
tions, and rapes from their parents, husbands, and the rest of society. As
in previous chapters, the private awareness of the disparity between
one's interior world and the external one results in an anxiety that
resurfaces in more or less dissective scenarios of punitive investigations, secrecy and exposure, guilt and innocence. These ingredients are
combined in Zayas's stories of women unable to prove their innocence
against orchestrated campaigns or overzealous husbands. They can
only appeal to the mute testimony of their bodies to prove their virtue,
but this is a private, unmediated knowledge that cannot be summoned
in their defence.[93] The aforementioned ingredients also appear in plots
of women's bodies sexually sullied without them having been aware of
or responsible for it. The description of women raped while they were
unconscious or hypnotized reappears in several stories and is central to
the plot of *La inocencia castigada* (*Innocence Punished*), in which the protagonist is deprived of her will through a magic spell.

At first sight, the torture and executions that the wives undergo do not
resemble dissections since no woman is literally "opened" by a knife.
Uncanny similarities exist, however, between some of these scenes and
the treatment of female corpses by contemporary anatomical science and
medicine.[94] For instance, lethal bloodletting is used to kill women in several stories, such as *El verdugo de su esposa* (*His Wife's Executioner*) and *Mal
presagio casar lejos* (*Marriage Abroad: Portent of Doom*). Critics have traditionally recognized the choice of this medical procedure as highly symbolic in a society obsessed with blood purity. Thus, the metaphorical

suitability of bloodletting for healing a wounded honour is fully developed in some plays of the period, such as Calderón's *El médico de su honra*. Putting aside the undeniable symbolism, bloodletting places women under the same medical knife with which dissections are performed. Furthermore, bloodletting acts as the first step in the embalming and reification of bodies, thus echoing the anatomical methods to stabilize the dissected corpses. But as we will see, dissective echoes are especially noticeable in how the executed wives' corpses become the centre of tableaux that bear an uncanny resemblance to the contemporary anatomical illustrations and instructional figurines.

## Female Anatomy under Scrutiny

Zayas's stories exemplify the suffocating scrutiny and the continuous danger that upper-class women had to endure in a social order that made them mere vessels that literally and figuratively reproduced the nobiliary system. In order to conserve and transmit privilege, the system restrained access to upper-class women's organs. Such restriction was a cornerstone in assuring legitimate paternity and, therefore, the transmission by birth of the qualities that noble blood was supposed to bestow upon the person. A consequence was that women were identified with and limited to their female anatomy – their hymens, vaginas, and uteruses – a prejudice that was supported by the medico-anatomical ideas passed down since antiquity. In the eyes of antiquity and early modernity, women were synonymous with their uterus, and their whole bodies were envisioned as enticing yet functional envelopes for the all-important reproductive organs.[95] These ideas resulted in the female body being conceived in spatial terms. Dopico Black, writing about the adultery-murder plays, affirms that the woman's body worked as "a mere *receptacle* for her husband's honour – or, if she is unmarried, her father's or her brothers," and women's crime was "allowing a sacrosanct interior – the house's or the body's – to be penetrated, sullied, contaminated even, by an Other."[96] As Clamurro has shown, this propensity is also detectable in the application of the discourse of empire and national integrity to women's bodies in Zayas's stories. Women's bodies were especially prone to be allegorized into a territory and, as such, subject to tropes of conquest and defence. Thus, many contemporary plots are about husbands struggling to defend their wives' and daughters' bodies against treacherous assaults by competing males. In some cases, the stories ended with the husbands' final departure from and destruction of the citadel they failed to defend.

Since antiquity, women's bodies were conceived as containing more empty space than men's bodies, with the female body often being conceptualized as a bottle or a jar.[97] This image was in part the result of the belief that female sexual organs were an inversion of their male counterparts. Women's anatomy included a penis turned inside out residing in the abdomen. The external space surrounding the penis was thought to be the internal cavity of the uterus. This organ was considered not to be fixed but in continuous movement throughout the abdominal and thoracic areas, which were believed to be also relatively hollow. Mouth and vagina were the two points of access to this empty space inside women. Accordingly, both orifices were used to administer good or bad odours to attract or repel the uterus when it hurt because it was situated too high or too low. Not only physical but also psychological disorders – later to be included under the umbrella term "hysteria" – were considered to be caused by these displacements.[98]

Women were thought to be more affected than men by their embodiment, which had negative and positive consequences. As Stallybrass has shown, a woman's body was considered grotesque in the Bakhtinian sense and, as such, had a tendency to escape regulations.[99] Because of their colder, dryer bodies, women were supposedly less rational and more given to pseudo-mystical visions. On the other hand, they were acclaimed as more finely attuned than men to their inner bodies and feelings. In *La más infame venganza* (*Most Infamous Revenge*), the narrator accuses men of feigning feelings they do not really have inside, because men "exaggerate and say more than they feel" (54, 71; publican más que sienten). The belief that women were more "interior" than men also played a role in the worship of the Virgin Mary, whose defining role in sacred history was precisely that of being a vessel in which the Son of God was begotten. Accordingly, she was often literally called a holy vessel, a reliquary, and other names associated with precious containers. Also, her entrails are part of her role as *La Dolorosa* or the pietà. Thus, the pain she suffered when she saw Jesus crucified is described by Fray Luis de Granada as "your heart is pierced by the spear and your entrails are torn by the nails" (penetra tu corazón la lanza, y rompen tus entrañas los clavos).[100] Mary's cousin Elizabeth is also a container finely attuned to its content during the Visitation, when she feels the jump of joy that the future John the Baptist makes inside her when he senses that Mary is carrying the Saviour.[101]

9 Title page of the first edition of Andreas Vesalius's *De humani corporis fabrica*
(Basilea: J. Oporinus, 1543). Vesalius is portrayed to the left of the cadaver.
(By permission of the History of Medicine Division, National Library of
Medicine of the National Institutes of Health)

In spite of the significance of its reproductive function, the worth of
the female body in anatomical studies was limited by the generalized
acclaim of the male body as the normative human model. Compared to
it, the female body was seen as an inferior variation whose only anatomical interest resided in the reproductive organs. Female corpses
were solely dissected for the study of these organs by anatomists, who,
being all males, were fascinated by their capacity to create life. The
interest that female anatomy raised is epitomized by the title page of
Vesalius's *De humani corporis fabrica* (see Figure 9). Although most of the
illustrations of the book are of male bodies dissected to exemplify
human anatomy at its best, the title page portrays Vesalius dissecting
the abdomen of a female corpse in front of a large audience of men. The

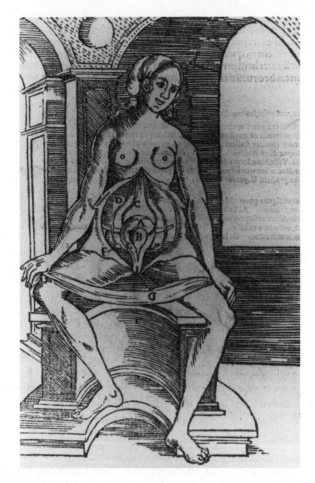

10  Nude woman sitting on a birthing chair with her abdomen exposed for
anatomical analysis. From *Anatomia Mundini* (1541). (By permission of the
History of Medicine Division, National Library of Medicine of the National
Institutes of Health)

widespread male curiosity for the female anatomy was the result not
only of its unique reproductive capacities but also of the halo of mystery surrounding it. Compared to their male counterparts, the female
sexual organs are internal and therefore invisible from the outside. The
voyeuristic curiosity that this hiddenness triggered manifested itself in
curious venues. For instance, some literature circulating at the time

11  Semi-reclined female figure in an alluring position with her abdomen
exposed for anatomical analysis. From Charles Estienne's *De dissectione partium
corporis humani* (1545). (By permission of the History of Medicine Division,
National Library of Medicine of the National Institutes of Health)

gave advice on how to read women's sexual intimacies from the outside. *De secretis mulierum,* a treatise falsely attributed to Albert the
Great, was originally written to help confessors advise women, but it
reached an extended readership. Next to truly gynecological chapters,
it dedicates a section to how to tell whether women are virgin from the
position they assume to urinate.[102]

But the male interest in female anatomy is not limited to spying on its reproductive capacities; rather, it often contains destructive, hubristic overtones. This is epitomized in the medieval legend of Emperor Nero ordering the opening of his mother's body so he could see the place where he had been conceived. This spurious anecdote, based on the historical event of Nero's assassination of Agrippina, wanted to convey the monstrosity of this enemy of Christianity by charging him not only with matricide but also with the ultimate sin of looking inside – and therefore tearing apart – the very place of his creation.[103] Similar sadistic, destructive impulses are detectable in the treatment of women's bodies in some early modern medical books. In a study of the anatomical engravings of these manuals, Traub proves that they reflect a voyeuristic and sadistic delight in taking apart and displaying the most recondite nooks and crannies of the female body. These illustrations were part of a "representational field in which the uncovering of the female body was taken to its physical limit."[104] Beginning in the late Middle Ages, anatomical books, such as those by Mondino de Luzzi and Berengario da Carpi, included representations of women whose abdomens had been cut open to show their reproductive organs (see Figure 10). These images of attractive young women, in positions that invite the male gaze into their most private organs through horrific wounds, contain a sadistic allure that anticipates later pornography. Some bodies are depicted in erotic poses of impudent abandonment, or sleep, as if they were nymphs caught by surprise in a meadow by a satyr. The best examples of eroticized dissections are eight figures illustrating female anatomy in Charles Estienne's *De dissectione partium corporis humani* (1545). This manual of inaccurate pre-Vesalian anatomy includes plates of naked women in their bedrooms and other private spaces, reclined in sensuous poses and immodestly showing the most intimate *secreta* that have been exposed by the dissecting knife (see Figure 11). The eroticized necrophilic appeal of these images is related to their origins: they are Estienne's adaptations for anatomical purposes of the engravings that illustrated the loves of the gods and their metamorphosis in *Gli amori degli dei* by Gian Giacomo Caraglio.[105] Their erotic background remains evident, since, as Mitchell has noticed, their "depiction of deeper levels of dissection into the organs of generation reveals the purported *telos* of heterosexual intercourse and the final cause of female sexual anatomy, the purpose for which it is designed and constructed."[106]

The images of dissected female bodies in these engravings were designed by and for men. They offered a combination of eroticism and sadism alluring to the male eye. But to the female eye, the images had a chilling effect because the unintended female viewers saw eroticized representations of women being punished for the same sexuality that they are invoked to illustrate. The images elicited the association between the gallows and the dissection table that was mentioned in previous chapters, but modified in a gender-specific way. While the male corpses used for dissections were those of executed felons, female corpses were those of the destitute women, many of them prostitutes, who died at charity hospitals.[107] An illustration of how women who ended up on the dissection table were often those whose sexuality was unprotected by the legal bonds of marriage is contained in an anecdote narrated by Vesalius. He writes that in Padua a monk's lover died suddenly from strangulation of the uterus. She was buried immediately to prevent the corpse from being used for anatomical purposes. But this cautionary measure was circumvented by Vesalius's clever students, who exhumed the corpse and flayed it promptly, so preventing its possible identification by the authorities if they came to reclaim it.[108]

The connection between illegitimate female sexuality, punishment, and dissection was only one of the aspects that made these images ominous to women's eyes. As Sawday writes, "[i]f the Renaissance anatomy theatre, in its modes of ritual and representation, offered the suggestion of redemption to the male cadaver, what it offered to the female was the reverse, a demonstration of Eve's sin."[109] A strong negative association between woman's sexuality and the Fall is integral to sacred history. Eve tempting Adam with the fruit of knowledge is often equalled to woman as the sexual temptress. Furthermore, in the post-lapsarian world into which humankind was exiled by Eve's sin, death becomes a reality that makes sexual reproduction necessary to replenish the decimated ranks. Female anatomy, in both its sexual and reproductive forms, is then a punishment and a consequence of Eve putting an end to an Edenic innocence that was often associated with the bliss of prelapsarian sexual ignorance. For upper-class women like Zayas, the anatomical engravings contained an added warning. By representing female bodies being simultaneously desired and punished for their sexuality, these images illustrated how the same organs that allowed noblewomen to perform the roles of wife and mother could easily become the agent of their demise. Noblewomen's social identity relied on two necessarily sexual functions: marrying a high-rank male and bearing his offspring. At the same time, the fulfilment of these tasks implied a controlled deployment of women's sexuality through chastity before marriage and spousal fidelity afterwards. If women were unable to curb their sexual desires and disobeyed these principles, they could be severely punished for breaking the rules. They became social pariahs and could not enter or maintain a respectable marriage, which was the only path for women to be constituted as subjects. In a few cases, it could even lead to them being murdered by their husbands or relatives.[110]

The control of women's bodies as the cornerstone in the maintenance and transmission of honour and privilege was especially important in a Spain obsessed with blood purity. As Dopico Black states regarding the situation of women in early modern Spain, "the wife's body served as a kind of transcoder of and for various types of cultural anxieties, a site on which concerns over the interpretation and misinterpretation of signs, and especially signs of Otherness – racial, religious, cultural – were at different times projected, materialized, codified, negotiated, and even contested."[111] If being from humble origins was not an insurmountable impediment to obtaining nobiliary titles, the suspicion of tainted blood was a major blow to any such aspirations. Talking about the importance of *limpieza de sangre* (blood purity) in the period and the institutions that took care of it, Brownlee claims that Zayas's stories explore

> the physical and psychological effects of these social institutions on the private citizen with a degree of obsessiveness and fascination that is hard to equal in that or any other period ... [W]hile Zayas does not explicitly allude to the Inquisition's regulatory zeal in religious terms (extending to racial repression as well), its effects on nationalism, race, and even religion are always a central focus of her writing.[112]

The prejudice that women were not capable of controlling their feelings and appetites was the justification for keeping them under constant surveillance. Where women went, how they dressed, what they did in their free time at home – all were highly regulated to prevent the possibility, even the suspicion, of unsanctioned sex. Several of Zayas's stories present upper-class women who are punished and killed for alleged sexual transgressions. The husbands, however, do not dissect their wives' bodies because they are aware that the sexual indiscretions they suspect do not leave physical traces, no matter how closely and deeply the bodies are scrutinized. Beyond the presence or absence of the hymen at the moment of marital contract – and the possibility of deception was notorious – later fidelity or unfaithfulness leaves no physical marks. As Dopico Black states, "where her chastity is concerned, the wife's body is illegible in ways that are not only specific to but requisite of her legal status as wife."[113] Symptomatically, the undeniable proof of unwanted pregnancies never happens in the stories in spite of the frenzy of illicit sexual activity.[114] But the most important reason for the husbands not to search for confirmation inside the bodies is that they are already convinced of their wives' guilt. In spite of the lack of tangible evidence, the husbands proceed to revenge their injured honour. They are executioners, not coroners.

The strongest echoes of dissection are to be found, then, not so much in the husbands' methods of execution and torture as in the female corpses. Unlike the anatomical engravings, in which women's guilty members (i.e., their sexual organs) take the cut of the knife directly, in Zayas's stories the whole body is punished. However, since the female body was understood as a mere envelope of the reproductive organs, punishment of any of its part stands metonymically for punishment of its sexuality. In any case, the results of the husbands' revenge are female corpses whose spectacularity rivals that of the female bodies in the anatomical engravings. The detailed description of the bodies of the executed wives has been repeatedly noticed by critics as one of the main ingredients of Zayas's aforementioned goriness. According to Greer, the aestheticized spectacularity of these corpses sets them apart from the sombreness of other dead bodies represented in the period: those of the *memento mori* iconography, the manuals of good death, and the martyrological literature.[115] Saints' and martyrs' miraculous dead bodies are, however, the undeniable origin of the pattern of extraordinary beauty that characterizes the wives' corpses. As the martyrological model prescribes, the innocent wives neither rebel against nor try to escape from their unjust sentences. After their execution, their bodies also follow the literary model in reaching an extraordinary beauty. In *El verdugo de su esposa*, Roseleta is subject to bloodletting to heal her sick throat. While she is asleep, her husband removes the band that keeps the wound closed. She bleeds to death, becoming a Sleeping Beauty who cannot wake up, "the loveliest sight human eyes have ever seen" (102, 221; la más bella cosa que los ojos humanos habían visto).

The post-mortem onset of extraordinary beauty goes beyond proclaiming the wives' innocence according to the martyrological pattern. It also triggers an erotic attraction in those who see their dead bodies that is comparable to the attraction anatomists feel towards corpses.

Similar erotic necrophilia is implied in the aforementioned story of Vesalius's students "eloping" with the body of the clergyman's lover, and near-romantic tones are detectable in Vesalius's descriptions of his secretive nocturnal excursions to obtain specimens for his experiments when he was a young man.[116] In Zayas's stories, dead women become even more sexually appealing to their husbands/executioners than they were while alive. In *Mal presagio casar lejos*, the beauty of Blanca's corpse is such that her husband, who had lost sexual interest in her to the point of replacing her for a male lover, finds her attractive again. A similarly morbid sexual attraction for unconscious, hypnotized, or barely alive women is present in several stories. In *Engaños que causa el vicio* (*Ravages of Vice*), Gaspar stares at the severely wounded, unconscious body of Florentina, which is qualified as "the almost dead beauty" (479; la casi difunta hermosura). In *La inocencia castigada*, Diego has intercourse with Inés's inanimate body while she is in a trance in which he is described as obtaining her "dead favours" (278; favores … muertos).[117]

Also connected to martyrology and hagiology is the corpses' resistance to decay. In *Mal presagio casar lejos*, the incorrupt state of Blanca after exhumation is identified as "a sign that her soul enjoys heavenly bliss" (237, 365; señal de la Gloria que goza el alma).[118] The incorruptibility of the executed wives reappears in several stories. Blanca's corpse is disinterred to be taken to Spain, and "she was as lovely as at the moment of her death" (237, 365; estaba tan lindo como si entonces acabara de morir). In *El traidor contra su sangre* (*Traitor to His Own Blood*), Ana's head, cut off and buried by her husband, is later recovered "as fresh and beautiful as if it hadn't laid buried for over six months" (267, 398; sacándola tan fresca como si no hubiera seis meses que estaba debajo de tierra). In *Tarde llega el desengaño* (*Too Late Undeceived*), the corpse of Elena, who succumbed to prolonged mistreatment by her husband, "with each passing hour looked more and more beautiful" (130, 254; cada hora parecía estar más hermosa). Like the corpses of the martyrs, the innocent wives' beautiful corpses talk back, proclaiming their innocence by not decaying, by exuding pleasant scents, or by healing their horrific wounds after death. In these cases, they are incorrupt in both meanings of the word, literally by not decaying and metaphorically by not being guilty of the adulterous relations of which they are accused.[119]

As well as serving as proof of their innocence in the martyrological tradition, the incorruptibility and beauty of the wives' bodies after their

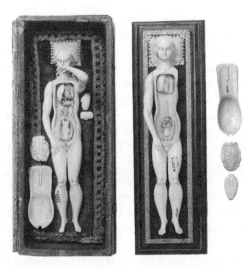

12  Two ivory figurines of anatomical Venuses dating from the seventeenth century. (R2351/1936, R2349/1966, reproduced by permission of the Wellcome Collection, London)

executions is also a manifestation of the process of reification to which they have been submitted by their husbands/executioners. The men act as anatomists who subject bodies to the destruction of the knife while turning them into lasting specimens whose decay is artificially stopped by the pencil of the artist or the embalming fluid.[120] Like the plates of the anatomical books of the period, the dead wives have been made into spectacular objects that are simultaneously appealing and horrifying. The reifying nature of the process that the wives undergo is perceptible in how their dead bodies do not seem to be made from flesh anymore. Their pale complexion – an attribute of female beauty in the Petrarchan tradition – is turned into a sign of their new nature as beautiful dolls made from wax or from a similarly inert material. References to dead women resembling statues appear several times in Zayas's stories. Thus, in *Engaños que causa el vicio*, Magdalena's dead body is lying on her bed "so beautiful that she looked like an ivory statue sprinkled with rosy petals" (348, 482; con tanta hermosura, que parecía una estatua de marfil salpicada de rosicler).

If we consider their wounds, colour, and general objectification, these spectacular dead women resemble the so-called anatomical Venuses, which were female figurines intended as instructional aids for doctors and midwives (see Figure 12). These were statuettes whose abdomens were cut out and could be removed to show the organs inside. Often they were displayed and kept in coffin-like boxes, as is the case with some of the few surviving ones, most made of ivory. Some made of wood still exist, but early statuettes made of wax have not survived given the fragility of the material. The anatomical Venuses are also evoked by a figurine made for magical purposes in *La inocencia castigada*. A nude doll in the likeness of Inés is made at the request of Diego, who, unable to obtain her favours, resorts to a Moorish sorcerer (154, 276). The figurine is probably made from wax, as was the case with a similar image described in *El desengaño amando y premio de la virtud (Disillusionment in Love and Virtue Rewarded)* (208, 404).[121] Like that image, the doll representing Inés has a dart that pierces through the left area of the chest, thus implying the existence of a heart inside the statuette.

The reification of anatomical and dissective practices is also evident in the immobilization and decentring to which Zayas's husbands subject their wives. The restriction of movement before and during their execution has been noticed by several critics, who attribute it to the male sadistic drive to make women into non-threatening erotic objects. Williamsen, for instance, writes that in *Mal presagio casar lejos* Blanca "becomes completely 'objectified' and she can serve as the perfect 'Other,' a passive canvas on which he can inscribe himself."[122] Repeatedly, the husbands tie up and confine their wives to narrow spaces before killing them or as part of prolonged torture. By restricting or impeding their movements, they are not only facilitating execution and increasing the suffering of the victims but also preparing their bodies to become the centrepieces of grisly tableaux. They want to frame their wives' bodies within a background that enhances their spectacularity in the same way the dissected corpses in the anatomical engravings are highlighted by carefully choreographed furniture and architecture.[123] In Zayas's stories the readers are shown the wives' corpses tied to the chairs in which they were garrotted or lying in the beds in which they were bled to death. Women are executed while sitting at the table, as in *El traidor contra su sangre*, in which Ana's head is cut off from behind while she is eating (264, 394). In *Mal presagio casar lejos*, Leonor is in her dressing room washing her hair, which her husband uses to strangle her after having entered the confined space through a window (212,

339). Motionless, surrounded by complicitous furniture and walls, Zayas's female corpses resemble dolls in a dollhouse of horrors. Connected to this immobilization is the decentring that female characters suffer. In *La inocencia castigada*, Inés is literally immured after she moves with her brother and sister-in-law to a house farther from Seville, outside of the new town, with no neighbours. The decentring imposed on Inés is accentuated because it originates from a nameless place, which is emphasized by how the story (echoing *Don Quixote*'s famous first lines) begins, "In a city near the great Seville that I choose not to name" (133, 265; En una ciudad cerca de la gran Sevilla, que no quiero nombrarla). Immobilization and decentring combine, as if the dissective narratives seek the centre of these "cavities" of displaced entities.[124]

Punitive reductions of mobility take varied forms in the stories. In *Mal presagio casar lejos*, Blanca's father-in-law, who will eventually be the agent of her death by bloodletting, threatens her: "I'll trim your wings" (228, 355; os cortaré yo las alas). This threat of immobilization evokes a butterfly pinned down to a board for display. The immobilization and confinement of the wives may encompass years of prolonged torture. In *Tarde llega el desengaño*, the invited dinner guests are horrified to learn how the supposedly unfaithful wife has been compelled to live in a confined space, from which she is only allowed to come out to eat the scraps with the dogs. Covered in rags, secluded within a small cubicle in which her only companion is the skull of her alleged lover, this wretched woman becomes a moving figurine in a macabre montage reminiscent of ascetics and penitents in their caves (113–16, 236–8). In her timed appearances to gather the leftovers, she resembles the mechanical figurines attached to clocks that strike the hour, acting as *memento mori* reminders of time passing. Similar motifs of immobility and automatism are present in other punishments that cruel husbands impose on their wives. In *Mal presagio casar lejos*, a woman jumps out the window to escape from the calculated orgy of blood her brother-in-law is perpetrating. As a result, she loses her legs and "[h]er bed became the theatre where, for the rest of her brief life, she was to live out the dreadful fate to which she had been born" (221, 348; la cama, el teatro mientras vivió representaba a todas horas la adversa estrella con que había nacido). As Williamsen appropriately remarks, she has become "half-woman, half-furniture."[125]

In spite of their spectacularity, the corpses resulting from the husbands' revenges are not intended for public display. In most cases, the lethal punishments are done and kept in private. Secrecy in purging one's honour is a commonplace in the literature of the period, as is evidenced by Calderón's choice of the title *A secreto agravio secreta venganza* (*Secret Vengeance for Secret Insult*). What is peculiar to Zayas is how the vengeful husband resembles the figure of the collector studied in the chapter on Quevedo, who patiently waits to obtain the specimen, then carefully preserves and displays it for his own private contemplation and that of a small group of intimates.[126] He turns a live woman into a dead body of statuesque beauty, so reversing Pygmalion's process of transforming a statue into a living woman.[127] More specifically, the husband evokes the peculiar collecting manners of the anatomist, who, while destroying bodies with his knife, turns them into displayable objects through drawings, castings, and other methods of preservation. Zayas's husbands make permanent displayable objects of their wives by killing and torturing them in ways comparable to the processes used in embalming and mummification. For instance, one of their preferred methods is bloodletting, which entails the removal of fluids and moisture from the body, considered the biggest cause of putrefaction of corpses.[128] Furthermore, in some stories the very punishments applied to the wives are a form of live embalming. In *La inocencia castigada*, Inés, immured in the house, is kept barely alive for years. When she is finally released from her confinement, the years of living in her own filth, insects, and maggots have consumed the lower part of her body. Her de-fleshed legs and emaciation make her resemble a corpse halfway through the artificial process of turning into a skeleton (164, 287).

## The Resistance of Beautiful Corpses

Although the wives' bodies resemble the combination of erotic appeal and horrific wounds of the female corpses in the anatomical engravings, Zayas's intention is not to produce a sadistic thrill to the male eye. Brownlee claims that Zayas's treatment of private matters in her stories "turns the readers into voyeurs."[129] This voyeurism must include both male and female readers since some women in Zayas's narratives do not show gender solidarity and are fully complicit in torture and murder, generally to protect their own interests. Their participation serves to detail the extent of the cover-up or veiling necessary for perceived infractions against the "holy" female body. Upper-class female readers would see themselves as complicit in what Zayas uncovers.[130] Vollendorf considers these images a form of resistance to violence, of "privileging the feminine perspective and displaying the dismembered body in order to re-member [*sic*] it again."[131] Zayas makes corpses talk back to their creators/executioners through a beauty and incorruptibility that reach the preternatural tones of the martyrological tradition. The prodigious persistent beauty of the corpses can only be attributed to the divine confirmation of their innocence. Thus, these bodies denounce the injustice, cruelty, and uselessness of their executions. The wives' dead bodies, which were opaque in their guilt or innocence while alive, become thus transparent in their innocence only after their death. The result is, as Jehenson and Welles have pointed out, that victims become also the victors in Zayas's stories.[132]

Zayas portrays jealous husbands' assaults on their innocent wives under the same discrediting light in which other inspections of interiority are presented by Granada, Cervantes, and Quevedo. Granada's treatment of the figure of the martyr is especially pertinent here. Zayas has mixed the portentous signs of the bodies of Christian martyrs with the beautiful female bodies of erotic poetry, and the result is disquietingly akin to anatomical engravings.[133] What makes some of Zayas's *Desengaños* like dissective narratives is not only the similarity of the dead bodies to these engravings, but also that her stories deal with interiority under external threat. The beautiful corpses resulting from the undeserved punishments symbolize upper-class women's anxiety about their difficult position within the social system. They are aware of playing a privileged yet dangerous role that relies on their sexualized body as the cornerstone for the maintenance and transmission of nobility. While offering them some advantages, this social identity places them at the mercy of an honour system rooted in old misogynistic and paternalistic prejudices that did not permit women to defend themselves against rumours and suspicions. They could easily be turned into social pariahs and, in some cases, be killed by their husbands or relatives. Zayas's stories narrate some of those cases from the woman's "inner" point of view. The prevalent scenario is one of unprovable inner innocence versus an external perception of guilt. In some cases, the defiling acts took place when the women were unconscious or asleep, or they were raped or seduced under the false impression that the men were their husbands or future husbands. In these situations, the woman's inner perception of innocence collides with the bluntness of an honour system unable to cope with subtle issues of free will and intent.[134] These cases too are other forms of dramatizing the unbridgeable gap between women's innocence and the

external opinion of husbands and society, between first-hand intro-
spective awareness of their unsullied interiority and a punishingly
inquisitive external world.

## Epilogue: Gracián's Performative Interior

Because dissective narratives may assume such diverse forms, I want to
guard against the possibility that any text dealing with interiority
through anatomical tropes could be classified as a dissective narrative.
To set boundaries that preclude such indiscriminate application of the
term, I will examine briefly the case of the Jesuit writer Baltasar Gracián
(1601–58). Although his texts deal profusely with interiority and contain abundant anatomical references, I contend that they do not qualify
as dissective narratives because they address a typically Baroque interiority that differs categorically from the cases previously studied. In
them interiority is not conceived as the intuition of a vague space that
may harbour thoughts felt by the authorities to be suspect and for
whose atonement propitiatory victims are to be sacrificed. Quite to the
contrary, interiority is perceived as a well-delimited, fully conscious
entity, the mastery of which is central to the personal quest for influence and power.[135] Gracián understands the inner realm in terms of a
theatrical space in which real and made-up scenarios are veiled or
unveiled according to the needs of the occasion, and faultless execution
is vital. Revealingly, the anxiety that interiority triggered with previous
authors has been replaced in Gracián by an obsession with adequate
performance. Also, the sacrificial victim of the dissective narratives has
been supplanted by the figure of one's adversary in the quest for power.
But the new object of dissection is not a voluntary or defenceless victim;
he is equipped with the same controlled interiority as the anatomizer,
and if the tables turn, he will be an equally proficient dissector. The
result is a duel that Checa appropriately compares to fencing.[136]

The exemplary characters praised by Gracián in El Político, El Héroe,
and El Discreto display an outstanding ability to ascertain their adversaries' most secret intentions. Equally, they know how to hide their
thoughts from their competitors through a variety of techniques, ranging from deception through false leads to the appearance of an unfathomable inner realm. As stated in El Héroe, "though by the means hereof
no man's merits can become inexhaustible, yet, which is the work of no
small genius, he must at least appear to be so" (3–4, 75; Esta primera
regla de grandeza advierte, si no el ser infinitos, a parecerlo, que no es

sutileza común). Interiority understood as competitive performance in the quest for ascendancy is also central to Gracián's allegorical novel *El Criticón*, as well as to his most famous work, *Oráculo manual y arte de la prudencia*. These books epitomize the Baroque world in which, because deceptive appearance rules, one must become a master at disguise while deciphering the intentions of others. For Egginton this attitude is part of the tendency of the period to privilege theatricality over presence in a society in which one must act, especially in the court, as a character in a play. In this society guided by self-interest, the idealistic ethos of the early Renaissance appears as outdated and naive.[137] In such a confusing and deceitful environment, the natural man is replaced by a cunning individual wearing "civilizing armours" for protection, writes Flor. The self, he adds, is a prisoner trapped inside the body, a feeling that is often compared to being in a labyrinth, the emblematic symbol of the period. Childers aptly summarizes this situation of inner exile by saying that, in the public sphere of the Baroque court, the opposite of public is not private, but secret.[138]

Gracián follows the well-established tradition of locating thoughts and feelings inside the body, as was the case with the previous authors, but he differs from them in his marked tendency to emphasize the vastness, remoteness, and inaccessibility of this location. Without specifying the organ, he often refers to it as "el fondo," "dentro," or "lo interior." His choice of metaphors, such as "secreto" or "llave" (213; secrecy, key), underlines the privacy of the inner locus. Vastness and remoteness are emphasized by his use of geographical terms, such as "océano" (124; ocean) or "ensenada" (397; cove).[139] In contrast to this secluded and spacious inner vault for thoughts and intentions, Gracián presents the outer body ("lo exterior," "la fachada," "la exterioridad") as a screen on which accurate or contrived signs of its contents are intentionally or accidentally projected. They are symptoms that offer the *discreto* – Gracián's epitome of the perfect man, always used in the masculine – the entry point to decipher his adversary's intentions. The *discreto*'s duty is to determine whether they are true representations of the opponent's real thoughts or merely smoke and mirrors. Gracián refers to the operation of deciphering the authenticity of external signs as an act of looking under the surface, which he compares to the task of a *zahorí* – i.e., to a diviner who, wand in hand, looks for underground water. Thus, in *El Discreto*, he speaks of "zahoríes del corazón" (322). Also, congruently with his use of ocean for interiority, he speaks of "sondar" (to probe or take soundings from a ship).[140]

In like manner to the authors studied in previous chapters, Gracián resorts to anatomical dissection as a trope to inspect thoughts and feelings.[141] The main difference is not in the images he chooses but in the intentions he implicitly attributes to the metaphorical dissective operations. Although the previous authors never presented dissection as a blatant manoeuvre for the selfish benefit of the dissector, Gracián recommends it as a powerful weapon in the daily struggle for personal supremacy. Thus, aphorism 49 of *Oráculo manual* calls for the ability to anatomize as an important skill for the *discreto*: "He knows very well how to make the anatomy of men's capacities, let him but look upon a man and he will dive into the depth of him, and know him thoroughly" (44, 358–9; Sabe hacer anatomía de un caudal con perfección; en viendo un personaje, le comprehende y lo censura por esencia). Situations as well as people must be anatomized: "It is a sort of curious anatomy thus to search and penetrate into things" (*El Discreto*, 278; Sagaz anatomía mirar las cosas por dentro).

As the dissector, the *discreto* – a word that comes from the Latin "cerno" (separate or sift) – has to use sharp instruments for his discriminating task; his sight, for example, must be as acute as that of the lynx, as stated in *El Héroe*, 77, or *El Discreto*, 322. The lynx is also one of the animals invoked by Gracián for its ability to access its prey's insides with its sharp fangs and claws. Just as lynxes and falcons tear their victims before devouring them, the *discreto* must dismember his opponent to obtain information. Chopping the opponent's body into discrete units – the etymology of *discreto* being pertinent again – permits him to notice and record minute changes, as in an *in vivo* autopsy. The symbolic piecemeal disassembly of rivals is performed through the scrutiny and decipherment of the gestures and behaviours of their limbs, face, and features. Thus, in *El Criticón*, Andrenio and Critilo run into the Acertador (He-who-is-always-right), who accurately judges peoples' characters based on their bodily features (1137). Not surprisingly, Gracián was conversant with the main texts of physiognomy, as many passages in his work evidence.[142] The abundant information that can be gathered from the analysis of an opponent's features explains what appears to be a contradiction in *El Discreto*, where Gracián dismisses the need to look inside to find the truth. Contrary to his repeated recommendation to look inside others to see their real motives, he disagrees with Momo's wish that human beings had glass windows in their breast so that their true thoughts were apparent. Gracián retorts that such a privileged access point is unnecessary because gestures and behaviours are true enough indicators of real intent (322). That Gracián precisely chose Momo, however, injects dissective overtones. Momo was, especially in Spain, the epitome of anti-exemplarity and satire.[143] This genre, as we saw, is associated with dismemberment because of the parodying potential in the isolating and exaggerating of specific features.

The conception of the body as a structure made up of discrete parts is also implied in Gracián's frequent allusions to the metaphorical replacement of one's specific organs.[144] The *discreto* has to know how to dismember not only others' bodies to obtain information, but also his own body to replace certain parts with those of animals reputed for their acute senses. As we saw, the *discreto* must adopt the eyes of the lynx or animal attributes such as the cunning of the fox or the inner obscurity of the cuttlefish. The *discreto* then becomes a sphinx-like creature, made up of human and animal organs that facilitate acute perception while obfuscating those of his opponents. This process may also include the co-option of accessory human organs to reinforce his own. Quevedo's treatment of the body politic implied similar advice when he recommended that the king resort to his ministers' bodies to supplement his own abilities. But Gracián goes further than Quevedo when he encourages not just the king but everybody to adopt symbolic auxiliary members and senses. For instance, in *El Criticón* (1, 956), he endorses uniting sight and touch by implanting eyes in one's hands, the better to navigate in the confusing world of the Baroque.[145]

Dissection and the assimilation of the limbs and organs of other bodies for personal gain are conspicuous in Gracián's *El Comulgatorio*.[146] This book in the Ignatian tradition consists of fifty meditations to be contemplated before taking Communion, which is presented as a literal banquet in which the body of Christ is consumed. Thus, meditation 16 advises the communicants to take morsels from Christ's feet, heart, or cheeks, according to their specific needs. Those in need of modesty should have a morsel from his feet, being the most humble part of the body because of their proximity to the earth. To extract all the salutary properties, the communicants are encouraged to chew on the morsels carefully after seasoning them to their taste (1310–11). By highlighting the sacrificial and cannibalistic aspects of the rite of Communion, Gracián emphasizes its resemblance to anatomical dissection, in which a sacrificial body is also dismembered for the benefit of the community. Although cannibalization of the corpse is not part of the anatomical quest, the learning obtained from it is internalized by the participants, who, somehow, incorporate the foreign body into their own as knowledge. *El Comulgatorio* also recalls Gracián's use of dissection in that it depicts Christ and the communicant mutually anatomizing each other, an image that, as we will see, appears in his books on worldly matters. Communion is presented as opening one's interior to Christ beyond the act of ingesting his body. The communicant has to rip open his entrails to allow Christ unhindered access to his interior. In return, Christ opens himself to shelter the communicant inside his soteriological bosom. The result is that both the communicant and Christ are simultaneously penetrating and penetrated: "He tries to enter the breast of those who will open his side" (1301; trata de metérseles en el pecho a los que le han de abrir el costado); "Let our Lord rest in your breast, and you in his bosom" (1326; descanse el Señor en tu pecho y tú en su seno).[147] Even mutual cannibalism is implied: "You should be so hungry for him and eat him as hungrily as he is hungry for your heart" (1349; Oh si le comieses tan hambriento como lo está el Señor de tu corazón).

Finally, an important peculiarity distinguishes Gracián's application of the anatomical-dissective metaphor from those of the other studied cases: although some vague identification with the sacrificial figure was detectable in the previous authors, Gracián is the only one who consciously assumes the position of the dissected with all its implications. He recognizes that the *discreto* must be ready not only to anatomize his opponents but also to be anatomized because they will also try to look for information inside him. Dissection is, after all, a weapon to which everybody has access. The *discreto* cannot escape being anatomized because his body is exposed through gestures and words while competing for pre-eminence in the court and other venues.[148] Given the unavoidable scrutiny to which the *discreto* must subject himself, Gracián advises the deployment of active and passive techniques of obfuscation to prevent opponents from gathering valuable information. The *discreto* must behave directly contrary to the sacrificial victim and the martyr, who, having nothing to hide, complied with the operation by volunteering their bodies. Such openness is recommended by Gracián for pious practices only, as seen in *El Comulgatorio*. In secular matters, the Ignatian advice of behaving as if the divine did not exist is to be followed. For this purpose, the *discreto* must systematize forms of passive resistance that recall the ones deployed by the *pícaro*, who, under pretence of compliance, yielded only contradictory answers to an inquisitive figure of authority. But instead of the *pícaro*'s mostly improvised pattern of resistance, Gracián endorses the strategic deployment of obfuscation. Such premeditated resistance is expressed in aphorism 98 through the adoption of specific animal behaviours: "To thwart lynx-like perspicacity, render your interior as obscure as that of a cuttlefish" (372; A linces de discurso, jibias de interioridad).[149] As the cuttlefish protects itself through a controlled release of dark ink that befuddles the predators, the *discreto* must render his intentions murky by pre-emptive operations, such as stating spurious intentions. Even more complex obscuring moves are presented, such as the occasional expression of one's true purposes so that the opponents will never be able to ascertain whether they are dealing with true or false expressions of intentions.

Another method of active defence recommended by Gracián is the near-predatory behaviour of luring opponents in order to entrap them, as in a cobweb, in the admiration of the *discreto*'s inner realm. For the setup, he must make his interior appear unfathomable. As it is stated in *El Héroe*, "the truth is, he who would preserve the admiration of the public has no other way of doing it but by concealing the measure of his capacity" (2, 75; excuse todo varón culto sondarle el fondo a su caudal si quiere que le veneren todos). Aphorism 299 of *Oráculo manual* recommends leaving the opponent eager for more, "to leave with an appetite" (271, 430; dejar con hambre). The kind of cannibalistic consumption of the *discreto*'s interior by the opponent implied in these and other passages differs from the one described in *El Comulgatorio*. There, both Christ and the communicants benefit from the mutual access to their respective interiors, whereas, in the deceiving strategy recommended by the *Oráculo manual*, only the *discreto* benefits from feeding his opponents enticing morsels cut from his interior. This practice of eliciting general admiration by making the interior attractive has been compared by Nelson to an act of eroticization of the self.[150] Indeed, the result is an inner desirability similar to that expressed in near-erotic terms by Vesalius, who depicted dissectors as drawn to the corpses they were cutting open. The difference is that, while the dead body is not consciously making itself desirable, Gracián instructs the *discreto* to elicit desire through the carefully orchestrated striptease of an interior that will never be completely unveiled.

The attraction to his interior fostered by the *discreto* contrasts with the unwanted male attraction to the inner female organs in Zayas's stories. There, the unsolicited attention resulted in negative, even fatal consequences for the women. But this is only one of the aspects in which Gracián's treatment of the human interior diverges from those of the other authors studied. Some of the differences point to a categorically altered conception of the world and its relation to the human interior. For instance, when the *discreto* is staging an interior that is both fascinating and confusing, he is reproducing inside himself two qualities characteristic of the Baroque vision of the world. The earlier image of the universe as an open book in which readers could discover God's well-thought-out plans had been superseded by a pessimistic outlook. In the Baroque era the expanding world came to be perceived as a labyrinth, an enigma, a set of puzzling signs that are difficult to decipher. Gracián's recommendation implies internally mirroring this confusion to one's advantage in a mimetic exercise in osmosis, resembling the equally reflective model defended by Fray Luis de Granada. But for Granada the human interior should reflect the same divine order that is easily readable in the rest of creation, therefore rendering it equally patent. Gracián agrees with this vision, but only as far as it is reserved for spiritual matters. In daily life, deception and false appearance rule society, so one's inside has to be a fascinating enigma. Gracián's advice to perfectly control one's interior diverges also from Cervantes's fear that an excessive or inappropriate cultivation of one's inner world might lead to isolation and insanity. This is not a risk for the *discreto*, who is expected to master his interior to the point of creating virtual inner worlds to confuse his opponents. The *discreto* is not in danger of getting lost in his own phantasmagorias, unlike the Glass Licentiate, Cañizares, and Don Quixote. Gracián equally deviates from Quevedo's concept of interiority. Quevedo, concerned for the survival of the body politic, was diffident with individuals who took advantage of the privacy that their bodies offered them for their personal gain. These reservations contrast with Gracián's model of highly private, secretive individuals who, like the king, incorporate external organs into their bodies not for the well-being of the republic but only for self-advancement.

This analysis of Gracián's complex treatment of interiority, even if limited to a few key points, reveals clear differences from the cases previously analysed. Since most of the dissective imagery he uses coincides with what we saw before, we must conclude that anatomical exploration had become an accepted metaphor that was mature enough to be deployed for many purposes. Gracián does not use it to express the anxiety of interiority that was characteristic of the previous narratives. He combines dissective imagery with sacred anatomy for the religious meditations of *El Comulgatorio*. But when he resorts to it as a heuristic method to find the truth, dissection becomes an offensive and defensive weapon in the contest for social pre-eminence to which the *discreto* and his opponents have access. Tactical mastery alone decides the victory. To dissect one's opponent and to know how to be dissected without revealing secrets has become a fully conscious practice to be deployed in a hostile world in which private interiority has been fully embraced without remorse, without a hint of the anxiety of interiority we saw in previous cases. If anything, it has been replaced by an anxiety of performance.

# Conclusion: Compliant Resistance

In spite of the clear differences in their tone and content, the texts by Granada, Quevedo, Cervantes, and Zayas examined in the previous chapters share clear traces of their authors' anxiety of interiority, of their awareness of having unfathomable interiors capable of harbouring dangerous contents. They create a sacrificial Other endowed with a complex interiority that is exposed by methods akin to those of contemporary anatomical dissection. The appeasement of anxiety in this Girardian exercise complies with what Hillman calls the sceptic's impulse "to open the body of others in place of – or as a cover story for– allowing access to his own interior."[1] Although the designated victims are condemned and punished, the verdict these narratives pass on interiority is ambiguous. It is presented as capable of harbouring ideas and psychological processes that can lead indistinctly to self-improvement or self-destruction. As Paige puts it discussing early modern France, interiority felt simultaneously good and bad, and it was considered both a haven and an exile.[2] The authors' relation to the sacrificial interiors they create is also ambiguous, even contradictory. In their overall punitive thrust, the narratives seem to reject the interiors. But they are not textual autos-da-fé in which the guilty party is burnt at the stake. The interiors are so vividly recreated and their descriptions so detailed that the authors' intimacy – even first-hand experience – with the thoughts associated with such interiors must be assumed. Thus, as in the contradiction-solving logic of dream work, the interiors presented in these narratives are simultaneously self yet alien, recognized as familiar but disallowed.

Some of the sacrificial characters are born to exemplify the dangers of deviant or excessively developed interiority and, as such, they are doomed to fail by their built-in flaws. Consequently, their interiorities do not pose a serious menace to the ideology from which they deviate because they never threaten the system as a whole, which can easily explain them away as exceptions to its universal validity. These interiors are described as isolated malfunctions resulting from the wrong implementation of the system's basic tenets, or from a morbid obsession for exploring its blind spots. Likewise, the characters and their interiors do not constitute a liability for their creators, who have volunteered them as sacrificial victims from which they distance themselves in introductions that warn the reader of their counter-exemplary intentions. Authorial detachment is reflected in the characters suffering abundant mishaps, some ending with them being punished for their built-in limitations. This procedure can be seen in Sor María de la Visitación, whose interior is excessively pious, and in the sorcerer Cañizares, whose interior is overtaken by witchcraft. In their isolated inner worlds, they have deformed contemporary religious orthodoxy into personal accommodations.

Zayas's women are different. Their interiority is limited to the sexual/ reproductive function that the honour system assigned to the females of the nobility. As with Granada's proper martyrs, they are doomed because they are subject to inquiries interested only in punishing, not in finding the truth. The result is that they die, unable to prove their innocence until their beautiful corpses reveal it. These women and the martyrs are, however, far removed from our modern sensibility because they are monolithic characters from two tightly scripted genres, hagiography and sentimental romance. Limited as they are to a narrow set of conventional behaviours, their unshakable righteousness makes them appear fanatical to our modern eyes. They accept awful, undeserved deaths without ever doubting the validity of the religious beliefs or the nobiliary code for which they are sacrificed. In the martyrological model, the victims' acceptance of gruesome punishments and the miraculous signs manifested in their corpses corroborate the validity of their beliefs. Zayas's women accept their unjust death with equal courage, without ever rebelling. Their fortitude comes from their pride of being members in good standing of the nobiliary system. In spite of their husbands' unfounded accusations, they know that they never infringed the honour code, which is the hallmark of their entitlement. The heroines' irreproachable behaviour during their torment and the beauty of their corpses both paradoxically act as a denunciation of the unfairness of the honour system towards women. But this system is never disqualified as a whole: it is, after all, presented as the creator of individuals of such high moral calibre that they have the strength to undergo heroic deaths.

The other sacrificial characters are presented in the dissective narratives in a negative light, but some of their features seem to herald modernity and so appeal to the modern reader. In the narratives, however, such features are never celebrated as positive or innovative; quite the contrary, they are presented as dangerous and abnormal. An example of a modern feature that is discredited is the attempt to claim a form of selfhood based on individual embodiment. The body – and in particular the inner body – is one of the pillars of the modern subject because it offers an unalienable location for the private feelings and thoughts that warrant autonomous individuality. In the dissective narratives, the use of embodiment for similar purposes is disqualified. Thus Richelieu's and Tomás Rodaja's reliance on their own intellect is presented as faulty, as excessive pride and ambition that lead them to disease and insanity. Revealingly, they are affected by physical symptoms that point to their strained interiority as the origin of their disease: Richelieu's head becomes an enormous free-floating entity hovering around Rome; Tomás Rodaja's body becomes a transparent and fragile container. Similarly, María de la Visitación's false stigmata are the manifestation of her singular interior as well as the main agent of her demise; and the drug-induced trances that draw Cañizares inside herself will eventually cause her body to be exposed, naked, in the plaza. The characters function as counter-examples of how interiority, if mishandled, leads to disaster. The situation is completely different in Gracián's writing, which recommends that one cultivate the ability, offered by individual embodiment, to hide secrets.

The negative role played by private embodiment and the claim to autonomy that it would imply in later periods confirm that the characters in these dissective narratives were never intended as dry runs or as Trojan horses of the modern self. To see them as failed heroes of modernity would be to fall into an evolutionary, teleological grand narrative of the self and modernity. Like many other practitioners of the field, I believe that early modern subjectivity and interiority have to be studied on their own terms, as specific products of a given time and place. They may present features that can be identified with the modern subject, but they are not necessarily its evolutionary ancestors. In this respect, I agree with Maus's reluctance to reify the concept of subjectivity. In her study of English theatre during the Renaissance, she sees the group of phenomena and behaviours that are usually included under the label of subjectivity as "a loose and varied collection of assumptions, intuitions, and practices that do not all logically entail one another and need not appear together at the same cultural moment."[3]

Dissective narratives are also connected to the oncoming of modernity by their possible influence on the development of the literary genre typically associated with this period, the novel. As we saw in the previous chapter, *Don Quixote*, a recognized stepping stone in the history of the modern novel, contains episodes, such as those of Maese Pedro's puppets and the Enchanted Head, that read as dissective narratives.[4] In addition to the presence of these passages, the figure of Don Quixote can be easily seen as a sacrificial victim, similar to the ones at the centre of many dissective narratives. In addition, the punishment that his body undergoes in his idealistic endeavours contributes to the enlightenment of those who witness it and of the readers. Not surprisingly, interpretations of Don Quixote as a Christ-like figure sprang up in later periods.[5] Also as in the dissective narratives, Don Quixote is endowed with an inner world whose uniqueness tempts the readers to look inside his body. Thus, Antonio Hernández Morejón, the doyen of the historians of Spanish medicine, ended his 1836 brief medical analysis of the book stating that "in my opinion, only one thing is missing in Cervantes's work [*Don Quixote*] to complete the story, namely, to open the corpse of Don Quixote." Hernández Morejón goes on to conclude that it was not done because Cervantes was aware that, if Don Quixote's body was opened, the results would be, as in the dissective narratives, inconclusive:

> But did [Cervantes] not include this episode because he knew that pathological anatomy was inconclusive in these kinds of ailments, or because, since Don Quixote had healed from his insanity, the dryness of his brains was not the cause or the seat of the disease, which had mutated into a different one, and all this would not have allowed Cervantes to find anything that matched Don Quixote's drifting imagination?[6]

Although Don Quixote is never anatomized properly speaking, some of his adventures contain hints of dissection, even of self-dissection. The detailed descriptions of the invasive traumatisms inflicted upon him and the subsequent cures that, as we saw in the previous chapter, abound in Cervantes's masterpiece can be interpreted as attempts to penetrate his body. Furthermore, some passages present specific dissective elements. An example is the episode in which Don Quixote is duped by Maritornes and the innkeeper's daughter to introduce his hand in a hole, high on the wall, while standing on his horse in the courtyard at the inn (1:43). While a fervent Don Quixote proceeds to describe the muscles and sinews of his mighty hand in anatomical terms to the two women hidden behind the wall, they tie it from the inside. The episode concludes with Don Quixote hanged from his wrist, in the same position in which the écorchés were often presented in anatomical manuals.[7] But in spite of these and other similarities between *Don Quixote* and the dissective narratives, I do not think that the whole book can be reduced to an instance of these narratives. The reason is that Cervantes's masterpiece is too complex and rich to be attributed *en bloc* to a manifestation of anxiety of interiority. As centuries of interpretation and scholarship have proved, there is much more to *Don Quixote*.

Interestingly, the feature that most noticeably connects *Don Quixote* to the modern novel is the highest-level similarity between this book and the dissective narratives, namely, the clash between a highly private inner world and the external reality. The conflict between an individual's thoughts and feelings with the outside reality, objectified in society, is central to the genre of the novel as it evolved in later centuries. Furthermore, also as in the dissective narratives, some varieties of the modern novel aim at exposing the embodied private sphere and its secrets through dissective methods. A case in point is the detective story or crime novel. This genre uncannily resembles the dissective narratives in their keenness on finding the mystery behind, or inside, a deviant character. Typically, an autopsy, not of the criminal but of the victim, uncovers disturbing secrets about the murderer, the victim, and society, which (often inadvertently) is an accomplice in the crime. In some cases, the killer, most often male, acts as a dissector by dismembering his female victims. What the slaughterer is trying to find inside these bodies is the explanation or resolution for some previous traumatic event in his life. The victims' bodies, however, resist yielding satisfactory answers, which compels the killer to an endless cycle of murder and dismemberment. Although other similarities between the many varieties of the modern novel and the dissective narratives could be posited, I think that an all-encompassing, indiscriminate conclusion about the influence of these narratives on the development of the novel should be avoided. The main reason for refraining from such hypotheses is that the anxiety of interiority that I claim informs them is specific of a time and place. All that can be safely said is that dissective narratives can be seen as one of the many influences on the development of the novel as a genre.

Continuing on the same theme of the relation among dissective narratives, anxiety of interiority, and modernity, I want to point out the resemblance between the dissenting voice characteristic of much modern literature and how some characters in the studied texts questioned the social order in whose defence they were conceived to be sacrificed. Some characters' behaviour seems to incarnate Foucault's famous statement that, wherever there is power, there is resistance – in this case, where there is surveillance, there is resistance.[8] But ascertaining the origin of such resistance is problematic. The actual position of the authors towards the contemporary order was ambiguous, often contradictory. Quevedo, the staunchest defender of the absolutist monarchy, is also notorious for his continuous quarrels with the political establishment, with which he disagreed on specific issues. Granada, although an exemplary member of the Catholic church, had disagreements on doctrinal matters with its higher echelons. Cervantes, the most enigmatic of the four in this respect, seems to have toed a thin line between apparent compliance and denunciation of the system. Famously, some of his passages seem to defend modern positions, while others can be easily defined as retrograde. Zayas's heroines, while submitting to the honour code, disqualify its treatment of women. Gracián's *discreto*, in spite of his very different approach to interiority, is still far from the modern subject. As Egginton remarks, Gracián's emphasis on self-interest is not compatible with the social altruism the Enlightenment will posit as one of the main characteristics of modernity.[9] All this variation is best captured by what, in his study of subjectivity in early modern Spain, Mariscal has called "contradictory subjects." Their subjectivity is not an entity but an endless process of discourses that compete in arranging and rearranging subject positions characterized by instability and contradiction.

The authors' fluid relationships with the system unavoidably handicap our attempts at understanding the resistance to power in the dissective narratives. A more fruitful approach is to examine the mechanics of this resistance in the narratives. Under this light, the oppositional stance appears as an epiphenomenon of the creative process itself. Indicating the need to go beyond Althusser or Maravall's visions of omnipotent state apparatuses and directed cultures, Cascardi writes that "the culture that emerged under Spanish Absolutism on the

Iberian peninsula itself turns out to be less the perfect mirror of state ideologies than it sometimes supposed … [Cervantes] demonstrates that those same discourses may undermine or reverse themselves in the process of shaping the subject who 'must' conform to them."[10] As was stated at the introduction, these narratives imply the construction of a sacrificial figure through a process comparable to self-fashioning. As in Greenblatt's famous formulation, the figures chosen for dissection share elements of "an authority and an alien" and display an excessive-ness that subverts the same authority in whose name they were cre-ated.[11] The characters' excessiveness originates in their versatile, even dislocated bodies and the corresponding interiorities revealed by the new anatomical dissection. Their behaviours result from allowing this multifarious new embodiment to develop and act along the traditional lines of the literary genres in which the narratives are inscribed. When the characters are exposed to the usual scenarios of the genres, the result is a vitality that overflows the narration. This is clearly visible in Quevedo's satirical dissective narratives. When submitted to the scatol-ogy and dismemberment typical of the genre, the characters' bodies can barely be contained. While the treatment that Quevedo applies to the *pícaro* may resemble the punitive disembowelment that was often part of the execution process through most of Europe, his chaotic inte-rior acts as a site of contestation to all logical constructions. The com-plex, disorganized interior has its own sense of purpose and agency, independent of the social order outside, even of the individual's own will. Its inspection becomes unpleasant and of questionable utility, since it is messy and the contagion may spread.[12]

The grotesque bodies of satire and its correspondingly hyperactive interiors are only one of the patterns though which the designated vic-tims of the dissective narratives resist power. Another pattern can be seen in the narratives inscribed within the martyrological model. In Zayas's stories, women's exemplary deaths and their beautiful corpses disqualify inquisitive processes that punish them to wash away affronts to male honour. In some of Granada's writing, the sacrificial victim fol-lows the pattern of the martyr's compliance with the torturer by pro-viding unrestricted access to her interior in the form of sincere responses to the interrogators. When the body is literally opened or dismembered during the torture, nothing other than the previously confessed belief is found, as in the cases of Saint Cecilia and Saint Catherine of Alexandria. Their compliance proves the search unnecessary in two ways. First, it shows that the outside and the inside are in agreement and that what is on the inside is also visible on the outside. Second, when the stigmata of Sor María de la Visitación, which were previously investigated and deemed true, are later proven to be painted, the validity of any search process is questioned. Granada's apologetic letter after the scandal makes the point that it is impossible to scrutinize interiors effectively because the outside, like the inside, may be artfully simulated. The same conclusion can be drawn from the story of Cañizares, who has managed to hide her wicked interior for years.

Like the martyrs, the Glass Licentiate's transparency pre-empts the need for a searching process. His insanity transforms him into a transparent machine that regurgitates its contents whenever prompted. But the interior that he voluntarily reveals mirrors the same prejudices, contradictions, and hackneyed truisms of the official ideology that he memorized in his bookish existence. He exemplifies what Maus has called the two fantasies of the early modern period: the belief that the self is interior, hidden, and ineffable, and the belief that, at the same time, it can be expressed and fully manifested.[13] When Richelieu's and Cañizares's interiors are exposed through a combination of accidental circumstances, their contents are also shown to be fragments of the predominant religious and political discourses. In their interiors, however, they have rearranged the current ideology into constructions that highlight its arbitrariness, blind spots, and ambiguities. This matches what Hillman states about how the recesses of the body were characterized by their ability to encapsulate contradictions, such as a being "the meeting point of the sacred and the abject."[14]

In all the aforementioned examples, dissective narratives act as anxiety-releasing exercises whose assuagement functions on a double level. On the one hand, the sacrificial model is clearly at work. The narratives are a secure exercise of fantasizing what is otherwise unthinkable by transferring it into an Other destined to be sacrificed. The authors are thus cooperating with the authorities by performing a pre-emptive exercise of (self-)denunciation in which a sacrificial alter ego is loaded with imaginary yet possible crimes and then exposed. On the other hand, the rhetoric of self-demonstrating or self-dissecting that Sawday connects to the model of Christ opening his entrails to allow his followers access and salvation is problematized in these narratives.[15] Although some of the characters seem to open themselves to allow us unimpeded access to their interior, as in some illustrations in the contemporary anatomical books, the reality is that it is mostly an obfuscating operation. The complicity in pursuit of the *nosce te ipsum* that Sawday sees as encompassing the dissector and the anatomized body is in these narratives more of a collusion to derail the investigation. The utility and even the feasibility of examining and exposing interiors are questioned. The findings of the dissective operations are always disappointing, no matter how forceful and thorough the operations might be. In some cases, the search is proven unnecessary since what is found inside turns out to be the same as that which was already visible on the outside. In other cases, the revealed interiors are too garbled to permit any conclusion as to their guilt or innocence. Even worse, the contents revealed may be aberrant, but a thorough analysis of their deviation only results in bringing to light the inconsistency and arbitrariness innate in the ideology that prompted the inspection.

# Notes

## Introduction: Dissective Narratives

1 I am using the word "anxiety" to signify a state close to fear, not in the Freudian technical meaning of unreleased sexual energy that has been repressed. It is this general meaning that has been most productively used as a tool by late twentieth-century and contemporary literary critics, such as Bloom in *Anxiety of Influence*. Anxiety in early modern Spain has been the subject of several studies, among them Dopico Black's *Perfect Wives, Other Women: Adultery and Inquisition in Early Modern Spain*, which deals with how the woman's body became the centre of scrutiny as part of the displaced anxiety over the *conversos*, the baptized Indians, and other marginal groups. For a basic definition of anxiety as pathology, see Wolman. For those interested in Freud's original writings on anxiety, the foundational texts are his "Inhibitions, Symptoms, and Anxieties" and "Anxiety and Instinctual Life." Although I am consciously avoiding a psychoanalytic reading of the texts, concepts of Freud that have become part of today's language can easily be detected in this book. Repression or transference, even if they are not formally called such, can be clearly seen at work in some sections of the book. For evident historical reasons, I am trying to be careful in my application of these concepts to the early modern period. The study of historical cases of anxiety is feasible if the peculiarities of the period are respected. In his classical study of a seventeenth-century painter who believed himself to be possessed by the devil, "A Neurosis of Demonical Possession in the Seventeenth Century," Freud implies that neurotic forces similar to present-day ones existed in previous eras. The main difference between our times, claims Freud, is that we have attributed the origin of our disturbances to our inner world, while the practice of previous days attributed it to external forces.

2 Sawday, *The Body*, viii, 2. An introductory bibliography of some of the many studies that use the concept of culture of dissection is in Calbi, xiii. For studies dealing with the culture of dissection in Spain, see Marshall, 24–5.

3 Paige, 1–3.

4 C.S. Lewis, 215. See also Guillén, 307, on the contemporary expansion of the inner realm.

5 For a phenomenological view of the transhistorical existence of some form of selfhood as access to inner experience, see Zahavi, 197. Finkelstein's initial chapter is an up-to-date summary of the problem in modern philosophy. The existence and the quality of some form of interiority prior to the early modern period – especially in the Middle Ages – is a much-debated topic; see, for instance, Morris on the onset of individualism in the twelfth century. For a specific example of a study in which a different form of interiority is attributed to the Middle Ages, see the chapter "Inside/Outside: Guillaume's *Roman de la Rose* and Medieval Selfhood" in Virz, 64–95. The classic source on the vision of a fully developed interiority as transhistorical is Aers.

6 This view of interiority matches the tenet of cognitive psychology that human behavior is a series of responses to external stimuli mitigated by our thoughts, perceptions, moods, and desires. Discussing the body as lived through culture, Paster writes, "[N]o matter what the physical facts of any given bodily functions may be, that function can be understood and experienced only in terms of culturally available discourses ... The operations of ideology upon the body may be even harder to detect than the operation of ideology upon emerging subjectivity because we experience our bodies as natural ..., often what goes on within the body 'goes without saying'" (4–5). Rorty summarizes the revolution that seventeenth-century subjectivity implied: "There were, to be sure, the notions of taking tacit thought, forming resolutions in *foro interno*, and the like. The novelty was the notion of a single inner space in which bodily sensations – 'confused ideas of sense and imagination' in Descartes' phrase – mathematical truths, moral rules and the rest of what we now call 'mental' were objects of quasi observation" (50). The next chapter will deal with this issue in more detail.

7 Weiss and Haber, xiv. "If embodiment is an existential condition in which the body is the subjective source or intersubjective ground of experience, then studies under the rubric of embodiment are not 'about' the body per se. Instead they are about culture and experience insofar as these can be understood from the standpoint of bodily being-in-the-world" (Csordas, 143). The specific role of embodiment in cognitive science and linguistics was studied by Lakoff and Johnson.

8 Wolfe, 4–9.

9 Aristotle, *Politics*, bk. 1, line 1253b.

10 *The Body*, 4.

11 Haggerty and Ericson, 605.

12 Although using different terminology, other critics have claimed the existence of feelings comparable to the anxiety of interiority I postulate. Maus speaks of the existence of "paranoia about hypocrisy and surveillance" in English theatre texts of the period (36). Talking about recent historical events, Los explains a similar anxiety in the terminology of today's surveillance studies: "For those living under a totalitarian regime, the knowledge of oneself (self-knowing) cannot be separated from the image of the file and the surmised process of its compilation. Any suspicion of internal freedom may mark one's file for special attention. Self-discipline is largely directed toward the negative goal of limiting any disclosure of the self, as any information can be a fodder for the file. Furthermore, given the fallibility of self-control and self-censorship it is prudent to avoid having the kind of self whose disclosure may get one in trouble" (75).

13 Hillman, *Shakespeare's*, 43.

14 Girard, 211. "Yet, a feature of our sense of interiority is that it can never be experienced other than at second hand. We may look into other bodies, but rarely are we allowed to pry into our own" (Sawday, *The Body*, 7). The direct observation of one's own inner body during the period was only possible as a fantasy or through the limited access that exploring one's own wounds offered, as was the case in some of Marlowe's compositions (Greenfield). For the view of anatomy as catharsis, see L. Wilson, 89.

15 At the request of an authority, the hero of the picaresque novel apparently complies and produces a confession. But much of what is confessed is obscured by rhetorical ruses that can even question the validity of the interpellating authority in whose name the confession is coerced; see Dunn, *Spanish*, 173. In his study of inwardness in early modern England, Schoenfeldt sees self-mastery of the internal processes as a claim to individuality in the face of power (*Bodies and Selves*). A study of the indirect forms of resistance to confessing to an authority in early modern Europe is in Zagorin, especially chapter 3, which deals with Jews and *conversos* in Spain (38–62). Specific forms of resistance will be treated in detail in the following chapters.

16 Greenblatt, 34. The idea of self-fashioning is anticipated in Orgel's study of role-playing in the genre of the masque in the Stuart court, in which performance and power interact. Greene's concept of the flexibility of the self during the Renaissance points in the same direction.

17 García Sánchez published a modern critical edition of the only 1564
   edition of Porcell's *Información y curación de la peste de Zaragoza y
   preservación contra peste en general*. A CD with the photographic images of
   the original book is also available; see Báguena. In addition to the more
   or less extended passages dedicated to Porcell in the manuals of the
   history of Spanish medicine, several monographs are dedicated to him
   (e.g., López Piñero and Terrada Ferrandis; and Mariscal y García).
18 Carlino, *Books*, 53.
19 The frontispiece and the portrait of Vesalius in his *De humani corporis
   fabrica* are reproduced and described in detail by O'Malley, 139–44,
   and by J.B. Saunders and O'Malley, 41–2. Complete analyses of the
   two engravings are Carlino, *Books*, 42–53, and Sawday, *The Body*, 66–78.
   L. Wilson, 69–74, and Ferrari, 62–6, are studies of the contrast between
   the representations of the anatomists in the act of dissecting and older
   practices. Portraits of physicians in similar poses became common in later
   periods. One of the best-known examples is Rembrandt's *The Anatomy
   Lesson of Dr. Joan Deijman* (see Gross).
20 On the authorship of the portraits of Vesalius, see O'Malley, 124–6. The
   authorship of the portrait of Porcell is unknown.
21 Sawday, *The Body*, 6–10.
22 In the frontispiece of Vesalius's *De humani corporis fabrica*, his figure is
   also a mirror image of the corpse being dissected. This is not the case in
   his portrait in the same book. However, it has been suggested that this
   portrait represents Vesalius in the pose characteristic of a drawing made
   from a mirror image (J.B. Saunders and O'Malley, 41). Sawday detects in
   the title page of Vesalius's *De humani corporis fabrica* (see Figure 9) the hint
   of a "shared conspiracy between anatomist and subject" (*The Body*, 112).

## 1. Dissection and Interiority: The Case of Spain

1 Fernández de Oviedo, 170–2. The translations are mine unless otherwise
  noted. A detailed study of this autopsy appears in Peña Chavarria and
  Shipley. The exact cause of their death is not stated, nor is whether the
  two girls were fed or starved. The *Gesta Romanorum* includes a similar
  case of a male child born with two breasts and heads: "After one year,
  one part of the boy died, and the other survived about three days" (340).
  Isidore of Seville explains that monstrous beings do not survive long
  after their birth because their only function is to announce imminent
  catastrophes (bk. 11, chap. 3; see also Daston and Park, 52). For a
  comprehensive study of the important role that monstrous births played

in the imagination of the period, see Bates, who includes several early
modern cases of conjoined twins, including the one in Hispaniola (154–6).

2 Fernández de Oviedo, 171. The problem of selfhood and individuality
posed by these Siamese twins was affected by theories about the location
of the soul in the human body, often in connection with the debate over
the exact moment the new soul entered the body during conception. A
good introduction to this matter is Dunstan. The contemporary orthodox
point of view was that two souls could not share the same body, as is
thoroughly explained by the Spanish Franciscan Juan de Pineda in his
influential 1589 *Diálogos familiares de la agricultura cristiana*, chapter 24,
entitled "Two souls cannot inform the same body, nor can one soul inform
two bodies at the same time or in succession" (Dos almas no pueden
informar el mismo cuerpo, ni una puede informar dos cuerpos junta
o sucesivamente [Pineda, bk. 2, p. 310]). The debate over the role that
shared organs play in selfhood is still open today and, although the terms
in which the discussion is conducted have changed, Siamese twins remain
a constant feature. Armstrong describes a modern thought experiment
involving conjoined twins, shared organs, and the concept of selfhood
and privacy in the following terms: "I do not think that the privacy of
our own thoughts and experiences is a logical privacy. The privacy is
contingent. We know that there are Siamese twins who have some portion
of their bodies in common. It seems a possibility, though it is not clear
if this is an empirical possibility, that there could be twins that have a
portion of their brain in common, and further can both introspect some
of the mental processes in this common portion" (107). In his *Philosophical
Investigations*, Wittgenstein asks, "Can conjoined twins with separate minds
but a partially shared body experience the same pain together?" (253).

3 Fernández de Oviedo, 171; English translation from Peña Chavarria and
Shipley, 301. Autopsies for judicial and medical purposes were common,
but the case narrated by Fernández de Oviedo is notable as the first
known autopsy performed in the New World. Other early autopsies in
the New World were studied by López-Ríos Moreno and López-Ríos
Fernández and by Hektoen. Dissective procedures to solve spiritual
matters were not uncommon. Dr Porcell mentions a case in which he
opened the body of a six-month-pregnant dead woman so that the priest
could baptize the foetus, which was still moving. For another testimony
of conjoined twins baptized as two individuals, see Daston and Park, 65.

4 Fernández de Oviedo, 172.

5 On the contemporary use of anatomical sheets, see Crummer as well as
Carlino, *Paper Bodies*.

6 An indication of the success of Vesalius's *De humani corporis fabrica* is that twenty-five legal editions appeared in the two centuries following its first publication (Singer, 134). Its illustrations were even more successful and took on a separate life, especially in illegal copies produced in many countries. For an overview of the influence of Vesalius on anatomical illustration, see Herrlinger.

7 Carlino, *Books*, 40–2; Ball.

8 García Ballester, 90.

9 Beltrán de Heredia, *Cartulario*, 484.

10 Granjel, 54–5.

11 The anatomical theatre of San Nicolás was built at the University of Salamanca in 1554 and was in use until 1904 (Prieto Carrasco, 25–31). O'Malley studied the years Vesalius lived in Spain in chapters 9 and 10, 187–268. An overview of the importance of anatomical dissection in Spain is found in Alberti López.

12 On Boniface's bull, see Brown.

13 Bynum, "Material," 270–1.

14 Prieto Carrasco, 30. Although the classical studies on the history of anatomical studies tend to pay little attention to Spain, they contain some examples that the Spanish universities were not behind the times in the teaching of anatomy (Choulant, 205, 218).

15 Carlino, *Paper Bodies*; Sawday, *The Body*, 85.

16 Sawday, *The Body*, 102. The perception that empty space exists inside the body was helped by the belief that void was a constituent part of matter. In his *De rerum natura*, Lucretius claims that empty space, even if intangible and therefore invisible, is a necessary condition for the operations of bodies in nature (1:329).

17 Panofsky, 27, 59. Perspective also plays an important role in the sensation of being a separate entity located in the space ("locatedness"), a sensation that characterizes early modern individuals (Bordo, 68). A history of perspective in drawing is given in Descargues; specifically for the early modern period, see Edgerton.

18 Hume, part 4, sec. 6, p. 252.

19 Wittgenstein, 106, §293.

20 Sánchez Valdés de la Plata, 91.

21 Isidore: "Duplex est autem homo: interior et exterior; interior homo, anima, exterior homo, corpus" (bk. 11, chap. 1, para. 6).

22 Sabuco and Sabuco, 110r. The metaphor of the body as a house or castle is old and transcultural and is found, for instance, among the Maori of Polynesia. One study of the image in Vitruvius, Grosseteste, and others is Barkan.

Barona specifically studies the use of the image of the body as a house among Spanish doctors of the fifteenth and sixteenth centuries. Even the etymological roots for "house" and "skin" come from the same Indo-European root "sku" (to cover); this relatedness is still notable in the similarity of the German words *Haut* (skin) and *Haus* (house) (Benthien, 26, 245).

23 On the implications that phantom limbs open as a metaphor for the concept of inner space and the self, see Melzack.

24 Hillman, *Shakespeare's*, 16–17.

25 Hillman writes an excellent analysis of how Freud's genesis of the ego implies a spatial relation between interior and exterior, from which I have summarized a few lines in my text (*Shakespeare's*, 11–15).

26 Leary, 12–13. The concept of the self is basically that of a spatial entity (Malpas, 36). Some form of spatial vocabulary is also used by authors who denounce the self as an illusion, as a series of processes impossible to pin down. For instance, Schopenhauer, following Hume's famous reflection on the impossibility of finding the self, claims that, when we try to find the elusive self, we get lost "in a bottomless void" (*in eine bodenlose Leere*) (371).

27 Crider, 50, 54. "The little one thinks of the belly as a hollow space in which what has been eaten is contained unchanged like the children in the fairy tales and myths who are swallowed by Kronos, the wolf, or the whale, etc., who are reborn by being vomited up" (Ferenczi, 325).

28 Homer, bk. 9, 312–13.

29 In book 10 of *Confessions*, Augustine follows the rhetorical tradition of the *loci of memory*, where things can be stored and then retrieved in a building-like environment: "When I am in this storehouse [of memory], I ask that it produce what I want to recall, and immediately certain things come out; some things require a longer search ... until what I want is freed of mist and emerges from its hiding places" (185). Echoes of this special conception of the self can be seen, for instance, in Cervantes's *Los trabajos de Persiles y Sigismunda*, where Periandro declares, "I am made like what we call a place, it is, where everything has a room and nothing is out of place" (Yo, señor Arnaldo, soy hecho como esto que se llama lugar, que es donde todas las cosas caben, y no hay ninguna fuera del lugar; *Obras completas*, bk. 2, chap. 13, p. 1605). Discussing Montaigne, Paige writes, "Reading autobiographically implies navigating this graduated topography, plumbing the depths of a subject who is not simply constructed of appearance and underlying reality, but who is layered, a human onion" (27). For a review of the metaphors of memory since antiquity, see Draaisma.

30 Bergson, 11.

31 Paige, 10, offers a brief summary of the evolution of the opposition
   inside/outside. Foucault claims that the rupture of inside/outside is a
   nineteenth-century phenomenon resulting from a break of the classical
   episteme (*Les mots*, chapters 7 and 8). However, this view of such late
   development of the inner sphere and its role in the formation of the self
   is contradicted by many studies – including Foucault's later work – that
   show a much earlier presence of the interior as one of the most powerful
   metaphors in the construction of the self.

32 Hillman, "Visceral Knowledge," 82.

33 Maus, 195; Hillman, *Shakespeare's*, 2.

34 Every period favours a different location for the spiritual element inside
   the human being. The debate over the location of the *anima*, whether in
   the head or the heart, goes back to antiquity. In the Bible, it is somewhere
   inside the breast (Jager, Nédoncelle); in classical antiquity, it is often a
   generic space inside the trunk (Onians, Starobinski). Aristotle and the
   Stoics preferred the heart, while Plato preferred the head. Christianity,
   via Aquinas, followed mostly the Aristotelian view. Vesalius had doubts
   about the location of the vital spirits, which he called animal spirits,
   but he tended to locate them in one of the three ventricles in the brain
   (Harvey, 4–30). A summary of Aristotle's three *animae* and their location
   can be seen in Des Chen. A brief account of the theories of the heart
   as centre of the soul appears in End and Wolner and in Erickson. The
   gradual displacement of the heart as the centre of human spirits, as well
   as the relocation of reason to the head and morality to the heart, is studied
   in Doueihi. Kearns offers an overview of metaphors of mind from the
   nineteenth century onwards. Rodríguez de la Flor studies metaphors
   of the inner space and the localization of the soul in sixteenth- and
   seventeenth-century Spain, with special attention to the mystics and the
   manuals of mnemonics.

35 Petrarch, 36: "di quei sospiri ond'io nudriva l'core."

36 Levisi, "La interioridad visualizable."

37 Cervantes, 841, 1471; part 2, chap. 58. Unless otherwise noted, the
   quotations of *Don Quixote* are by page number of Cohen's translation,
   followed by page number of *Obras completas*, then part and chapter.

38 I take the term "proprietary interior" from Rowe, 174, who is elaborating
   on Sutton, 41. Several scholars have pointed out that it was precisely
   during early modernity that the inner space became a place of curiosity
   and inspection for the person (see, for instance, Bordo, 54). Rorty,
   commenting on the pre-existence of an inner realm implied in expressions

such as the rhetorical *in foro interno*, specifies that what is characteristic of early modernity is "the novelty of the notion of a single inner space in which bodily and perceptual sensation ... and all the rest of what we now call mental were objects of quasi observations. Such an inner arena with its inner observer had been suggested at various points in ancient and medieval thought, but it had never been taken seriously" (50).

39 Ferry, 33–60. Especially influential is Saint Augustine's conception of the soul as an entity that can be conceived only in spatial terms. His concept of interiority is greatly indebted to Saint Paul's image of the *homo interior*. The concept of *homo interior* in Saint Paul and the Christian tradition is summarized in Derville and Solignac. On the interpretation of *homo interior* in Saint Paul as a form to express its opposition to the body as the sinner, see Paige, 51, and Sandnes.

40 Shuger, 100.

41 Hanson, 16. The view of the interior of the human being as a private space is related to the conception of the human being as an entity categorically separated from the rest of the universe. For many centuries, the relation between the human being and the universe was encapsulated in the unifying metaphor of the microcosm, or miniature representation of the cosmos, the implications of which are examined in detail in the next chapter. Early modernity gradually replaced this image with that of the human being as an exceptional entity categorically separated from the rest of creation (D.B. Martin, 17). Le Breton claims that a radical rupture at the end of the Middle Ages separated man from cosmos and, therefore, from others (*Anthropologie*, 8). He also speaks of a break between the self and the body that culminates in Descartes (*Corps et sociétés*).

42 Belsey, 36.

43 Cervantes, 19, 1032. Here I follow John Ormsby's translation because Cohen translates this saying freely as "under my cloak a fig for the king" (25). A brief commentary on the origins of the saying and its possible meanings as part of Cervantes's penchant for satire is in Reichenberger, 13n3.

44 Hanson, 16, 39.

45 Montaigne, 411–15.

46 Paige, 8.

47 Another peculiarity of Spanish society was the system of purity of blood, which was a religious issue in its origin – old Christian blood vs. suspected descendants of Muslims and Jews. Castro is the classical authority on the importance of blood in Spain (*De la edad conflictiva*). One summary of the implications of blood for the formation of early modern

subjects in Spain is Mariscal, 39. On Spain's being the first European
country to develop a modern state, see Maravall, "The Origins"; also
Bataillon, *Érasme*, 530.

48 Sawday, *The Body*, chapter 5, "Sacred Anatomy and the Order of
   Representation." Unfortunately, Sawday's book does not include many
   examples from Spanish culture.

49 Apart from Bataillon's famous book (*Érasme*), see Andrés Martín. The
   subject of the new forms of private religious practice will be covered in
   detail when dealing with Fray Luis de Granada's education in the next
   chapter.

50 Hillman qualifies the "disembodied" nature of the inner turn in
   Protestantism: "Protestantism may be said to resituate faith from a
   transcending of the somatic division between the inside and the outside
   to an (increasingly 'excarnated') interior self … It is only through the
   language that God enters the human being … The alliance between
   anatomy and Protestantism is based, I suggest, on an attempt to replace
   mystery with mastery" (*Shakespeare's*, 39–40).

51 Metaphors such as the inner house of conscience, often associated with
   the older forms of confession, did not imply so much a private inner
   space for the self as a common space in which confessor and penitent
   met and spoke (Denery, 13–17, 44). On the institutionalized inner turn
   that confession took after the Counter-Reformation, see Bossy and Lea, *A
   History of Auricular Confession*, vol. 1, chap. 8 and 11. More recent studies
   are Myers and Sabean, the latter dealing primarily with Protestantism but
   also applicable to Catholicism.

52 Myers, 176–80.

53 Maravall, *Culture*, 57–79. On the evolution of confession and its value
   as a social controlling mechanism, see Tentler. Although confession is
   a religious practice, it can be seen as related to what Foucault called
   "governmentalization" or modern states' change of focus from controlling
   territories to controlling citizens ("Governmentality," 103).

54 Fernández-Santamaría, *Reason*, 6, and *State*, 6–7.

55 Kamen, *Spanish Inquisition*, 138.

56 Kamen, *Spanish Inquisition*, 162. A description of the torture sessions of
   the Inquisition and its pre-established limits appears in chapter 7 of Lea,
   *A History of the Inquisition*, and in Kamen, *Spanish Inquisition*, 170–5. See
   also Pérez, who describes the process and specifies that 90 per cent of the
   accused were never tortured (146–8). On the importance of confiscations
   for the financing of the Inquisition, see Kamen, *Spanish Inquisition*, 146–7.

57 Bennassar, 180–2.

58 Juan de Mariana quoted in Pérez, 121. On the role of the *familiares*, see Kamen, *Spanish Inquisition*, 145, and *Inquisition and Society*, 142–6. University professors and other groups that today are identified as intellectuals were, if one takes into account their reduced number, the most persecuted by the Inquisition. The masses did not have much to fear since they did not produce documents that could be scrutinized (Lynch, 357–60). On the specific issue of the ideological control imposed on Spanish society by the Inquisition, see Pinto Crespo, *Inquisición*.

59 Pérez, 87.

60 Lea, *History of the Inquisition*, 2:99.

61 Kamen, *Spanish Inquisition*, 162.

62 Pérez, 86. This is the kind of paranoia that Quevedo parodies in *El Buscón*, when Don Pablos compels the devout owner of the inn where he is lodging either to self-denounce or to hand over to him chickens that she has summoned with the customary onomatopoeic Spanish sound "pío pío," which happens to be the word used for "pious" (*La vida del Buscón*, 154).

## 2. Fray Luis de Granada's Ill-fated Defence of the Inner Man

1 Although she is talking about the English Renaissance, Shuger's description of religion as the main discourse of the period is applicable to Spain: "Religion during this period supplies the primary language of analysis. It is the cultural matrix for explorations of virtually every topic: kingship, selfhood, rationality, language, marriage, ethics, and so forth. Such subjects are, again, not masked by religious discourse but articulated in it; they are considered in relation to God and the human soul" (6).

2 Granada is often not included among the Spanish mystics, or only treated as a minor figure, as in Peers, 27–61. This is one of the few extended treatments of his figure available in English, together with John A. Moore's *Fray Luis de Granada* and Oechselin's *Louis of Granada* (1954, originally in French). Much of the bibliography in Spanish is specialized, often written by Dominicans and members of other religious orders on specific topics and in a pious tone. This is the case of the most authoritative biography, the one published by Cuervo in 1895. One of the few figures of the twentieth century to deal extensively with Granada was Azorín, who published an essay in which he compares Luis de Granada and Luis de León. See also the introductions to the editions of his works that are mentioned in this chapter, as well as the collection of articles in Spanish about Granada edited by Balcells, *Fray Luis*.

3 A study of the success of Granada's *Libro de la oración y la meditación* in the period can be found in Rhodes, "El Libro." The translations of his two manuals into other languages were many and the books circulated widely, even in Protestant countries such as England, where Granada was the most popular Spanish writer in the Elizabethan period (Peers, 14). According to Mansberger Amorós, whereas in France Granada was a source of continuous study and translation, in Spain his manuals were not used for religious education after the sixteenth century.

4 The *Index* of 1559 is one of several published in the century, the previous one in 1551. One of its characteristics is that it pays special attention to spiritual literature, which is not the case in other *Indexes* (Kamen, *Spanish Inquisition*, 90–103). On this *Index* and its relation to previous ones, see Pinto Crespo, "Censorship," 313.

5 Biographies of Fray Luis de Granada started to appear immediately after his death, such as the one by the Dominican Francisco de Oliveira, who knew Granada well since he had been Granada's assistant in his old age. Several were published in the final years of the sixteenth century and in the beginning of the seventeenth century. All are written in the tradition of exemplary, nearly hagiographic narratives. Later, several others were written, such as the one by Justo Cuervo at the end of the nineteenth century already mentioned and the more recent one by Álvaro Huerga, *Fray Luis de Granada: Una vida al servicio de la Iglesia*. These biographies are equally pious in the treatment of Granada but contain abundant data. A brief critical evaluation of Granada's main biographies can be seen in Balcells, "Introducción" (1989), 13n1. In English, the most extended biography is the one contained in John A. Moore's monograph.

6 Because of his *cristiano viejo* origins, Granada does not belong to the group of Spanish mystics of *converso* descent – Saint Teresa of Avila, Saint John of the Cross, Saint John of Avila – who turned inwards, disenchanted by a society obsessed with blood purity that made their success in the outside world impossible (Castro, *Teresa*, 81).

7 See Kamen, "Toleration and Dissent."

8 Beltrán de Heredia, *Las corrientes*, 483.

9 The prestige that Granada had in the Portuguese court and in ecclesiastical circles is explained in detail in Resina Rodrigues, 477–661.

10 An example of how closely Granada followed traditional teachings, such as Aristotle's distinctions on the nature of objects and animals, can be seen in Strosetzki, 344–6.

11 The classic study on the *alumbrados* is vol. 5 of Menéndez Pelayo's *Historia de los heterodoxos españoles* and, more recently, Márquez.

12 See Hyma.

13 Specific passages in Granada's writings that come from northern mystics, such as Louis de Blois and Pseudo-Tauler, have been identified by De Ros. The influence of Savonarola on Granada was proven by Bataillon, who pointed out several passages in Granada's *Libro de la oración y la meditación* that are taken from Savonarola; see Bataillon, "De Savanarola." Also, the first edition of the *Guía de pecadores* (1556) includes a treatise of Savonarola added at the end; see Pérez Villanueva and Escandell Bonet, 1:805.

14 Granada's writings include many references to the Pauline concept of the inner man – "our inner man" (nuestro hombre interior; *Guía de pecadores*, 1:27) – or to the idea that "in one man there are two very different men that are the inner and outer man, i.e., spirit and flesh, passions and reason" (en un mismo hombre hay dos hombres tan contrarios entre sí, como son el interior y el exterior, que son espíritu y carne, pasiones y razones; *Guía de pecadores*, 1:75). Many of these references seem to be taken directly from chapter 6 of Erasmus's *Enchiridion*, entitled "Of the Inward and Outward Man and of the Two Parts of Man, Proved by Holy Scripture" (De homine interiore et exteriore et de duabus partibus hominis ex litteris sacris). Bataillon's study of Erasmus's influence on Spain contains numerous references to Granada; see the index of his *Érasme et l'Espagne*, 875. Other passages taken by Granada from Erasmus's *Enchiridion* are pointed out by Alonso. All the quotations and references by volume and page number are to *Obras del V.P.M. Fray Luis de Granada, con un prólogo y la vida del autor por Don José Joaquín de Mora*. I have chosen this edition because it is the most readily available. I have regularized the punctuation to modern Spanish use since this is a mid-nineteenth-century text and was not updated in the subsequent editions. The translations into English are mine unless otherwise noted.

15 The trial of Carranza and Granada's role in it is well documented. I follow Huerga's works *Fray Luis de Granada: Una vida al servicio de la Iglesia* and "Fray Luis de Granada entre mística, alumbrados e inquisición."

16 Huerga, *Fray Luis de Granada*, 144.

17 2:16. In his *Memorial de la vida cristiana* Granada is specific about the role that *entendimiento* (reason) plays in the meditative inner exercises that he advocates, and it is basically the role of an assistant to raise the sentiments (2:332). The importance Granada attributes to feelings during prayer and meditation shows his admiration of the Ignatian exercises, in which the raising of feelings is paramount. Like Ignatius, Granada recommends practices such as the detailed contemplation of the Passion of Christ. See Balcells, "Introducción" (1986), xvi.

18 2:147.

19 2:153. Saint Bernard's words are actually a reference to Isaiah 24:16: "Secretum meum mihi, secretum meum mihi." See Bernardus, col. 0889A.

20 1:46.

21 In spite of all the changes, on two separate occasions during Granada's lifetime his two republished manuals were denounced to the Inquisition again for fostering *alumbrismo*, and the Spanish *Index of Forbidden Books* of 1583 still included his *Guía de pecadores*. In 1576, Fray Alonso de la Fuente denounced Granada's books because he considered them responsible for the rebirth of *alumbrismo* in Andalusia and Extremadura in those years. Later, in Portugal, Jorge da Silva denounced them for similar reasons. In both cases the charges did not have consequences, but to be denounced to the Inquisition was not a matter to be taken lightly; see Huerga, *Fray Luis de Granada*, 555–60. A curious case involving Granada's books and the Inquisition took place after his death. In 1596 the Mexican branch of the Inquisition burnt a *judaizante* who claimed that the reading of Granada's *Introducción al símbolo de la fe* had made him convert to Judaism; see Castro, "Luis de Granada," 441. The Jews expelled from Spain who lived in Amsterdam in the sixteenth century read Granada's work for certain passages that they considered supported their beliefs; see Mechoulan.

22 1:651. Granada's respect for the Inquisition is evident in the fact that for many years he was the confidant of Cardinal Henry, Inquisitor General of Portugal. At the beginning of the book, in the dedicatory letter to the archbishop of Toledo and the Inquisitor General at the time, Gaspar de Quiroga, Granada writes, "The Kingdom of Spain is free from the pestilence of the Protestant heresy thanks to God's mercy, and to his Royal Highness and the Inquisition's dedication under your singular supervision, and we hope that this will always be the case" ([E]stos reinos de España, por la misericordia de Dios, y amparo de la Católica y Real Majestad, y por la providencia del Santo Oficio, de que V. S. Ilustrísima tiene singular cuidado, estén puros y limpios de esta pestilencia, y así esperamos que siempre lo estarán). This letter is not included in the BAE edition of *Introducción al símbolo de la fe*, but it is in Balcells's edition of *Introducción del símbolo*, 103–4, which I follow.

23 Letter quoted in Huerga, *Fray Luis de Granada*, 144.

24 Although Granada's emphasis on the normalcy and orthodoxy of the human interior burgeoned after his books were included in the *Index* of 1559, some instances can be found in his previous works. The original version of *Guía de pecadores* (1556) – not to mention the corrected version of 1567 – is full of passages in which the human being's interior is

presented as accessible for inspection and the contents as completely orthodox and in agreement with the rest of God's creation; see, for instance, 1:119.

25 See Justo for a detailed analysis of the inner desert in Granada.

26 Heninger, *Cosmographical*, 23, 144–51. On the use of "individual," see Fowler, 12. The importance of the harmony of universe is studied in several of the articles included in Balcells, *Fray Luis*.

27 Le Breton, "Dualism," 54–7. This idea goes back, at the least, to Saint Augustine, who, in spite of his debasement of the body and elevation of the soul, shows an urgency to present the unity between body and soul as a Christian ideal – something not seen in earlier patristic authors – and the need to present this unity as a consequence of the incarnation of Christ; see Miles.

28 Laín Entralgo, 28, 100–1. Laín Entralgo defines Granada as a modern anatomist who does not want to abandon the old school (138). The fact that modern Vesalian and traditional Galenic anatomy are simultaneously present in Granada matches the reality of anatomical studies in sixteenth-century Spain as described by López Piñero and Calero. On the popularity of Juan Valverde de Amusco's *Anatomía del corpo humano*, sometimes preferred to Vesalius's *De humani corporis fabrica* within and outside Spain, see Choulant and see Cushing, 146. It cannot be established for certain if Granada became familiar with anatomy during his formative years in the convent of San Gregorio of Valladolid or later. In this city and in other cities later in life Granada had opportunities to read anatomical books and even to witness first-hand dissective practices in the so-called anatomical theatres of the universities. Laín Entralgo categorically denies that Granada attended a dissection (131). He does not explain why he has reached this conclusion. The University of Salamanca built a permanent anatomical theatre in 1552 in which the professors opened bodies in front of the students, and often a lay audience was allowed to attend these lessons (Beltrán de Heredia, *Cartulario*, 484; and Pardo Tomás and Martínez Vidal). The sculptor Juan de Arfe Villafañe states in 1585 that, as part of his professional training during his youth, he went to Salamanca to witness the dissection of corpses (Alberti López, 184). Ferrari and Winkler are both detailed studies of the anatomical theatres.

29 Part 2 of *Introducción al símbolo de la fe* is a comparison of Christianity to other religions that are missing the revealed element and are imperfect, unlike Christianity, whose perfection is proven by the testimony of martyrs, which Granada presents in detail; parts 3 and 4 explain redemption from the point of view of reason and faith respectively; part

5 is a summary of all the previous parts. The most available edition of *Introducción al símbolo de la fe* is the one included in Granada's complete works I have used. A more recent edition, but only of part 1, was published by Balcells, *Introducción del símbolo de la fe*. There is no modern English edition available of this book, which never reached the popularity of Granada's other manuals.

30 Using the hexaemeral or six-days-of-creation format to present the marvels of the world as proof of the existence of God and His providence had been a convention since antiquity and was already present in the Book of Wisdom 13:5: "For by the greatness of the beauty, and of the creature, the creator of them may be seen, so as to be known thereby" (Sap. 13:5: A magnitudine enim speciei et creaturae cognoscibiliter poterit creator horum videri) (Heninger, *Cosmographical*, 20–5). To have this type of demonstration of the existence of God culminate with the complexity of the human being is also part of the apologetic tradition. Granada's direct source for the hexaemeral description is Theodoretus's *De providentia* and also Saint Ambrose and Saint Basil, as well as medieval *bestiaria*. On these sources see Balcells, "Introducción" (1989), 46–51. For an example of ending the description of creation with the human being, see Lactantius's *De opificio Dei*.

31 In his writings Pineda was careful to avoid problems with the Inquisition. This caution shows, for instance, in the caveat he includes at the beginning of the list of the authors mentioned in his *Diálogos familiares de la agricultura cristiana*: "Catalogue of nearly seven hundred authors included in this book ... and if by chance, any of them were an author forbidden by the Holy Inquisition, I repudiate this author too, but this book was written before the *Index of Forbidden Books* was published" (Catálogo de quasi setecientos autores de la obra presente ... entre los cuales, si acaso fueren algunos prohibidos por la Sancta Inquisición, yo los condeno también, sino que se compuso esta obra antes de salir los catálogos; bk. 1, chap. 9). The few known details of Pineda's life can be deduced from references in his writings. The best biography and only extended study of his figure is by Meseguer Fernández.

32 Kurtz, 191.

33 Although Pineda and Granada are both familiar with the old anatomical works of Galen, Pineda is much closer to the Galenic text, which he quotes repeatedly, while Granada barely mentions it. Pineda includes the names of Vesalius and Valverde on a few occasions but does not mention the new methods of anatomical dissection.

34 1:246.

35  1:243. For the tradition of the image of man as a microcosm, see Heninger, *Cosmographical*, 144, and Barkan. For an overview of this image in Spain, see Rico. This medieval conception of man's interior as being of the same nature as the rest of creation survives well into the Renaissance. For instance, John Donne still defends the conception of the body as an open system permeable to the outside world and functioning through the balance of fluids of Hippocratic medicine; see Selleck. This conception of man as a microcosm is present even today in some forms of alternative medicine, such as homeopathy.

36  On the widespread metaphor of the book of nature and its medieval use, see Curtius, 321.

37  1:246. This image of the body as a house or republic appears in other passages in Granada, such as *Guía de pecadores*, 1:29. The principles of harmony and hierarchy, which are central features in the representations of the cosmos and the human being as a microcosm, are equally present in the image of a house. The division of the body into rooms is connected to the tradition of cosmographical origins of apportioning it within a circle, square, or other geometrical figures, which are subdivided into equal areas by lines. The results are symmetric parts that correspond to the rational order that rules the universe (Heninger, *Cosmographical*, 144–6).

38  For the church as the body of Christ, see Hillman, *Shakespeare's*, 19n89. The metaphor of the body as a castle is present not only in Valverde's *Anatomía del corpo humano* but also in the *Libro de anatomía* (1542) by Lobera de Ávila, which Granada uses profusely. The second part of this pre-Vesalian anatomical text is entitled "Brief exposition of the organic and marvellous composition of the microcosm or small world that is man" (Declaración en suma breve de la orgánica y maravillosa composición del microcosmos o menor mundo que es el hombre). It is narrated as a dream by the author, who falls into a deep sleep and sees an *alcázar* (castle), which, in an extended allegory, he describes as the human body.

39  Heninger, *Touches*, 193.

40  1:246.

41  "Know ye not that ye are a temple of God, and that the Spirit of God dwelleth in you?" (1 Cor 3:16). Saint Paul is following the common usage of the image of the house in Hellenistic Greece to represent the city or the state as a body made of separate parts standing together in harmony; see D.B. Martin, 92. Such a metaphor can be found in both Buddhist and Hindu texts; see Collins, 167. The pervasiveness of this metaphor may indicate that it belongs to the group that occur originally

in thought, innate conceptual metaphors to understand the world that are later expressed in language. This is a mechanism akin to Jungian archetypes described in Lakoff. For a study of this metaphor in Spain, see David-Peyre.

42 The physiognomic practice of reading the character in the external bodily features is also part of this tradition; see D.B. Martin, 17.

43 Images representing the human body connected to the planets, the zodiac, or the seasons of the year can be seen in Heninger, *Cosmographical*, 147–53.

44 1:262.

45 1:245.

46 Granada explains this malfunction as a temporary disruption because, eventually, the same laws and hierarchical order that keep in motion the heavenly spheres should prevail inside the human body too: "It should also be noticed that, although some of the affects and natural passions that we have mentioned can be named vices or virtues, they are neither but natural passions that are good or bad depending on how we use them. Because when these passions that are in the lower part of the soul follow the rules of the upper portion of the soul, where intelligence and will reside, and embrace what reason offers them, then we can say that we are properly using these passions, i.e., we are using them for the purpose they were given to us. And Aristotle says that this movement is similar to the one of the lower heavenly spheres, which move according to the motions of the higher sphere, which is called the *primum mobile* and moves from East to West around the world in a day. As the lower heavenly spheres follow the motions of the upper heavenly spheres, it is also to be recommended that the passions of the lower part of our soul follow the commands of the upper part. But when these passions follow a different lead – i.e., when they abandon reason and are moved by imagination and the attachment to the very blind guide of sensuality – they lose their bearings" (También se debe aquí advertir que aunque algunos de estos afectos y pasiones naturales que aquí hemos contado tengan nombres de vicios o de virtudes, no son lo uno ni lo otro, sino pasiones naturales que son indiferentes para bien y para mal, según bien o mal de ellas usáremos. Porque cuando estas pasiones que están en la parte inferior de nuestra ánima siguen el dictamen de la parte superior de ella, donde está el entendimiento y la voluntad, abrazando lo que la razón les pone delante, entonces usamos bien de ellas, que es sirviéndonos de ellas para aquello que nos fueron dadas. Y este movimiento dice Aristóteles que es semejante al movimiento de los cielos inferiores, los cuales se mueven conforme al movimiento del cielo superior, que llaman

el primer móvile, el cual se mueve de Oriente a Occidente, dando una vuelta al mundo en un día natural. Porque así como es cosa conveniente que los cielos inferiores sigan al movimiento del superior, así lo es que estas pasiones de la parte inferior de nuestra ánima sigan el regimiento e imperio de la parte superior de ella. Mas cuando siguen otro norte, que es cuando, dejada la razón, se mueven por la imaginación y aprensión de las cosas sensuales, que es una guía muy ciega, entonces van descaminadas por seguir este adalid tan ciego; 1:262). This conception of sin was common at the time. For instance, the first week of Saint Ignatius's exercises call for "deformata reformare," or to reform what has been deformed by sin.

47 Sawday, *The Body*, 113.

48 This engraving in Valverde's book is a copy of Vesalius's *De humani corporis fabrica*, but it has been modified completely given that Vesalius's male figure has not removed his own skin; the image may be inspired by Michelangelo's depiction of Saint Bartholomew in the Vatican and by paintings of Marsyas flayed by Apollo (Binet, 28, and Wells).

49 Sawday, "The Fate of Marsyas," 113, 114, 118.

50 Ángeles, 225; my translation.

51 See Jacobs and Barnes. For the popularity of this image in Spanish art and its presence in *Don Quixote*, see De Armas, *Quixotic Frescoes*, 85–7.

52 Topoi of hagiography, especially the presence of humour during martyrdom, can be found in the chapter "Jest in Hagiography" in Curtius, 425–28.

53 1:651.

54 See Gregory, 287–90. Although the Catholic and Protestant uses of martyrology as a propagandistic weapon are similar, there are fundamental differences in how the two sides envision the testimony of the martyrs and the devotion to them (Coats).

55 1:653.

56 1:658.

57 A complete summary of Philip II's manoeuvres to become the king of Portugal is to be found in the chapter "Years of Triumph, 1579–1588" in Parker, *Philip II*, 142–58.

58 Balcells, "Introducción" (1989), 26–7.

59 A detailed description of the role of Granada in the Portuguese dynastic crisis is to be found in Cuervo, 36. In 1580 Granada may have written a sermon in which he tried to convince the Portuguese to accept Philip II as their monarch, but the authenticity of this lost sermon has not been established; see Balcells, "Introducción" (1989), 26–7, 28.

60 For the political overtones of visions during this period, see Kamen, *Philip of Spain*, 281–2; Parker, *Grand Strategy*, 104; and Kagan, "Politics" and his monograph *Lucrecia's Dreams*.

61 One of the most detailed studies of Sor María de la Visitación is Huerga, "La vida seudomística." MacInnes offers a more recent article that studies her figure within the context of the abundance of stigmatized women in this period.

62 San José Salazar, Weber, and Powell, 59n51.

63 Huerga, "La vida seudomística," 97.

64 The text of this report and a shorter but equally favourable judgment of her case also written by Granada can be seen in Huerga, "La vida seudomística," 118–24. Granada's correspondence from the period reveals his strong support of María de la Visitación; see Robres Lluch and Ortola.

65 Granada wrote on the life of María de la Visitación in 1584. The text was included as part of a letter to the patriarch of Antioch and the bishop of Valencia as "Vida milagrosa de Sor María de la Visitación, de la orden de Santo Domingo en el convento de la Anunciación en Lisboa," and was printed in Rome in 1585; see Granada, *Obras*, 1:xxxv. This work is not included in this edition, but Huerga has published it as Granada, *Historia de Sor María de la Visitación y sermón de las caídas públicas*. Granada had experience in narrating the life of pious and religious people since, among his vast production, he had written on the lives of saints of antiquity and of some of his contemporaries. He wrote the biography of his friend, the also Dominican archbishop of Braga, Fray Bartolomé de los Mártires (1514–90). He also wrote the biography of another friend, the preacher and religious writer Juan de Ávila (1500–69). Granada wrote biographies of other contemporary nuns, such as the missing manuscripts *Vida de Felicia Fernández* and *Vida de Doña Elvira de Mendoza*; see Granada, *Obras*, 1:xxxv.

66 *Historia de Sor María de la Visitación* includes the miraculous events attributed to the nun that Granada related to the pope. This makes this biography look like evidence in a canonization process. For a study of the humility and obedience that was required of women to be considered saintly, see Ahlgren. For a detailed study of how Teresa of Avila subverts these norms of humility and obedience in her writing while pretending to submit to them, see chapter 1, "Little Women: Counter-Reformation Misogyny," in A. Weber.

67 Granada, *Historia de Sor María de la Visitación*, 176–7. The resemblance that Granada saw between Sor María de la Visitación and Catherine of Alexandria is curiously notable in the report he was asked to write

by the Master General of the Dominicans, Sixto Fabri, in 1587. In this favourable report, which he signs together with the nuns' confessor and a third priest, the point is made that the three religious men examined her stigmata precisely "on November 25, 1587, the anniversary day of martyr Saint Catherine [of Alexandria]" (en 25 de noviembre de 1587, día de S. Catharina [de Alejandría] mártir); Huerga, "La vida seudomística," 118.

68 Huerga, "La vida seudomística," 124.

69 Granada, *Historia de Sor María de la Visitación*, 149–50.

70 The stigmata are connected to the devotion to the five wounds of Christ during crucifixion beginning around the eleventh century; see MacInnes, 385–6. For the connection between the devotion to the five wounds of Christ and devotion to the Sacred Heart of Jesus, see Gougaud. Chapter 5, "Sacred Anatomy and the Order of Representation," in Sawday, *The Body*, deals extensively with the wounds of Christ and their cult, as well as with how these practices found their echoes in the anatomical and dissective practices of the period, and vice versa. For an overview of how the devotion to the body of Christ differed between Catholics and Protestants, see Stevens. See also MacInnes, 390–2.

71 The fact that the stigmata are an internal process to which the external wounds are accessory is evident in the case of Catherine of Sienna. She was compelled by her natural humility to ask God to suppress the visible external part of her stigmata, which became internal and invisible until after her death. In other cases, as that of Saint Clair of Montefalco (1268–1308), sainthood is manifest internally in forms that can be found only after death. She never had stigmata in life but, when the nuns of the convent where she died opened her chest to extract her heart to keep as a relic, a small cross and a whip, two of the *arma Christi* (or instruments of his Passion) were found inside her heart; see Camporesi, 3; see also chapter 2 in Park, *Secrets*.

72 *Historia de Sor María de la Visitación*, 240. The reference to Solomon is to Prov. 10:9, "Qui ambulat simpliciter ambulat confidenter; qui autem depravat vias suas manifestus erit."

73 Ibid., 294, 393, and 294 respectively. It must be noticed that female mystics are more prone to imitate the behaviour of the flesh of Christ – bleeding, sweating – given the fluidity that characterizes the female body; see Bynum, "Female," 204–22.

74 A copy of the Inquisitorial sentence in Portuguese can be seen at Huerga, "La vida seudomística," 124–5, and in Imirizaldu, 187–8.

75 Granada, *Obras*, 3:43. An example of Granada's use of this psalm to indicate that there is nothing hidden inside the human being has already

been mentioned, when, in *Introducción al símbolo de la fe*, the psalm is put
in the mouth of Thomas Ford (*Obras*, 1:653).

76 It is accepted that religious practices, specifically the form of pietism
common during the Renaissance, "nurture habits of mind that encourage
conceiving of human inwardness" (Maus, 2). Religious practices
nurturing interiority are not exclusively a Protestant phenomenon but
are also present in Catholic countries, as is the case with the Ignatian
exercises, which rely on the systematic formation of mental images.
Evennett says, "All this [Counter-Reformation] technique of regular
mental prayer, with its demands on the powers of the mind and its
requirements in the way of preparatory and concomitant asceticism,
was conceived and practiced in highly individualistic terms, to the
diminution of stress on communal or liturgical values. Surely, we
see here the individualism of the age taking its appropriate form in
Catholic spirituality – something, perhaps, not wholly unconnected
with the process by which, as medieval society dissolved, the mystic
interpenetration of Church and society faded and the individual was
left to face by itself the problem raised by the mutual confrontation of
Church and state as separate perfect societies" (58). Another religious
practice of the period that has been connected to a fostering of the self
is confession. The practice of confession changed not only in Protestant
countries but also, after the Counter-Reformation, in Catholic countries,
where more private forms of confession, different from its understanding
as communal act in previous times, were implemented; see chapter 12 in
Lea, *A History of Auricular*, and Bossy.

### 3. Quevedo and the Interiority of the Body Politic

1 Serrano Poncela, "Formas," 123.
2 See, for instance, González Fernández de Sevilla and Hoover.
3 The character of Quevedo is notoriously complex. I follow here the
generally accepted view of Quevedo as a conservative writer. He was
an erudite composer of treatises that supported the status quo, a witty
critic of those who opposed the system, and a denouncer of those who
did not live up to the high standards he set for the system. This image is
summarized in Jauralde Pou's description of Quevedo as an example of
"ortodoxia militante" (28). Tierno Galván, on the other hand, sees certain
characteristics of Quevedo as an anticipation of modern interiority, a view
that I do not find convincing. However, it is true that Quevedo was riddled
with contradictions. He has been defined as a defender of the established

order, even as a propagandist, but also as somebody who often said and did things that did not match the narrow mold of an intellectual who acted as a cogwheel in the apparatus of political propaganda. As Maravall puts it, Quevedo is a conservative who from time to time says things that do not follow the established model ("Sobre el pensamiento," 76). On the contradictory character of Quevedo, see Ettinghausen, "Quevedo." On the difficulty and the practicality of trying to define the real Quevedo, see Mariscal, 102. For a summary of how the critics have seen Quevedo as a figure over the centuries, see Jauralde Pou, 895–8.

4 For the biographic details of Quevedo's life, I follow the exhaustive study of Jauralde Pou. Roger and Clare Moore maintain an ongoing bibliography with more than 2,000 items on Quevedo, some of them with information on his life. Contributions, some on biographical aspects, appear in scholarly journals, especially *La Perinola*, which since 1997 has been publishing articles exclusively on Quevedo.

5 Quevedo points out on several occasions the problems that the king's embodiment implies. In *Grandes anales de quince días*, Quevedo praises Philip II, who "knew how to entertain his youth and dissimulate his old age" (Supo entretener la mocedad, supo disimular la vejez) (*Obras completas*, 1:760). All subsequent references, unless otherwise noted, are by volume and page number to Quevedo, *Obras completas*. I chose this edition, in spite of its shortcomings, because it is easily available and contains Quevedo's works in two convenient volumes. The translations into English are mine unless otherwise noted.

6 *City of God*, bk. 19, chap. 13, p. 515.

7 On Quevedo's conservative political views, see Baum. A brief summary of Quevedo's political ideas is found in Serrano Poncela's "Quevedo, hombre político."

8 Maravall, "Sobre el pensamiento," 112–13.

9 Conceits are often divided into Petrarchan and metaphysical. Petrarchan conceits are mostly associated with love poetry and are comparisons between two strikingly separate entities through metaphorical imagery, typically the suffering of the lover versus the serenity of the beloved. Metaphysical conceits are associated with John Donne's poetry and are witty comparisons from different sources, such as theology, alchemy, or everyday objects. These, while closer to the Spanish terms *concepto* and *conceptismo*, are not exactly the same. The Spanish terms apply to a wider range of tropes that play with the sound and meaning of single words, something of which Quevedo is a master. For the association between allegory, conceit, and wit, see Dundas.

10 Accumulation is a well-known rhetorical device that may have many
   different effects. Curtius studies it as part of what he calls "formal
   mannerisms" but cites many examples from earlier periods (282–91).
11 Frye, 308–14. See also an analysis of the grotesque body and its potential
   for satire in the chapter "The Grotesque Image of the Body" in Bakhtin,
   303–67.
12 Sawday, *The Body*, viii, 4.
13 Quevedo also uses the word *anatomía* in the burlesque sense, frequent in
   the period, of a skinny or wretched person. One of his parodic *Canciones*,
   in which the extreme skinniness of a woman is parodied, begins, "do not
   find it shocking, Lady Anatomy" (2:398; no os espantéis, señora Notomía).
   For other instances of the word *anatomía* in Quevedo, see Moreno Castillo,
   152.
14 The authority of sight over other senses is often undermined in Quevedo,
   who, in typical *desengaño* fashion, frequently mentions that one should
   not even believe one's eyes. For instance, after seeing the fake mourning
   of a widower who is ready to remarry immediately after his wife's death,
   he writes in *El mundo de por dentro*, "After today I will not believe my own
   eyes any more" (1:168; desde hoy perderán conmigo todo crédito los ojos).
15 In other writings of Quevedo, the water and blood that the wound in
   Christ's side exuded reappear and are subject to different interpretations.
   For instance, in *Homilía a la Santísima Trinidad*, the water is symbolically
   connected to baptism, and the wound and blood to God's extraction of
   Adam's rib to create Eve (1:1170).
16 Wiener, 1:68.
17 Barkan, 4. Chroust: "The premise of all socio-political thinking of the
   Middle Ages, namely the idea of a single and uniform but nevertheless
   articulate whole, presupposed an organic interrelation between this
   divinely ordained universal whole and its equally divinely ordained
   parts, members, or individuals on the one hand; and between the various
   parts, members, or individuals themselves on the other hand. And since
   every part of the whole must be connected with the whole as well as with
   every other part, such a universal order of all created things presupposed,
   again, a divinely instituted harmony, which pervades this whole as well
   as each and every part of it" (424). A variation of this image, in which the
   societal order reflects the natural order of the cosmos, is the comparison
   of the four elements to the different social groups. Quevedo uses this
   image when he compares earth, water, fire, and air to the four social
   groups: peasants, nobility, clergy, and judges. For him the king is the
   subtle *quintum esse* or quintessence (1:1077).

18 On the prehistory of the body politic, see Barkan, 62. On the dance of Shiva Nataraja and its symbolism, see Coomaraswamy and a more recent evaluation in Kaimal.

19 "Quid si nocere uelint manus pedibus, manibus oculi?" (translation by Basore, 236–7). Quevedo expresses the need for internal harmony of the body politic as the need for the balance of the humours, so important in the Stoic writings: "The health of the kings and kingdoms is like the health of the human body, because the opposition of the different humours, while not good in themselves, through their opposition keep the body in harmonious health" (1:1055; La conservación de reyes y reinos es como la del cuerpo humano, que humores, aunque no buenos, por contrarios unos a otros tienen en concierto al cuerpo).

20 In spite of the many similarities, the image of the body politic in Saint Paul and the Stoics developed independently of each other; see Hale, 28n41.

21 Maravall, *Estudios de historia*, 185–9, points out many uses of the image of the body politic before the sixteenth century in texts such as the *Siete Partidas*. He thinks that this transformation allowed its use outside a religious context and, at least in Spain, it appears as early as the fourteenth century, thus contradicting Bataillon's well-known idea that it is present in Spain only after Erasmus (*Érasme*). On the widespread use of the image and its many occurrences in the Spain of the period in which Quevedo lived, see Davis, as well as the other articles contained in the same volume.

22 Archimbault, 25.

23 Aquinas, quoted and translated by E. Lewis, 858–9. A detailed analysis of how the image of the collective body of Christ evolved within its original religious context is to be found in Lubac.

24 The implications of the position of a medieval king as the head of the state are reflected in what Gierke named "monarchy as office": the simultaneous position of a king as the sovereign head of the political body and as a ruler obliged to consult with the rest of the body (Gierke, 34). Not everybody agrees with Gierke's interpretation; see, for instance, E. Lewis.

25 "The image one paints of the human body in this type of (political) literature is a direct consequence of one's political orientation: to a large extent, the author's political color determines the shades of the image" (Archimbault, 21). Maravall considers that the ambiguity and even egalitarian overtones of the image are the reason why, during the Counter-Reformation, the theory of the *corpus mysticum* was often ignored (*Estudios de historia*, 197).

26 On the final stage of the image of the body politic and the mechanization implied in Hobbes's *Leviathan*, see Barkan, 114; Hale, 129; and Harris, 141; see also chapter 8 in Sawday, *The Body*. Quevedo refers to the "máquina del estado" (machinery of the state) in his writings – for instance 1:1028 – but *máquina* is used not in the modern sense, which emphasizes the self-moving aspect, but in the old one of a complex construction made up of many elements, i.e., to emphasize the collective aspect of the state.

27 The difference between society as an organism and a machine is not clear-cut. The mechanization of the image of the state is implied in Aristotle's conception, which is more mechanistic than Plato's (Barkan, 64). For a discussion of the problems of trying to establish a qualitative difference between the conception of society as an organism and as a machine, see the chapter "Organisme, mécanisme et le langage de l'harmonie" in Schlanger, 47–54. An overview of the history of these images of society, with emphasis on the modern period, is to be found in Stark.

28 An analysis of the connection between the political and the religious sphere of the body politic in Quevedo's *Política de Dios* is found in Riandière la Roche, "Corps politique." The embodied nature of the king and the sacred nature of his position makes the use of sacred rhetoric – i.e., the kind used for religious sermons – the ideal method to reach him; see Peraita, "La oreja," and García-Bryce.

29 Although the image of the body politic is frequent in Quevedo, it is not the only image he uses to represent the state and its relation with the king. For instance, he uses other images of clear religious origin when he says in his *Migajas sentenciosas*, "The king and his kingdom are like a marriage, the king is the husband and the kingdom is the wife; a kingdom that does not have a proper king is like a widow" (1:1053; El rey y el reino un matrimonio formado, el rey el varón, el reino la mujer. Reino viudo el que no tiene rey de valor).

30 In a similar way, he plays with the double meaning of "venas" as blood vessels and as underground mineral deposits when he refers to the extraction of gold in America as a bloodletting of its veins in *La Fortuna con seso* (1:252).

31 Harris, 19, 142.

32 For cases of the medicalization of the metaphor by Spanish political writers, see Aguilar-Adan. Davis, 36–7, deals with uses of humoural medicine in the metaphor. Images of the French and Italian bankers and traders as lice or leeches that suck blood out of Spain are frequent in Quevedo; see, for instance, 1:252. The metaphor of illness in the meaning of social problems has survived the image of the body politic, and the figurative association is still made, although in a more general sense; see Sontag.

33 Donne has many aspects in common with Quevedo. The most extended study that compares the two writers is Hoover. See also González Fernández de Sevilla. Although Hoover's book concentrates on specific aspects of their poetic creation, the introductory section points out many similarities in their lives and pessimistic Baroque *Weltanschauung*. There are also several shorter studies of themes and treatments shared by the authors, such as Pando Canteli.

34 Barkan, 51–60. On the atomistic ideas of Donne, see Hirsch. On Donne's perception of the self as an open entity that participates with the rest of creation not in a harmonic but in a grotesque way, in the Bakhtinian sense, see Selleck. In addition, the strong connection between John Donne's writings and anatomy is mentioned several times by Sawday, *The Body*, viii; see, for instance, 126–9. Coincidentally, Granada may be one of the points of departure for Quevedo's view of the image of the world as a microcosm. See Fernández Suárez and Barkan, 51–60.

35 Donne, Meditation XI, 430–1; Meditation XII, 434.

36 The history of the fable of the belly and of its use in England is summarized in Schoenfeldt, "Fables." See also Barkan, 95–109.

37 On the influence of Lucian of Samosata on Quevedo, see Morreale. On other genres that deal with dreams and their influence on Quevedo, see Nolting-Hauff, 104–7.

38 Mark 9:47: "And if thine eye offend thee, pluck it out: it is better for thee to enter into the kingdom of God with one eye, than having two eyes to be cast into hell fire." See also Matthew 18:9. In the *Sueños* and other writings by Quevedo, many elements of the Christian tradition are used to introduce dismemberment. For instance, in the initial description of *El sueño del infierno*, the path to heaven is presented as a narrow path of sharp thorns and rocks. Some lose their limbs, others their skin or their heads while trying to walk this difficult route, which is a clear allusion to dismemberment and its association with martyrdom (1:141). Also in the first *Sueño*, several biblical characters are metonymically reduced to the body parts that represent their fundamental role. So Judas is presented as "the one who, with his hand, pointed at Him, whom John the Baptist had pointed at with his index finger, and he is the same who slapped Jesus's face with his hand" (1:128; Éste es el que señaló con la mano al que San Juan con el dedo, y fue el que dio la bofetada a Cristo).

39 The word *camarín* is used in the Spanish of the period to indicate a small room or closet in which porcelain, glass, and other precious containers were kept, as well as a small private, secluded room that served as a study for men. For the different images of the devil in Quevedo, see Duarte.

40 On the cabinet of curiosities, see Impey and MacGregor, as well as Bennett.

41 All the references are to Ynduráin's edition of Quevedo's *La vida del Buscón llamado Don Pablos.*

42 Barbers acted as surgeons in many countries and performed, among many other minor procedures, bloodletting. A specific study of their practice in Spain during the period is in Martín Santos.

43 The persistent presentation of the characters in *El Buscón* not as in unity but as a series of poorly articulated limbs and organs that do not follow the same purpose was first pointed out by Spitzer, 147. This technique of describing the characters as an accumulation of parts is so graphic in Quevedo that it has been compared to the Italian painter Arcimboldo's famous portraits of human figures as a collage made out of vegetables and other objects (Levisi, "Las figuras").

44 On the cannibalism implied in this episode, see Ricapito, "Los pasteles."

45 Quevedo derides not only those who resort to this kind of literal bodily modification but also those who indulge in transformation of a textual nature, such as the poets, who turn the teeth of their loved women into pearls with their worn-out metaphors (1:59). Also included among the deceiving transformers of real nature are the pastry cooks. On several occasions, Quevedo parodies their alleged stuffing of pies not with the expected meats but with that of cats and dogs, even with human flesh. He also criticizes the alchemists because their principal endeavour is to transform the immutable nature of matter by making gold out of lead (1:158).

46 The theatrical company where Pablos works is presented as a concrete manifestation of the world upside down, which is a topos that Quevedo uses frequently in his writings. In his romance "Los borrachos," the topos appears in its basic formulation: "The world is distorted / the world is upside down / women are soldiers / and men are virginal maids" (1:128; Todo se ha trocado ya / todo al revés está vuelto / las mujeres son soldados / y los hombre son doncellos). *La Fortuna con seso* can be considered an extended development of this topos. Quevedo uses it so much that it has been said to be implicitly present in most of his satirical work (Vaillo, 368). For the evolution of the topos, see the study by Cocchiara. For an overview of its use in Spanish literature, see Grant.

47 Many instances of this attribution of agency to the intestines and the stomach are present in *El Buscón* and other texts by Quevedo. For instance, the digestive tract often appears as a stubborn third party that has to be engaged in rhetorical argumentation: "persuade one's guts"

(123; persuadir a las tripas). Displaced cases of incontinence are presented in the form of uncontrollable externalization of mental states, such as Pablos's inability to contain his laughter when the situation calls for it, or his blushing when, disguised as a wealthy gentleman, he runs into his old friend Diego Coronel and tries to deny his true identity (265).

48 Kamen, *Iron*, 389.

49 The words "privado," "valido," and "favourite" are not freely interchangeable since they are loaded with political nuances, even if they are often used as synonyms. In general, *privanza*, like the English term "favourite," is used to refer to the position of the person chosen by the king among his courtiers. The term emphasizes the singularization of an individual and implies a personal relationship akin to friendship. *Valimiento* is often associated with the Habsburgs' institutionalized practice of placing a member of the nobility in a function similar to that of a prime minister. It emphasizes the power and influence that the person (the *valido*) has with the king. Quevedo and Olivares show their preference for one or other of the terms at different points; see Elliott, "Staying in Power," 115. I will predominantly use the term *privado*, the most common in Quevedo, and I will take the liberty of extending its use to Richelieu.

50 Curiously, Richelieu's real head has attracted much interest over the centuries. When he died in 1642, his body was dissected and, according to the doctors, his head was truly peculiar: it had no sutures between the different bones of the skull, the ventricles were double, the brains were thicker than usual, and it emanated an uncannily pleasant smell. In 1793 the head was stolen from his desecrated tomb and was not recovered until 1886. In 1895, to avoid future defilements, it was immersed in a cubic metre of cement that was included in the mausoleum sculpted by Girardon in the Church of the Sorbonne (Jouhaud, 33–48).

51 In his mock epic poem "Toma de Valles Ronces," Quevedo calls Richelieu a "formless hydra" (hidra disforme) because he has become a second unnatural head on the body politic of France (2:454).

52 The uneasiness the *privado* triggered in many, like Quevedo, shows in the abundant writing on the *privado*'s education and improvement. Whereas in the past such literature had always been dedicated to the improvement of the prince, now the *privado* is considered more reachable and malleable than the king. On the *privado* as a closer, easier-to-influence person than the king, see MacCurdy, 55–6. The king is also reachable, for which the use of rhetoric, especially sacred rhetoric, is necessary (Peraita, "La oreja").

53  Parker, *Europe*, 58.
54  Rupp, 94–6.
55  Elliott, "Introduction," 19. For a review of the favourite as the alter ego of the king, see Marvick.
56  Elliott, "The Court."
57  Tomás y Valiente, 55, 63, 65. Maravall, *La teoría*, is a detailed study of the *privanza* in Spain and especially of how it could be accommodated within the political theories of the period.
58  Feros, "Images of Evil," 211, 215. On the importance of friendship between the monarch and the *privado*, see Feros, "Twin Souls."
59  Bradner. See also Muñoz Palomares. For the figure of the *privado* Don Álvaro de Luna's influence on later literature, see MacCurdy. For the treatment of the *privado* in Calderón's theatre, see Rupp, 77–125.
60  Quevedo's relationship with the Duke of Osuna followed a pattern similar to his relationship with Olivares, evolving from initial friendship and protection to hostility and even denunciation. Olivares's complex figure has been studied in depth in extended monographs, which often include a chapter or extended section on his relations with Quevedo, such as the psychological profile in Marañón and such as Elliott, *The Count-Duke of Olivares*. Another detailed study of the relations between Olivares and Quevedo is in Elliott, "Quevedo and the Count-Duke of Olivares." On Olivares's and Richelieu's relations to their men of confidence, see Elliott, *Richelieu and Olivares*, 53.
61  "Privado: ser favorecido de algún señor … porque se particulariza con él y le diferencia de los demás" (Covarrubias Orozco, *Tesoro de la lengua*, 1212; my translation).
62  On the limits of political power in Quevedo, see Arellano. In his *Migajas sentenciosas*, Quevedo gives another meaning of *privado*: "They are called *privado*s in Spanish maybe because, in their position, they are *deprived* of their natural security" (1:1051; Privados llama la lengua española, quizá porque en siendo privados se hallan privados de la seguridad natural; emphasis added).
63  This play was never published in its day and it has only survived in a single manuscript. For the textual history of the play, see Somers, 266nn1–2. See also the introduction by Artigas. For some of the literary sources of the play, see Iglesias, "Las fuentes literarias." The vast majority of critics see the play as an adulatory document. Only a few claim that the play contains some criticism of the weakness of Philip IV and the excessive power of Olivares, such as De Armas, "En dos pechos," and Iglesias, "El imposible."

64 "A la muerte de Don Rodrigo de Calderón, marqués de Siete Iglesias, capitán de la guardia Tudesca" (2:70). MacCurdy describes the impact of Rodrigo Calderón's fall on the contemporary literature (38–47).

65 The visit of the Prince of Wales to Spain was much commented on in the period. See Elliott, "Quevedo," 235–6.

66 See Cicero's *Tusculan Disputations* on the loss of a daughter (3, 63) and on the loss of a child (4, 40). Partially because most of the Stoic tradition and Christianity disagreed only on specific issues, which became less crucial over the centuries, by the 1600s Stoicism had become the fashionable ideology of educated men. Quevedo was interested in the revival of Stoicism at least since the time when, as a young man, he wrote to Justus Lipsius, the most important figure of the neo-Stoic movement in Europe. Although in some aspects, as in his belief in the divine monarchy, Lipsius belongs to the past, in others he has been said to anticipate the modern capitalist world, even a Weberian turn towards efficiency and rationalization (Oestreich, 7, 30). On the influence of Stoicism, neo-Stoicism, and Lipsius in Spain during the period – and in particular in Quevedo – the classic study is Ettinghausen, *Francisco de Quevedo and the Neostoic Movement*. See Ramírez's introduction to Lipsius's letters; see also J.L. Saunders and Oestreich.

67 Stoicism includes one of the first systematic descriptions of human psychology. It is based on a highly embodied conception of the human being in which emotions are the result of excessive pressures within the body. Stoicism embraces a definite physiological view of the inner working of the human being, which goes back to Erasistratus and other doctors of antiquity. For a description of the understating of emotions and their functioning in Stoicism, see chapter 21, "Posidonius on Emotions," in Cooper. On the medical theories associated with Stoicism, in particular the theory of the *pneuma*, see Hankison. Other discourses on passions were also present in the period, some of them denouncing the emotional control of Stoicism as impossible and non-productive, as Erasmus does in his *Praise of Folly*; see Paster, Rowe, and Floyd-Wilson.

68 For the implication of perfection in the word *compuesto*, see the entry in the *Diccionario de autoridades* of the Real Academia. An example of the word used to refer to the union of body and soul is Boscán in his translation of *El cortesano de Baltasar de Castiglione*: "del cuerpo y del alma resulta un compuesto más noble que sus partes, el cual es el hombre" (361; man is a compound of body and soul, nobler than his ingredients).

69 Hillman, *Shakespeare's*, 3.

70 The image of the body as a tomb is recurrent in Quevedo, not only in his poetry but also in his prose. For instance, *La cuna y la sepultura* is based on this idea. In *La virtud militante* the body is presented as the walking tomb that contains the five ages of man (1:1282).

71 Quevedo's political writings often mention John the Baptist as an example of a *privado* because of his ideal relation to Christ (Rupp, 114–17). Often he mentions the role played by specific parts of John the Baptist's body when he was close to Christ, which Quevedo interprets allegorically to teach the *privados* how to relate to their kings (Fernández, "Fragmentación"). Judas and his body are presented by Quevedo as counter-examples of the good *privado* (Vilar). In *La cisma de Inglaterra*, Calderón presents Adam as God's favourite in charge of Eden, an image that was common in writings of the time (Rupp, 141).

72 *Visita y anatomía de la cabeza del Cardenal Armando Richelieu* was not published in its day. In the early twentieth century several manuscript copies, none in Quevedo's hand, were discovered in the National Library in Madrid. Riandière la Roche, "Francisco de Quevedo," contains a transcription of the pamphlet based on a study of the manuscript of the text. The text can also be found in the complete edition of the works of Quevedo from which I am quoting (*Obras completas*, 1:903–9). There are four studies dealing with specific aspects of this pamphlet: Riandière la Roche, "La folie"; Valdés; Artal; and Fernández, "La grotesca." The most recent is the identification of the doctors mentioned in the pamphlet in Tato Puigcerver.

73 A list of other anti-French pamphlets published in Spain is found in Astrana Marín, 495. Pamphlets against Richelieu circulated also in France, and Richelieu himself was the origin of pamphlets attacking his enemies, often through his protégés, such as Renaudot, the publisher of the *Gazette*. On this kind of propaganda in France, see Solomon, 100–61. In the same period, Quevedo wrote several similar satirical works that are strongly anti-French, such as "Carta al cristianísimo Rey Luis Deciomotercio." In it Quevedo accuses the French troops of connivance with the Protestant troops and of sacrilegious acts, such as the rumoured feeding of the communion wafers to their horses during the looting of a church. From the same period comes the anti-French parody of the Romance of Roncesvalles entitled "Valles Ronces" and *La sombra del Mos de la Forza*. Another of Quevedo's anti-French writings is *La Fortuna con seso y la hora de todos*, which contains accusations against Richelieu similar to the ones in *Visita y anatomía*. Also, he wrote a parodic sonnet in Italian, "Al cardenal Richelieu, movedor de las armas francesas."

Richelieu is Quevedo's target in later writings as well, such as in his *Relación en que se declaran las trazas con que Francia ha pretendido inquietar los ánimos de los fidelísimos flamencos a que se rebelasen contra su rey y señor natural* (1637), in which Quevedo denounces Richelieu's intentions to be crowned king of France and his Machiavellian manoeuvres. As in many other aspects of Quevedo's life, his relationship with France is not as simple as these propagandistic pamphlets may make us think. Quevedo, who knew French, among other languages, respected and even admired the successful way in which state matters were handled in the France of Louis XIII and Richelieu. This was probably part of the charges used to imprison him because he was most likely a member of a group of conspirators around the Duke of Lerma, who aimed to replace Olivares with a more pro-French *privado*. On the alleged pro-France conspiracy, see Elliott, "Quevedo and the Count-Duke of Olivares" and *The Count-Duke*, 553–9. A recent review of this French aspect of the mysterious accusations against Quevedo is Jauralde Pou, 775–6

74 Lucian of Samosata, 284–303. On the influence of Lucian on Quevedo, see Morreale. For the image of hell as the stomach of an animal, see G.D. Schmidt. References to Jonah swallowed by a whale appear several times in Quevedo. In his satirical song "A una mujer gorda" ("To a Fat Woman"), he writes, "I wish I could be inside your breast / burning with love / since I would be satisfied / in such a big house / and I could easily come out / as Jonah on the third day" (2:402; Quién fuera el que en tu pecho / pudiera estar cuando de amor se abrasa / puesto satisfecho / que no tuviera en él estrecha casa / y sin daño podría / salir, como Jonás, al tercer día). Also, in the burlesque romance "Pinta lo que le sucedió con una fregona" ("Description of What Happened to Him with a Cleaning Woman"), he writes, "I compared myself to Saint Anthony / facing such temptation / when an elephant / approached me disguised as a cleaning woman. / She opened her mouth to laugh. / I thought that this dirty whale / was going to swallow me / as if I were poor Jonah" (2:354; Túveme por San Antón / al ver tentaciones tales / porque en traje de fregona / se me acercó un elefante; / abrió la boca y rióse, / creí que quería tragarme, / ballena del golfo sucio, / como a un Jonás miserable).

75 "Poema heroico de las necedades y locuras de Orlando enamorado" (2:412–32). On the date and sources of this poem, see Jauralde Pou, 732.

76 Barahona de Soto, 241–50. A detailed study of the episode of Zenagrio inside Orco, especially of its implications regarding the epic tradition, is found in Ganelin.

77 For a study of Montaña de Monserrate's and Lobera de Ávila's use
of the image of the body as a castle or city, see David-Peyre. Ferreras
has a detailed analysis of the dreams of Lobera. See also Barona. For
Bernardino Montaña de Monserrate, see López Piñero, "Vesalian," 77–81.
The transcription of these medical texts can be found as an appendix in
Alberti López.
78 Merola. A study of the book is in Barona, 27.
79 Valdés contains a detailed description of the influence of Boccalini on
Quevedo. For the influence of Boccalini in Spain, see Williams.
80 Riandière la Roche, "La folie," 164.
81 Kamen, *Inquisition and Society*, 165; Pérez, 137. The text about Juan de
Ovando is taken from Parker, *The Grand Strategy*, 9.
82 In spite of the fantastic tone of the passage, the separation of the head
from the rest of the body used here for political satire matches the actual
dissecting practice at the time. The historical Vesalius advises in his
*De humani corporis fabrica* to separate the head from the body the better
to study it. For this purpose, he recommends the heads of decapitated
convicts and gives detailed instructions on how to saw the top of the
head while an assistant holds it by the ears (Vesalius, bk. 7, chap. 18) The
idea of decapitation as punishment for the bad *privado* is implied here.
Decapitation is a traditional outcome in the case of the fall of a *privado*,
both in history and in its traditional literary treatment. For instance, in
Damián Salucio del Poyo's *La privanza y caída de Don Álvaro de Luna* (c. 1601),
the queen convinces the king that he has to cut off the head of Don Álvaro
de Luna, using the analogy of the diseased member of the body politic
that has to be amputated to save the rest (in MacCurdy, 120). The famous
execution of Rodrigo Calderón in 1621, who was the man of confidence
of the Duke of Lerma and therefore the *privado* of the *privado*, was not
by decapitation; instead, he had his throat slit, as testimonies of the
period and his mummy, kept at the convent of Porta Coeli in Valladolid,
evidence (F. Díaz-Plaja, 96).
83 Quevedo's choice of the ears as the point of entry does not correspond to
any real dissective practice but instead refers to the widespread notion
that the ears – sometimes competing with the eyes – are the point through
which envy enters the human being. The ear as a point for access to
the inside of the human being has an old tradition in the Fathers of the
Church and other religious writers, such as Aquinas, who considers
hearing the sense chosen by Faith because it inspires a salutary mistrust
in the matters of the world (Rupp, 141). In *Virtud militante*, Quevedo
describes hearing as a sense ambitious by nature that fights with sight for

the highest position in the court of head and also as the point of entrance of all the adulation that vain and ambitious people covet (1:1129). A similar view of ambition and greed as a suctioning force inside the body is in Quevedo's *Política de Dios*, where he speaks of "codicia hidrópica" (1:611; dropsical greed).

84 Huarte de San Juan, 133.

85 The influential Spanish anatomist Valverde agrees that there are four ventricles in the brain. However, he doubts that we can really know anything of the psychological functions that take place inside the ventricles (fols. 79v and 80v).

86 Quevedo's description, however fantastic, is based in the anatomical findings of the period, which noticed the abundance of liquid inside the brain. Valverde writes, "Both sides of the brain and the ventricles are soft and filled with liquid, most noticeably in the bodies of those who died recently. Because of this, I find it ridiculous that many [doctors], after performing an autopsy, explain a sudden death as the result of the abundance of liquid in the brain. They do not realize that this liquid is normal, which is proven by how easily and copiously we can cry" (fol. 80r; Entrambos sesos y ventrecillos son lisos y cubiertos de un humor acuoso, principalmente en los que están recién muertos, por lo cual me suelo yo reír mucho de algunos que queriendo ver la causa de alguna muerte súbita, abren la cabeza, y viendo dentro esta agua piensan que ella ha sido la causa, no mirando que esto es cosa natural, como manifiestamente nos muestra la facilidad que en el lloro tenemos, juntamente con la gran copia de agua que un momento vemos salir por los ojos).

87 It is not certain that Quevedo had read Rabelais or if he knew him only second-hand through other authors' commentaries on Rabelais's impiety. On this possibility, see Artal. Writing marginal annotations and underlining passages is a common reading practice in the period that Quevedo also followed; several of his books have survived and are profusely annotated (Peraita, "Mapas de lectura").

88 As an example of the equation of Tacitus and Machiavelli, in his *Política de Dios*, Quevedo writes, "Who could deny that the pompous disciples of Tacitus and the modern impious follower [Machiavelli] do not drink from the same fountains of Pilate's poison?" (1:602; ¿Quién negará de los que son pomposos discípulos de Tácito y del impío moderno que no beben en estos arroyuelos el veneno de los manantiales de Pilatos?).

89 See Schiffman. Montaigne also uses the anatomical method as a heuristic device; see both Demonet and Panichi.

90 Chartier, 103.
91 Also in *Política de Dios,* this Latin phrase is quoted as an example of the way of speaking that characterizes a tyrant (1:533). The passage is actually adapted from Juvenal's famous *Satire VI* against women, since these are the words of a capricious woman who asks her husband to crucify an innocent slave (v. 223) (quoted in Arellano, 24n1, and in Crosby, 520).
92 The same expression "Yo me entiendo" appears also in a negative context in *Discurso de todos los diablos* (1:211). This kind of attack on the autonomy of personal judgment is frequent in Quevedo and in other writers of the period.
93 For a definition of *morbus regius* and its symptoms, see Riandière la Roche, "Francisco de Quevedo," 70n29.
94 The usurpation of the king's senses by the favourite is also present, for instance, in *La Fortuna con seso y la hora de todos,* where Quevedo claims that the favourite who usurps these functions transforms the king into a living corpse (1:176). He mentions the dangerous effects of excessive praise of the favourite in front of the king: "More favourites owe their fall to praise than to denunciation. The more one praises the favourite to the king, the more one equates him [to the king], eliciting therefore unavoidable envy in the king" (1:232–3; Más privanzas han arruinado las alabanzas que las acusaciones. Quien alaba en presencia del rey a su valido, cuanto más le alaba, lo contrasta más, porque produce la envidia donde no puede ser evitada).
95 I am using Max Weber's concept of disenchantment (*Entzauberung*) of the world in the sense that calculation and rationalization can be applied to all aspects of nature, including the human being (Germain, 34–41).
96 Quevedo's *Doctrina de Epicteto* explains this division between external and internal: "External and internal things are those that are our own and those that are not ... Body, wealth, worldly honours, rewards and high positions are not in our hands" (2:788; Las cosas, exterior y interiormente / se dividen en propias y en ajenas /... No están en nuestra mano / el cuerpo, la hacienda, ni el profano / honor, las dignidades y los puestos). This matches the negative image of the body as a delicate organism, prone to imbalance. The Christian and Stoic depiction of the body and flesh as decaying substances is frequent in Quevedo, who, in his *De remedios de cualquier fortuna,* comments on the idea that disease is the natural state of the human being (1:960). In the same tradition, he presents the embodied nature of the human being as a negative, humbling factor that begins at the moment of conception in his *Discurso de todos los diablos.* There the process of conception and the nine months inside the mother's body are

described as a sobering first experience of interiority, in this case that of the body of the mother, which Quevedo sees as a dirty place where the foetus has to feed from her unclean menstrual blood and live close to her urine (1:202).

97 The image of the human body as clockwork is extensively treated in the next chapter.

## 4. Cervantes's Mechanical Interiors and Zayas's Female Anatomies

1 The only contemporary medical treatise that Cervantes mentions (*Don Quixote*, part 1, 18, 1095) is Andrés Laguna's Spanish translation of Dioscorides's *De materia medica*, first published in 1555 and republished several times in the second half of the sixteenth century. However, Cervantes's familiarity with medical theories of the period, especially with those of Juan Huarte de San Juan, is commonly acknowledged (Puerto).

2 In his short play *El juez de los divorcios* (*The Divorce Court Judge*), Cervantes emphasizes the difference between doctors and surgeons. The stage directions specify that a surgeon, dressed in the fashion associated with doctors, enters the scene with his wife. She alleges that "when we got married, I was deceived, because he claimed to be a physician and, overnight, he turned out to be a [barber-] surgeon, one of those men who tie bandages and cure some diseases" (*Obras completas*, 543; fui engañada cuando con él me casé, porque él dijo que era médico de pulso, y remaneció cirujano, y hombre que hace ligaduras y cura otras enfermedades; my translation). On the importance of illustrated images for the instruction of barber-surgeons, see Crummer, and Carlino, *Paper*. A specific study of barber-surgeons in the city of Valladolid during the period is Martín Santos.

3 García Barreno, 164. On the medical care that Cervantes may have received, see both López Alonso and Eisenberg.

4 The references to *Don Quixote* are to the page number in Cohen's translation, followed by the page number in *Obras completas*. The references to the *Exemplary Novels* are by page number in *Obras completas* and in Lipson's English translation. This passage of *Rinconete and Cortadillo* is freely translated by Lipson as "I'd rather be married to a pile of dead and rotting bones" (95).

5 Lipson freely translates the word *notomía* as "sack of bones" (289).

6 The encounter with Cañizares is the culmination of the descent into the abyss that is Berganza's life. Afterwards, his life becomes a slow ascent

that leads him to the practice of charity as one of the dogs who escort the pious Mahudes to collect alms for the needy in the hospital of Valladolid. Partially because of this, Berganza's encounter with Cañizares has been identified by the critics as the central episode of *El coloquio de los perros*. "Berganza's story, in an unpicaresque fashion, rushes toward the witch's episode like iron filings to a magnet" (El Saffar, *Cervantes*, 39). Forcione also considers this encounter the centre of the story: "We have reached the monster at the centre of the labyrinth" (*Cervantes and the Mystery*, 59).

7  On the unity of *El casamiento engañoso* and *El coloquio de los perros*, see, for instance, Waley. Detailed attention to this issue is also given in Woodward and more extensively in El Saffar, *Cervantes*. An up-to-date summary and new argumentation on the relation between the two stories can be found in Aylward.

8  Forcione, *Cervantes and the Mystery*, 135. Forcione also remarks how Campuzano's trunk becomes a tomb in "the descent into the grave" and the subsequent rebirth that *El casamiento* and *El coloquio* are (139). Also, the small room into which Campuzano and Estafanía moved after the true owner of the house returns is presented as a narrow tomb in which there are two sepulchres and shrouds: "She led us to a narrow room in which the two beds stood so close together that they looked like one, because there was no space between them and the sheets were touching" (243, 994; Llevónos a un aposento estrecho, en el cual había dos camas tan juntas, que parecían una, a causa de que no había espacio que las dividiese, y las sábanas de entrambas se besaban).

9  El Saffar, *Novel*, 76.

10  The importance of *tropelías* or *eutropelías* in Cervantes's work has been acknowledged by many scholars after Wardropper pointed it out. For instance, Reed writes that "Cervantes sees a clear relationship between the entertainment value of *eutrapelia* and its didactic power to reveal truth through illusion" (207). A summary of recent scholarship on Cervantes's use of *tropelías* can be seen in Colin Thompson.

11  In his analysis of the two stories in *Cervantes and the Mystery of Lawlessness*, Forcione repeatedly uses the terms "dismemberment," "disarticulation," and "fragmentation."

12  On the significance of the "colas de pulpo," see Forcione, *Cervantes and the Mystery*, 5–6.

13  "The world of the beast is a world of savagery, depredation and mutilation, and in the Cañizares episode there is a striking concentration of the imagery of dismemberment and violence which runs through the entire work, from the initial descriptions of the ravages of syphilis and the

carnage of the slaughterhouse to Berganza's concluding confession of his desire to rip to pieces the lap dog which epitomizes parasitic favorites" (Forcione, *Cervantes and the Mystery*, 84–5).

14 Prieto Carrasco, 25. Covarrubias is also clear about the origin of the bodies used for the anatomy lessons: "Anatomy is the removal of the flesh and the opening of human bodies in order to look inside ... and sometimes it is done on the bodies of those executed or of those who die in charity hospitals" (*Tesoro*, 117; Anatomía es la descarnadura y abertura que se hace de un cuerpo humano para considerar sus partes interiores ... y se ejecuta algunas veces en los cuerpos de los ajusticiados y otras en los que mueren en los hospitales y en algunas otras personas particulares).

15 The importance of Marsyas in art and anatomy as an aid for the artists is studied by Jacobs. Sawday mentions several concrete cases of anatomical books that represent the scene or refer to it. He also comments on the use of the story to symbolize hubris (*The Body*, 184–8, and "The Fate").

16 Ribera is famous for the painting of martyrs, and his treatment of the flaying of Marsyas connects with some of his religious paintings. Another version by him can be seen at the Museo Nazionale di Capodimonte, Naples. Other paintings representing the scene resort to a similar disposition, the so-called "hanging" or "red" type, in which Marsyas is tied to a tree by his heels upside down while Apollo starts to flay him (Jacobs, 429). Many of these paintings represent figures of onlookers who are horrified by the procedure. Berganza, who shows his disgust at having to bite the repulsive body of Cañizares, incarnates the role of both Apollo and the horrified spectators.

17 A detailed account of the technology in the Spain of the period, with special attention to wind and hydraulic technology, is in García Tapia, "Los molinos."

18 Mayr studies in detail how the clock metaphor became frequent, especially in the seventeenth century; see chapter 2, "The Rise of the Clock Metaphor." There are some specific but partial studies of the influence of the clock in Spanish culture, such as Heiple, who includes a section dedicated to clock images in poetry. A concise description of the new mechanistic conception of the world, with special attention to the ideas of natural philosophers such as Robert Boyle, can be seen in Shapin.

19 Sawday, *Engines*, 97.

20 Grafton, 11–18.

21 Daston and Park, 284.

22 Rivadeneira, *Tratado*, 530–1. A good example of the overtones of (self-) guidance implied in the word "clock" at the time is the title *Reloj de*

*príncipes*, which Antonio de Guevara chose in 1529 for his book on the edification of rulers.

23 Other uses of the word 'clock' as a metaphor for government and control were common; see, for instance, Vega Carpio, 440, and Saavedra Fajardo. More examples can be seen in Mayr, 102–14. The metaphor of the clock was also deployed to illustrate other important concepts of the period. It served, for instance, to illustrate the new attitudes towards certainty in matters of hypothesis and observation. In this sense, the clock was the antecedent of today's black box or a device in which only input and output can be studied since the internal works are unknown. Equally, the relation between clock and clockmaker became one of the arguments to support the existence of God in the new mechanistic paradigm that envisioned the universe as a machine (Shapin, 101–2, 142–4).

24 Timoneda, 145.

25 *Cigarrales de Toledo*, 129.

26 Arce de Otálora, 2:921.

27 Rufo, apotegma 99, 47.

28 "*Reloj desconcertado* is a form of referring to people who do not keep the proper decorum in their actions and words" (Covarrubias, *Tesoro*, 561; Reloj desconcertado llaman al sujeto desordenado en sus acciones o palabras).

29 In the diagrams of the cosmos of the time, as well as in the theories that explain its functioning, the concept of harmony is central. God is the creator of a vast system that, in spite of its complexity, eternally follows a rational pattern of movement epitomized by the precise regularity of astronomical movements (Heninger, *Cosmographical*).

30 A detailed study of the complex problem of making clocks accurate can be found in von Bertele. Cipolla's classic monograph contains a detailed description of the invention and evolution of mechanical clocks beginning in the fourteenth century.

31 López de Úbeda, 2:517–18.

32 The idea of man as a clock that fell out of sync with the rest of the created world after the Fall was a commonplace. A similar example can be seen, for instance, in Alemán, 433.

33 *El juez de los divorcios* in *Obras completas*, 543.

34 Granada, *Obras*, 2:107.

35 Juan Bautista de la Concepción, 878.

36 *Aucto de la prevaricación de nuestro padre Adán*, 145. Similar metaphorical uses of clocks that do not work properly can be found in the chapters "El reloj en la poesía lírica," "El reloj en el teatro," "El reloj ascético," and "El reloj en los prosistas clásicos" in Herrero García, 67–164.

37 Much has been written about the structure and the possible unity or lack thereof in *El licenciado Vidriera*; see, for instance, Casa, Edwards, and Ruan.

38 Doctor Frankenstein and the Glass Licentiate are victims of the dangers of too much external knowledge. The Glass Licentiate is "one of the numerous fools that fascinated the Renaissance" (Forcione, *Cervantes and the Humanist*, 232n16) and exemplifies the negative side of the Renaissance obsession with learning, whose dangers Haydn showed.

39 Cadalso, 80.

40 Descartes, 7:19. On several possible real-life models for Cervantes's *El licenciado Vidriera*, see Speak. There are also studies dedicated to the specific kind of insanity that may have affected Tomás Rodaja, such as Redondo; Munguía García; and Reiss, 29. The influence of the aphrodisiac on his insanity has also been studied; see Schleiner and also El Saffar, *Novel*, 57.

41 The old association of glass with pure spirit is also present in the mystics, who saw glass as an element between matter and spirit. Some forms of crystallomancy – crystal ball reading – have their origin in the belief that crystals are open windows into another dimension; see E.G. Wilson, 8–14, and Egido, 75nn72–6. For man's essence as being made of glass and therefore knowledge being an optical display in *foro interno*, see Rorty, 37. Through the widespread metonymy of referring to a mirror as a "reflecting glass" or simply as a "glass," glass can be seen as a heuristic device that permits observers to see the truth in its reflection. This use is behind the exemplary meaning of glass and mirrors in such cases as when Don Quixote is called the "mirror of the errant knights" (espejo de la caballería andante). The word "mirror" is also used in the anti-exemplary sense of the true reflection or the realistic portrait of an ugly reality. This is the case of Quevedo's *Buscón*, a book that on its title page is called "example for bums and a mirror glass for cheapskates" (ejemplo de vagabundos y espejo de tacaños). Symptomatically, in the England of the period "mirror" and "anatomy" were common in the titles of satirical books to indicate that they were a realistic description of mores, but anatomy eventually prevailed; see Grabes, 230–3.

42 Although originally "glass" was reserved to refer to the hourglasses made from this material, later it was extended to mechanical clocks, which included a glass to protect the dial and part of the complex mechanism while displaying it. A mechanical clock in a glass box (the *cristalino*) that Turriano made for the emperor Charles V is described in the inventory of possessions left by Philip II at his death. See Junquera, 14, and Montañés Fontenla, *Capítulos*, 105.

43 Although it does not appear as an entry in Covarrubias's earlier
   dictionary, the word *rodaja* is included indirectly in its definition of the
   word *carrillo* (little cart) as the turning wheel in a pulley. Also, Nebrija's
   Spanish–Latin dictionary of 1495 defines "rodaja" as "rolling instrument"
   (instrumento para rodar) and "small wheel" (rueda pequeña). That *rodaja*
   is a diminutive of *rueda* (wheel) is manifest, for instance, when Sancho
   Panza comically refers to the "rueda de la fortuna" (wheel of Fortune) as
   the "rodaja de la fortuna" (1337, 591, 2:19). Appropriately Tomás, once
   cured, changes his name from Rodaja (little wheel) to Rueda (wheel). Also
   common in the period, the word is used in the meaning of the rowel in
   a spur, a name that matches the irritating role that Tomás's provocative
   statements have on the whole of society.

44 A similar sense of reification is implied in another name applied to Tomás
   during his insane period, the nickname Licentiate Redoma. This choice
   of a name adds to Tomás's characterization as an object since *redoma* is a
   flask or container made from folded glass, as the one that Don Quixote
   uses to keep the famous balsam of Fierabrás. To refer to Tomás as
   Licentiate Redoma (glass flask) is a pun since *redomado* is used in the early
   modern Spanish to refer to a rascal. As Covarrubias's dictionary explains,
   "*redoma* is a glass flask made of two layers of glass that have been shaped
   two times in a furnace. Because of this we called *redomado* a man who is
   very astute, because his cunning has several layers" (1233; Redoma: …
   Díjose redoma, porque ultra de ser doblada en el grueso del vidrio, se
   mete en el fuego, y se doma y recuece dos veces. De aquí llamamos
   redomado al hombre cauteloso y astuto, porque está recocido en malicia).
   Much has been said about the different names that the protagonist of the
   story adopts as he changes during his adventure; see, for instance, García
   Lorca.

45 Forcione, *Cervantes and the Humanist*, 236, 242, 273, and 313; El Saffar,
   *Novel*, 56; Shipley, 96.

46 Forcione, *Cervantes and the Humanist*, 242.

47 Shipley, 68. For a study of Cynical philosophy in *El licenciado Vidriera* and
   *El coloquio de los perros*, see both Riley and Oliver. Zappala is a study of the
   influence of Lucian of Samosata and Cynical philosophers on Cervantes.
   Forcione's *Cervantes and the Humanist* and *Cervantes and the Mystery*
   contain many references to the influence of Cynical philosophy on these
   two novels.

48 The legend of the Hombre de Palo originates with a wooden statue that
   holds a box to collect alms in a street of Toledo – called the Calle del
   Hombre de Palo today (Porres Martín-Cleto, 465).

49 Cardboard is the quintessential material of deception. This meaning can be seen, for instance, in Cervantes's famous sonnet to the tomb of Philip II in Seville. For its ironic effect, the sonnet relies on the fact, well known at the time, that the funerary monument, although apparently made from luxurious marble, was in reality contrived from painted cardboard (A.L. Martín, 107).

50 Oracular machines have a long tradition in European folk stories and literature. In addition to the aforementioned head attributed to Albert the Great, other talking artificial heads, often made from bronze, are present in many legends and poems (Sawday, *Engines*, 193–4).

51 Shipley, 73.

52 Haley's influential article points out the importance of dehumanization in the episode. Although he does not refer to mechanization per se, he emphasizes the importance of the "mechanics of telling" (146) and "the mechanics of the performance" (156).

53 In his history of puppetry in Spain, Varey documents the display of automata and puppets in dramatic performances at public festivities or in the royal palace (41–90).

54 Varey, 232–8.

55 Haley, 151, 152.

56 Varey, 45–51. On origins of the vocabulary of puppetry in Spain, see also Castro, "La palabra."

57 Mechanical and religious ingredients are also combined with purity of blood in the Spanish legend of a brazen head in the church of Távara (Zamora), which supposedly came to life and spoke every time a Jew entered the building (Sawday, *Engines*, 194).

58 Haley, 163. Other critics see political intentionality in the episode. According to Gaylord ("Pulling"), to make the puppets act out the legendary kidnapping of Melisendra by a Moor would question the contemporary discourse of the Reconquest.

59 Dissective elements are detectable not only in the detailed description of the puppets' horrific wounds but also when Maese Pedro refers to his destroyed puppets as "relics" (643, 1365), which, as we saw in previous chapters, are part of the culture of dissection.

60 In the essay entitled "Of the inconstancy of our actions," Montaigne quotes the complete form of this maxim: "ducimur ut nervis alienis mobile lignum" (bk. 2, chap. 1, p. 375). The maxim is an adaptation of a passage taken from Horace, *Satires*, bk. 2, satire 7, v. 82.

61 Several critics have identified Ginés de Pasamonte as a trickster; see, for instance, El Saffar, "Tracking." Dunn, "Cervantes," 117–21, analyses

Ginés de Pasamonte as a *pícaro* and expands on the implications that his treatment by Cervantes has on his concept of the picaresque as a genre.

62 Covarrubias's dictionary describes marzipan as "a sweet *paste* of sugar, almonds, and other ingredients" (1258; una *pasta* dulce, de azúcar y almendras y otras cosas; emphasis added).

63 Villalón, 174–5 (the spelling has been regularized to modern Spanish).

64 Arce de Otálora, 2:1113.

65 Quiñones de Benavente, 210.

66 López de Úbeda, 2:714.

67 Other automata were attached to this clock before the Papamoscas. Surviving documents confirm that the chapter of the cathedral intended to install a mechanical friar that would strike a young sleepy student every hour and display a notice board with a call to awakening; see Aracil, 464–5. A detailed enumeration of automata in the Spain of the period can be seen in Herrero García, 21–4. Many facts about the initial years of the clocks in Spain, some with automata, can be found in the six volumes of *Biblioteca literaria del relojero* edited by Montañés Fontenla.

68 Cervantes mentions Turriano's famous water machine of Toledo in *La ilustre fregona* as "el artificio de Juanelo" (*Obras completas*, 926; Juanelo's artefact). For a study of Turriano's machines, see García-Diego.

69 There are testimonies speaking about Lastanosa owning a mechanical pigeon and miniature reproductions of landscapes with artificial birds that sang (Gil Encabo, 114).

70 See García Tapia, *Tecnología*, 35–6; and Aracil, 314–15.

71 Ricapito says that "[Vidriera] has made a spectacle of himself, [i]n fact, Vidriera is a 'spectacle' – I use the word in a theatrical and dramaturgical sense" (*Cervantes's* Novelas, 92).

72 Covarrubias's definition of the word "machine" indicates that it was commonly used to mean a war machine: "A machine is a sizable construction designed by human wit, the name comes from the Latin *machina*. War machine is the one designed to destroy the enemy. There are many of this type; see Vitruvius, lib. 10, cap. 19" (1096; Máquina [es una] fábrica grande, ingeniosa, del nombre latino *machina*. Máquina bélica, es la que hace el ingeniero para dañar a los contrarios: éstas son muchas y varias, *vide* Vitruvius lib. 10. cap. 19). Several fabulous automata of antiquity served military purposes, such as warning of impending attacks (Daston and Park, 89–90). Reiss considers the meaning of rowel of a spur implied in the name Rodaja to be connected to Tomás's joining the army and dying at the end of the story (28).

73 In the modern period, the risks inherent in knowledge acquisition took the form of scientific development, as Mary Shelley's *Frankenstein or the Modern Prometheus* (1818) exemplified. This fear emerges in other, apparently unrelated areas as well, such as the recent field of surveillance studies, which deals with the potential of new technologies to endanger privacy and individuality. Seminal works of the field are those by Groebner, by Haggerty and Ericson, and by Los.

74 *Metamorphoses*, bk. 6, line 385, p. 166. Translation by Dryden, 182.

75 Greene, 264.

76 Several critics point out Cervantes's depictions of characters that do not see their limitations. For instance, Hart writes that "[b]oth Berganza and Don Quixote fail because they cannot or will not see themselves as they really are and accept their limitations" (197).

77 Greenblatt, 2. Saint Augustine's commentary on the Psalm reads, "We will not reach true justice except from grace. Hands off etc." (*Sermo 169*, cap. IX, 11, col. 0921; Justitia nobis vera non est nisi ex gratia. Tolle te, tolle, inquam, te a te, impedis te).

78 "Thou mayest fashion thyself in whatever shape thou shalt prefer. Thou shalt have the power to degenerate into the lower forms of life, which are brutish. Thou shalt have the power, out of thy soul's judgment, to be reborn into the higher forms, which are divine" (quoted in Greene, 243).

79 Detailed biographies of Zayas can be seen in Greer, 17–35, and Yllera, 11–21. A summary of the popularity of Zayas's novels in her and later centuries are Greer and Rhodes, 28–32, and Olivares, 28–32.

80 Goytisolo, "El mundo," 72. The importance of the conflict between honour and desire is also emphasized by other critics, such as Clamurro, 43, 46.

81 On the problem of the true titles of Zayas's two books, see Rhodes, *Dressed*, 10–12.

82 Studies of violence against women in Spanish theatre include Stroud and Carrión, especially her chapter 4, "Foundational Violence and the Drama of Honour"; Levisi connects the popularity of martyrology at the time to the rediscovery of the Roman catacombs in 1578 ("La crueldad," 454); Maravall, *Culture*, 106, 162–3.

83 Greer, 142. A summary of the different critical opinions on the abundant violence in Zayas's stories is Vollendorf, 77–8. Two detailed tables of the violent events in Zayas's texts can be seen in Vollendorf, 97, 108–9.

84 Goytisolo calls Zayas's detailed accounts of goriness "truculencia granguiñolesca" (histrionic goriness; "El mundo," 86). Greer, 24, 114; Brownlee, 89; Matos-Nin, 118; and Rhodes, *Dressed*, 84, express similar

opinions. Grieve connects the grotesque violence of Zayas's stories with the influence of the hagiographic model (103). Levisi speaks of sadism and considers the attention that the stories pay to violence structurally unnecessary ("La crueldad," 449).

85 Amezúa y Mayo speaks of *costumbrismo* in Zayas's detailed descriptions (xv). A summary of early critics' attributions of realism to Zayas can be seen in Yllera, 40–3.

86 Brownlee, 11. Cases of women murdered by jealous husbands taken from contemporary legal and historical sources can be seen in Sánchez and, more recently, in Barahona and in Taylor. Stroud revises how accurate the *comedias* were in representing the reality of uxoricide.

87 Vollendorf, 118; O'Brien, 244; Clamurro, 44; Boyer, xxxiii. See also Vollendorf, xiv.

88 Mariscal emphasizes the importance of class in the formation of subjectivities in early modern Spain but ignores gender. A convenient summary of the role that critics have attributed to gender in the formation of subjectivities can be seen in Voros, 158–60. The subject of *honor* and *honra* in early modern Spain has a long tradition of study, among which Castro, "Algunas"; Honig; Larson; and Maravall, *Poder*, are fundamental. The position of Zayas regarding nobility, its privileges, and its obligations is complex. Zayas is aware of the faulty attitudes of noblemen not only towards women, but also towards king and country (Clamurro, 48).

89 The translation of this passage of the prologue is taken from Greer and Rhodes's edition. The Spanish texts of the *Desengaños* are quoted by page number in Boyer's English translation, followed by page number in Yllera's edition, unless otherwise specified. The references to the *Novelas amorosas y ejemplares* are to Olivares's edition. Convenient summaries in English of the plots of the *Novelas amorosas* and the *Desengaños* are in Greer, 361–80, and of the *Desengaños* in Rhodes, *Dressed*, 177–83.

90 I add the English title used by Boyer in her translation next to the Spanish title the first time one of Zayas's stories is mentioned. For the *Novelas amorosas y ejemplares*, I use the translation of the titles in Vollendorf, 13.

91 Jehenson and Welles expand on the significance that the stories in the second volume are narrated on the days preceding Lent (178). Rhodes writes that Zayas designed the female characters "to fail, dressing them in specific features the better to kill them and thereby deliver the sharpest disillusion to her public," for which she calls them "perfect victims" (*Dressed*, 8, 82, 89).

92 The most common references to viscera in the stories are conventional allusions to the heart, which is invoked several times as the location of

men and women's feelings. Next to the numerous cases of the loss of
virginity, only a few vague references to female anatomy are implied in
matters related to giving birth. Thus, in *La fuerza del amor* (*The Power of
Love*), we are told that Laura's mother died while giving birth (Zayas,
*Novelas amorosas*, 345).

93 Classical medical authorities believed that women experienced sensations
about their reproductive status that could not be expressed in words:
"pregnancy was supposed to be something which women 'knew' from
their own sensations on conception" (King, 45).

94 Castillo points out the resemblance between Zayas's description of
violence and anatomical illustrations, although he does not give specific
examples (111–35).

95 Sawday, *The Body*, 215.

96 Dopico Black, 16, emphasis added, and 19. On women considered
receptacles of male honour, see Vollendorf, 130.

97 King, 28, 34.

98 Laqueur, 5. Schiebinger, 46–66, has a summary of the perception through
history of the anatomical differences between men and women.

99 Stallybrass, 126. See also Sawday, *The Body*, 9–10, and Vollendorf, 140.

100 Granada, *Memorial de la vida cristiana* in *Obras*, 2:563, my translation.

101 The worship of the Virgin Mary and its origins and evolution is studied
by Warner. See also Winstead.

102 Lemay, 127. An example of the popularity of *De secretis mulierum* is that
Fernando de Rojas, the author of *La Celestina*, owned a copy that he left to
his son in his will (Valle Lersundi).

103 Park, "Dissecting," 32–4.

104 Traub, 81–2.

105 Carlino, *Paper Bodies*, 23–6. For a description of Estienne's figures, see
Choulant, 150–5. A detailed account of the authorship of the images is in
Kellett.

106 Mitchell, 273.

107 The practice of using the bodies of executed felons and prostitutes for
dissections continued until much later. In 1713, the English physician
William Cheselden reported that he had anatomized "executed bodies
and ... a common whore that died suddenly" (Schiebinger, 49).

108 Vesalius, 538 (also cited in O'Malley, 113). Richardson is a study of
bodysnatching.

109 Sawday, *The Body*, 224. Sawday presents the Virgin Mary as the
quintessential figure of what he calls "sacred anatomy." Statues or
paintings that show the foetus of Jesus inside Mary's womb or of John

the Baptist inside Saint Elizabeth's were common in the Middle Ages (Sawday, *The Body*, 104).

110 Dopico Black, xv. Entering a convent was another option permitted to noblewomen. It is repeatedly chosen by several characters in Zayas's stories, including Lysis at the end of the second volume. Several critics have pointed out that the convent offered women a shelter from the dangers of the honour system.

111 Dopico Black, 4.

112 Brownlee, 2, 12–13. Dopico Black refers to the social control of women as "inquisitorial hermeneutics" in a period, the Counter-Reformation, in which matters such as marital transgressions – adultery, bigamy – were included in the category of heresy (11–12). Vollendorf defines wife-murder plays as "dramas in which wives' bodies and desires become the subject of a kind of self-fulfilling inquisitorial surveillance" (xvi). On the connection between the inquisitorial methods and the control of women, see also Carrión, 80–1.

113 Dopico Black, 25.

114 A parody of the undecidability of wives' bodies regarding their fidelity is the medieval story of the painter Pitas Payas in the *Libro del buen amor*. A painter by that name has to leave his wife alone for an extended period. To ensure her chastity during his absence, he paints a lamb on her belly. Soon after his departure, however, she takes a lover, and the image of the lamb is worn away in the course of regular sexual activity. When she learns of her husband's imminent return, she asks her lover to restore the erased image of the lamb. In his haste, he paints a ram with a big set of horns. The punchline of the story is the explanation she gives to her husband when he sees the ram: the little lamb has grown up during his long absence (Ruiz, 177).

115 Greer, 268.

116 Sawday, *The Body*, 197.

117 I am using here my own translations since neither Boyer's ("her beauty so close to dead," 344) nor Greer and Rhodes's translations ("her all but expired loveliness," 296) convey the exact meaning of the original. The same applies to the second passage: Boyer's translation ("empty favors," 153) fails to translate the point I want to emphasize; Greer and Rhodes's translation ("he took those things, although they were favors, as dead ones," 272) is closer to the original but still inadequate for my purposes. Paun de García points out the necrophilia in Diego's intercourse (50). In *El imposible vencido (Triumph over the Impossible)*, one of the novels of the first volume, we have a similar situation in which Rodrigo goes into the chapel where his beloved Leonor's dead body is buried to embrace it (473–4).

118 Greer mentions the importance of a good death as testimony of salvation
and calls Zayas's presentation of death "a spectacle in which ultimate
truth is written in the body" (268). An extended analysis of the similarities
between Zayas's stories and the martyrologies is Levisi, "La crueldad."
Although female corpses are prevalent in the stories, several male corpses
appear. These bodies are not presented in the same uniform way as their
female counterparts, although they are also treated according to Christian
and martyrological traditions (Greer, 269).

119 "Corruption" was also the word used to indicate the loss of virginity
(Covarrubias, *Tesoro*, 618).

120 A concern of the anatomists in the period was to prevent the scarce
dead bodies from decaying while they were studying them. Thus, the
dissections were performed mostly in the cold months of the year, and the
inner organs were examined first since they decayed faster. Embalming
dead bodies was a common practice in the period. An example is Pérez
Fadrique's *Moda práctica de embalsamar cuerpos defunctos para preservarlos
incorruptos y eternizarlos en lo posible* (Sevilla, 1666). The author makes
several interesting references to Vesalius and Valverde, and he claims to
have performed dissections himself.

121 In *La esclava de su amante* (*Slave to Her Own Lover*), the protagonist describes
her feeling as "my heart was softer than wax" (18, 135; mi corazón más
blando que cera). Anatomical Venuses and similar male figures are
described by C.J.S. Thompson and by Russell, the latter including several
images. Stephens mentions that the manufacture of wax figures was
originally connected to religious observance (29). She also studies the wax
figurines exhibited in the Natural History Museum at the University of
Florence, the Josephinium in Vienna, and the Museo di Anatomia Umana
in Bologna (26–52). See also "Bodies on Display" in Bronfen, 95–109.

122 Williamsen, 621. With respect to the aestheticization of dead women,
Welles notices that Zayas's "chilling details prefigure the effects sought in
the gothic novel of late eighteenth century" (304). Dead women's bodies
have been attributed aesthetic value in the West since antiquity. Good
introductions to the subject are to be found in Bronfen and in the articles
contained in the monograph edited by Lord and Burfoot.

123 As mentioned in the chapter on Granada, it was customary for anatomical
engravings to represent the dissected bodies interacting with their
surroundings, often standing in front of architectural features or natural
backgrounds (Sawday, *The Body*, 113).

124 Such decentring can also be compared with what happens in the story of
the ensign Campuzano in *El coloquio de los perros*. He is released from a

hospital located on the outskirts of the city and his narration, a kind of life dissection, eventually leads him out of sight: "Let's be off" (305, 1026; Y con esto se fueron). I want to thank one of the anonymous reviewers for pointing out this coincidence and its implications.

125 Williamsen, 620.

126 Wives become monsters in the etymological meaning of the word, i.e., of something worth showing (Latin *monstrare*). Aronson considers the resulting dead wives as monsters that act as scapegoats in the Girardian sense, although, she adds, they are "not intended to be viewed but are hidden away, replicating in an extremely perverse form the social imperative that advocated the enclosure of women within the home, the convent of marriage" (543).

127 Bronfen notices repeated instances in Poe's texts in which men create beautiful corpses from living women, thus reversing Pygmalion's story (112). Several critics have connected the beautiful corpses of Zayas's stories and those in the Gothic novels and in Poe's stories in particular. Zayas's texts, however, do not intend the erotic thrill that dead women elicit in the Romantic period: "Unquestionably, when inscribed by Zayas, the death of a beautiful woman has a very different 'poetical' force from the one Poe envisioned" (Williamsen, 623).

128 The aforementioned book by Pérez Fadrique on embalming corpses specifies that humours, such as blood, are the main cause of the putrefaction of corpses, for which he advises the drying out of the corpses (29).

129 Brownlee, 77.

130 I want to thank one of the anonymous reviewers for this clarification.

131 Vollendorf, 281.

132 Jehenson and Welles, 189. The victory of the victims is typical of the paradoxical nature of Zayas's work. On the importance of inner contradictions in Zayas's stories, see Brownlee, xiii; Mujica, 129; and Rhodes, *Dressed*, 8, 91.

133 Both Grieve and Nieman consider that Zayas subverts the hagiographical and martyrological models in her writing. I agree with Brownlee's nuanced vision that Zayas is using the penchant for violence of these sacred models in innovative ways (27–8, see also 189n49). A similar view is expressed by Jehenson and Welles.

134 Whitenack points out how Zayas's stories present several cases of women unconscious during sexual assaults and notes that this scenario is common to other honour dramas of the period (176).

135 An indication of how interiority has been assumed as an entity in Gracián is that, unlike the other authors studied, he uses the abstract noun

"interioridad," as in *Oráculo manual*, aphorism 49 (359), or in *El Criticón* in *Obras completas*, bk. 3, chap. 5, p. 1167. Expressions such as "el interior" and "lo interior" are also common, as in *Oráculo manual*, aphorism 48 (358). Also, the opposite abstract term, "exterioridad," is used, as in aphorism 130: "A good outside is the best recommendation of internal perfection" (125, 382; La buena exterioridad es la mejor recomendación de la perfección interior). Page references to Gracián appear with the English translation first, followed by the Spanish. The Spanish quotations of Gracián's works are from *Obras completas* edited by Santos Alonso. Unless otherwise indicated, the English versions are by page number from the translations in the bibliography. I have regularized the spelling of the English translations.

136 Checa, 268. Childers compares the situation to a game of chess (169). In *El Discreto* Gracián extols the spectacle of two equally astute opponents confronting each other: "It is when two adepts of this kind attack one another upon equal terms, mutually resolving not to quit until they have gazed at least upon some part or other, what dexterous artifice and management on both sides in order to sound one another, what subtle fetches and delicate efforts to get the first hold, what wariness and circumspection in their words!" (167, 323; Si recíprocamente dos juiciosos se embisten a la par, con armas iguales de atención y de reparo, deseando cada uno dar alcance a la capacidad del otro, ¡con qué destreza se acometen, qué precisión en los tientos, qué atención a la razón, qué examen de la palabra!).

137 Egginton, *How*, 60–1. The image of the world as a stage, although popular in the period, has older origins and it can be used for different purposes, as Calderón's famous *auto sacramental* proves. A revision of the use of the image in Gracián can be found in Forastieri Braschi.

138 Flor, 23–45; Childers, 170.

139 Gracián deploys other words that imply vastness in a positive meaning: "caudal" (358, 371; flow), "capacidad" (371, 125; capacity), "ensanche" and "profundidad" (322, 373; expansion and depth). Egginton connects the use of "caudal" and "fondo" to the stage techniques of the period ("Of Baroque Holes," 64).

140 The image of the *zahorí* reappears in *El Criticón*, III, 5, when Critilo and Andrenio meet the "Veedor de todo" (the Seer of Everything), who identifies himself as a *zahorí* (1167). An example of the use of "sondar" can be seen in *El Discreto*, XIX: "Sonda atento los fondos de la mayor profundidad" (322).

141 The abundance of anatomical imagery in Gracián has been noticed by several critics, such as Blüher, 211.

142 As Laplana Gil remarks, the fact that Gracián makes very precise physiognomic statements does not imply that he believed the person's physiognomy to be deterministic of the character, only indicative (106).

143 Egido, 56.

144 The image of eyes in the hands is based on an emblem of Andrea Alciato (Cacho, 121).

145 Gracián resorts to a similar image in his treatment of the body politic. In *El Político*, III, Gracián praises wise Nerva for adopting courageous Trajan so that "the two became a body in which the first acted as the head and the latter as the arms" (111; hacían un cuerpo entrambos; que aquél era cabeza y éste brazos).

146 On the influence and adaptation of the Ignatian exercises by Gracián, see Neumeister.

147 The translations of *El Comulgatorio* are mine.

148 The scenario in which one must be prepared to play alternately, or even simultaneously, the roles of the dissector and the dissected is not properly represented in any of the images included in the medical books of the time. The closest illustration is the already mentioned engraving of a man with an open thorax dissecting the same area of a cadaver in Juan Valverde de Amusco's *Anatomía del corpo humano* (Figure 7). However, to represent exactly the reciprocity of the situation described by Gracián, the recumbent corpse in the engraving should also be cutting into the body of the dissector.

149 I am using my translation of this aphorism because other translations are not literal enough for my purpose here.

150 "Gracián configures a series of machine-like, intellectualized organs of taste designed to tactfully attract, provoke, and manipulate the desire of other subjects in the public representation of the 'hombre con fondos'" (Nelson, 170). A commodification of the body, which becomes thus a ware in the market, is also pointed out by Nelson as another implication of the operation of making one's interior attractive (183).

## Conclusion: Compliant Resistance

1 Hillman, *Shakespeare's*, 57.

2 Paige, 3, 4.

3 Maus, 29.

4 A recent review of the implications that *Don Quixote* had for the theories of the novel and their relation to modernity can be seen in Rachel Schmidt's monograph.

5 For the interpretation of Don Quixote as a Christ-like figure, see Ziolkowski.

6 Una cosa falta en mi concepto en la obra de Cervantes para el complemento de la historia; a saber: la abertura del cadáver de Don Quijote. ¿Pero dejó de ponerla porque estuviese penetrado de la insuficiencia de la anatomía patológica en estas enfermedades; o porque habiendo vuelto en sí de la locura, ya no era la secura del cerebro la causa próxima, ni el asiento de ella cambiada en otra enfermedad, y no hubiera hallado cosa alguna que coincidiese con los extravíos de la imaginación? (Hernández Morejón, 21–2; my translation).

7 Fernández, "Sola." See also Gaylord, "Whole Body," 126.

8 Foucault, History, 95.

9 Egginton, "Gracián and the Emergence," 165–7.

10 Cascardi, 147, 152.

11 Greenblatt, 34.

12 Paster points out the similarity between the internal and the grotesque Bakhtinian body, but makes the important distinction that the Bakhtinian body is collective, not individual (10, 15). For the image of the inner body as something grotesque that simultaneously triggers fear and laughter in the Spain of the period, see Iffland. Goytisolo identifies what he calls the excremental obsession of Quevedo with the resurfacing of repressed sexual impulses ("Quevedo").

13 Maus, 28. Hillman agrees with the impossibility of visceral knowledge: "There is no certain knowledge to be found within the body, except the knowledge of doubt, disease, and ultimately, death" ("Visceral Knowledge," 97).

14 Hillman, Shakespeare's, 15.

15 Sawday, The Body, 110–29.

# Works Cited

Aers, David. "A Whisper in the Ear of Early Modernists, or Reflection on Literary Critics Writing the History of the Subject." In *Culture and History 1350–1600*, ed. David Aers, 177–202. New York: Harvester Wheatsheaf, 1992.

Aguilar-Adan, Christine. "Métaphores du corps politique malade autour des années 1620." In *Le corps comme métaphore dans l'Espagne des XVI$^E$ et XVIII$^E$ siècle*, ed. Augustin Redondo and André Rochon, 61–71. Paris: Publications de la Sorbonne, 1992.

Ahlgren, Gillian T.W. "Negotiating Sanctity: Holy Women in Sixteenth-Century Spain." *Church History* 64.3 (1995): 373–88.

Alberti López, Luis. *La anatomía y los anatomistas españoles del Renacimiento.* Madrid: CSIC, 1948.

Alemán, Mateo. *Segunda parte de la vida de Guzmán de Alfarache, atalaya de la vida humana.* Ed. J.M. Micó. Madrid: Cátedra, 1975.

Alonso, Dámaso. "Sobre Erasmo y Fray Luis de Granada." In *De los siglos oscuros al de oro*, ed. Dámaso Alonso, 218–25. Madrid: Gredos, 1964.

Amezúa y Mayo, Agustín G. "Introducción." In *Desengaños amorosos*, ed. Agustín G. Amezúa y Mayo, vii–xxiv. Madrid: RAE, 1950.

Andrés Martín, Melquiades. "*Alumbrados*, Erasmians, 'Lutherans' and Mystics: The Risks of a More 'Intimate' Spirituality." Trans. Esther da Costa-Frankel. In *The Spanish Inquisition and the Inquisitorial Mind*, ed. Ángel Alcalá, 457–94. Highland Lake, NJ: Atlantic Research and Publications, 1987.

Ángeles, Fray Juan de los. *Diálogos de la conquista del reino de Dios.* Ed. Ángel González Palencia. Madrid: Real Academia Española, 1946.

Aracil, Alfredo. *Juego y artificio: Autómatas y otras ficciones en la cultura del Renacimiento a la Ilustración.* Madrid: Cátedra, 1998.

Arce de Otálora, Juan de. *Coloquios de Palatino y Pinciano.* Ed. José Luis Ocasar Ariza. 2 vols. Madrid: Turner, 1995.

Archimbault, Paul. "The Analogy of the 'Body' in Renaissance Political Literature." *Bibliothèque d'Humanisme et Renaissance* 29 (1967): 21–53.

Arellano, Ignacio. "El poder político y sus límites en la obra de Quevedo." *La perinola* 12 (2008): 17–33.

Aristotle. *The Politics, with an English Translation.* Trans. H. Rackham. Cambridge, MA: Harvard University Press, 1967.

Armstrong, D.M. *Sketch for a Systematic Metaphysics.* Oxford: Oxford University Press, 2010.

Aronson, Stacey L. Parker. "Monstrous Metamorphoses and Rape in María de Zayas." *Revista canadiense de estudios hispánicos* 29.3 (2005): 525–47.

Artal, Susana G. "Quevedo y Rabelais en la cabeza del cardenal." In *Actas del XIV Congreso de la Asociación Internacional de Hispanistas,* ed. Isaías Lerner, Robert Nival, and Alejandro Alonso, vol. 2, 43–9. Newark, DE: Juan de la Cuesta, 2001.

Artigas, Miguel. "Introducción." In *Teatro inédito de Don Francisco de Quevedo y Villegas,* ed. Miguel Artigas, 1–80. Madrid: Tipografía de la Revista de Archivos, 1927.

Astrana Marín, Luis. *La vida turbulenta de Quevedo.* Madrid: Editorial Gran Capitán, 1945.

*Aucto de la prevaricación de nuestro padre Adán.* Ed. Miguel Ángel Pérez Priego. Madrid: Castalia, 1988.

Augustine of Hippo, Saint. *The City of God.* Trans. Marcus Dods. Lawrence, KS: Digireads.com Publishing, 2009.

– *Confessions.* Ed. Henry Chadwick. Oxford: Oxford University Press, 1998.

– *Sermo 169, de verbis Apostoli, Philipp., cap. iii, 3–16.* Vol. 38. Paris: Migne, 1880.

Aylward, Edward. "The Peculiar Arrangement of *El casamiento engañoso* and *El coloquio de los perros.*" In *A Companion to Cervantes's Novelas ejemplares,* ed. Stephen Boyd, 235–60. London: Tamesis, 2005.

Azorín. *Los dos Luises y otros ensayos.* Madrid: Austral, 1961.

Báguena, María José. *La naturaleza de la peste a través de las obras de Juan Tomás Porcell y Luis Mercado.* Valencia: Universitat de València, 2002.

Bakhtin, Mikhail. *Rabelais and His World.* Trans. Helene Iswolsky. Bloomington: Indiana University Press, 1984.

Balcells, José María. "Introducción." In *Guía de pecadores, Fray Luis de Granada,* i–xliv. Barcelona: Planeta, 1986.

– "Introducción." In *Introducción del símbolo de la fe,* 11–98. Madrid: Cátedra, 1989.

– *Introducción del símbolo de la fe.* Madrid: Cátedra, 1989.

– *Fray Luis de Granada: Una visión espiritual y estética de la armonía del universo.*
   Barcelona: Anthropos, 1992.
Ball, James Moores. *Andreas Vesalius, the Reformer of Anatomy.* Saint Louis:
   Medical Science Press, 1910.
Barahona, Renato. *Sex Crimes, Honour, and the Law in Early Modern Spain:
   Vizcaya, 1528–1735.* Toronto: University of Toronto Press, 2003.
Barahona de Soto, Luis. *Las lágrimas de Angélica.* Ed. José Lara Garrido.
   Madrid: Cátedra, 1981.
Barkan, Leonard. *Nature's Work of Art: The Human Body as Image of the World.*
   New Haven: Yale University Press, 1975.
Barnes, Bernadine. "Metaphorical Painting: Michelangelo, Dante, and the Last
   Judgment." *Art Bulletin* 77.1 (1995): 64–83.
Barona, José Lluís. "El cuerpo alegórico: Claves renacentistas para una
   interpretación de la naturaleza humana." *Medicina e historia* 47 (1993): 5–28.
Baronio, Cesar. *Martyroligum Romanum cum notationibus.* Rome: Dominici
   Basae, 1586.
Bataillon, Marcel. "De Savanarola à Louis de Grenade." *Revue de littérature
   comparée* 16 (1936): 23–9.
– *Érasme et l'Espagne: Recherches sur l'histoire spirituelle du XVI$^E$ siècle.* Paris:
   Librairie Droz, 1937.
Bates, Tony. *Emblematic Monsters: Unnatural Conceptions and Deformed Births in
   Early Modern Europe.* Amsterdam: Rodopi, 2005.
Baum, Doris L. *Traditionalism in the Works of Francisco de Quevedo y Villegas.*
   Chapel Hill: University of North Carolina Press, 1970.
Belsey, Catherine. *The Subject of Tragedy: Identity and Difference in Renaissance
   Drama.* London: Methuen, 1985.
Beltrán de Heredia, Vicente. *Cartulario de la Universidad de Salamanca.* Vol. 5.
   Salamanca: Universidad de Salamanca, 1972.
– *Las corrientes de espiritualidad entre los dominicos de Castilla durante la primera
   mitad del siglo XVI.* Salamanca: Biblioteca de Teólogos Españoles, 1941.
Bennassar, Bartolomé. "Patterns of the Inquisitorial Mind as the Basis for a
   Pedagogy of Fear." Trans. Esther da Costa-Frankel. In *The Spanish Inquisition
   and the Inquisitorial Mind,* ed. Ángel Alcalá, 177–83. Highland Lake, NJ:
   Atlantic Research and Publications, 1987.
Bennett, Tony. *The Birth of the Museum: History, Theory, Politics.* New York:
   Routledge, 1995.
Benthien, Claudia. *Skin: On the Cultural Border between Self and the World.*
   Trans. Thomas Dunlap. New York: Columbia University Press, 2002.
Berengario da Carpi, Jacopo. *Isagogae breves.* Bologna: Benedictus Hectoris, 1522.

Bérenger, J. "Pour une enquête européenne: Le problème du ministériat au XVII^E siècle." *Annales (Économies, Sociétés, Civilisations)* 29 (1974): 166–92.

Bergson, Henri. "L'idée de lieu chez Aristote." In *Mélanges*, ed. André Robinet, 1–56. Paris: Presses Universitaires de France, 1972.

Bernardus, Sanctus. *Sancti Bernardi Abbatis Clarae-Vallensis operum tomus quartus complectens sermones in Cantica numero LXXXVI.* Ed. Migne. Vol. 183. Paris: Patrologia Latina, 1855.

*Biblia de Jerusalén.* Spanish edition by José Ángel Urbieta. Bilbao: Desclée De Brouwer, 1975.

Binet, Jacques-Louis. *Dessins et traités d'anatomie.* Paris: Chênes, 1980.

Bloom, Harold. *The Anxiety of Influence: A Theory of Poetry.* New York: Oxford University Press, 1973.

Blüher, Karl Alfred. "Mirar por dentro: Análisis introspectivo del hombre en Gracián." Trans. F.G. Povedano. In *El mundo de Gracián: Actas del Coloquio Internacional, Berlín, 1988*, ed. Dietrich Briesemeister and Sebastian Neumeister, 203–17. Berlin: Colloquium Verlag, 1991.

Boccalini, Trajano. *Ragguagli di Parnaso e scritti minori.* Ed. Luigi Ferpo. Bari: G. Laterza, 1948.

Bordo, Susan R. *The Flight to Objectivity: Essays on Cartesianism and Culture.* Albany: State University of New York Press, 1987.

Boscán, Juan. *El cortesano de Baltasar de Castiglione.* Ed. Mario Pozzi. Madrid: Cátedra, 1994.

Bossy, John. "The Social History of Confession in the Age of the Reformation." *Transactions of the Royal Historical Society* 25 (1975): 21–38.

Boyer, H. Patsy. "Historical Background." In *The Enchantments of Love*, ed. H. Patsy Boyer, xxxii–xxxv. Berkeley: University of California Press, 1989.

Bradner, Leicester. "The Theme of *Privanza* in Spanish and English Drama 1590–1625." In *Homenaje a William L. Fichter: Estudios sobre teatro antiguo hispánico y otros ensayos*, ed. David Kossoff and José Amor y Vázquez, 97–106. Madrid: Castalia, 1971.

Bronfen, Elisabeth. *Over Her Dead Body: Death, Femininity, and the Aesthetic.* New York: Routledge, 1992.

Brown, Elizabeth A.R. "Death and the Human Body in the Later Middle Ages: The Legislation of Boniface VIII on the Division of the Corpse." *Viator* 12 (1981): 221–70.

Brownlee, Marina Scordilis. *The Cultural Labyrinth of María de Zayas.* Philadelphia: University of Pennsylvania Press, 2000.

Bynum, Caroline Walker. "The Female Body and Religious Practice in the Late Middle Ages." In *Fragmentation and Redemption: Essays on Gender and the*

*Human Body in Medieval Religion*, ed. Caroline Walker Bynum, 181–238. New York: Zone Books, 1992.

- "Material Continuity, Personal Survival, and the Resurrection of the Body: A Scholastic Discussion in Its Medieval and Modern Contexts." In *Fragmentation and Redemption: Essays on Gender and the Human Body in Medieval Religion*, ed. Caroline Walker Bynum, 239–98. New York: Zone Books, 1992.

Cacho, María Teresa. "'Ver como vivir': El ojo en la obra de Gracián." In *Gracián y su época (Actas de la I Reunión de Filólogos Aragoneses)*, 117–35. Zaragoza: Institución Fernando el Católico, 1986.

Cadalso, José. *Cartas marruecas*. Ed. Nigel Glendinning and Lucien Dupuis. London: Tamesis, 1966.

Calbi, Maurizio. *Approximate Bodies: Gender and Power in Early Modern Drama and Anatomy*. London: Routledge, 2005.

Camporesi, Piero. *The Incorruptible Flesh: Bodily Mutation and Mortification in Religion and Folklore*. Trans. Tania Croft-Murray and Helen Elsom. Cambridge: Cambridge University Press, 1988.

Carlino, Andrea. *Books of the Body: Anatomical Ritual and Renaissance Learning*. Trans. John Tedeschi and Anne C. Tedeschi. Chicago: University of Chicago Press, 1999.

- *Paper Bodies: A Catalogue of Anatomical Fugitive Sheets 1538–1687*. London: Wellcome Institute for the History of Medicine, 1999.

Carrión, María M. *Subject Stages: Marriage, Theatre, and the Law in Early Modern Spain*. Toronto: University of Toronto Press, 2010.

Casa, Frank P. "The Structural Unity of *El licenciado Vidriera*." *Bulletin of Hispanic Studies* 41 (1964): 242–6.

Cascardi, Anthony. "Beyond Castro and Maravall: Interpellation, Mimesis, and the Hegemony of Spanish Culture." *Ideologies of Hispanism*, ed. Mabel Moraña, 139–59. Nashville: Vanderbilt University Press, 2005.

Castillo, David R. *Baroque Horrors: Roots of the Fantastic in the Age of Curiosities*. Ann Arbor: University of Michigan Press, 2010.

Castro, Américo. "Algunas observaciones acerca del concepto del honor en el siglo XVI y XVII." *Revista de filología española* 3 (1916): 357–86.

- *De la edad conflictiva*. Madrid: Taurus, 1974.
- "La palabra 'títere.'" *Modern Language Notes* 57.7 (1942): 505–10.
- "Luis de Granada y los conversos." In *La realidad histórica de España*, 441–2. Mexico: Editorial Porrúa, 1971.
- *Teresa la Santa y otros ensayos*. Madrid: Alfaguara, 1972.

Cervantes Saavedra, Miguel de. *The Adventures of Don Quixote*. Trans. J.M. Cohen. New York: Penguin, 1950.

— *Don Quixote*. Trans. John Ormsby. Lawrence, KS: Digireads.com Publishing, 2009.

— *Exemplary Stories*. Trans. Lesley Lipson. Oxford: Oxford University Press, 1998.

— *Obras completas*. Ed. Ángel Valbuena Prat. Madrid: Aguilar, 1967.

Chartier, Roger. "Leisure and Sociability: Reading Aloud in Early Modern Europe." In *Urban Life in the Renaissance*, ed. Susan Zimmerman, 103–20. Newark: University of Delaware Press, 1989.

Checa, Jorge. "*Oráculo manual*: Gracián y el ejercicio de la lectura." *Hispanic Review* 59.3 (1991): 263–80.

Childers, William. "The Baroque Public Sphere." In *Reason and Its Others: Italy, Spain, and the New World Order*, ed. David Castillo and Massimo Lollini, 165–85. Nashville: Vanderbilt University Press, 2006.

Choulant, Ludwig. *History and Bibliography of Anatomic Illustration*. Trans. Mortimer Frank. New York: Hafner, 1945.

Chroust, Anton-Hermann. "The Corporate Idea and the Body Politic in the Middle Ages." *The Review of Politics* 9.4 (1947): 423–52.

Cicero, Marcus Tullius. *Tusculan Disputations*. Trans. J.E. King. Cambridge, MA: Harvard University Press, 1950.

Cipolla, Carlo M. *Clocks and Culture, 1300–1700*. London: Collins, 1967.

Clamurro, William H. "Ideological Contradiction and Imperial Decline: Toward a Reading of Zayas' *Desengaños amorosos*." *South Central Review* 5.2 (1988): 43–50.

Coats, Catherine Randall. "Reconstituting the Textual Body in Jean Crespin's *Histoire de martyrs*." *Renaissance Quarterly* 44.1 (1991): 62–85.

Cocchiara, G. *Il mondo alla rovescia*. Turin: P. Boringhieri, 1963.

Collins, Steven. *Selfless Persons: Imagery and Thought in Theravada Buddhism*. Cambridge: Cambridge University Press, 1982.

Coomaraswamy, Ananda Kentish. *The Dance of Shiva: Fourteen Indian Essays*. Bombay: P.S. Jayasinghe, 1948.

Cooper, John M. *Reason and Emotion: Essays on Ancient Moral Psychology and Ethical Theory*. Princeton: Princeton University Press, 1999.

Covarrubias Orozco, Sebastián de. *Emblemas morales, 1610*. Yorkshire, England: The Scolar Press, 1973.

— *Tesoro de la lengua castellana o española*. Ed. Martín de Riquer. Barcelona: S.A. Horta, 1943.

Crespin, Jean. *Histoire des martyrs persécutés et mis à mort pour la vérité de l'Évangile*. Ed. Matthieu Lelièvre and Daniel Benoit. Toulouse: Société des Livres Religieux, 1887.

Crider, Cathleen. "Children's Conception of the Body Interior." *New Directions for Child Development* 14 (1981): 49–65.

Crosby, James O. "Citas eruditas." In *Francisco de Quevedo, política de Dios, gobierno de Cristo*, 519–45. Madrid: Castalia, 1966.

Crummer, Leroy. "Early Anatomical Fugitive Sheets." *Annals of Medical History* 5.3 (1923): 189–209.

Csordas, Thomas. "Embodiment and Cultural Phenomenology." In *Perspectives on Embodiment: The Intersections of Nature and Culture*, ed. G. Weiss and H.F. Haber, 143–64. New York: Routledge, 1999.

Cuervo, Justo. *Biografía de Fray Luis de Granada*. Madrid: Librería de Gregorio del Amo, 1895.

Curtius, Ernst Robert. *European Literature and the Latin Middle Ages*. Trans. Willard R. Trask. London: Routledge, 1953.

Cushing, Harvey. *A Bio-Bibliography of Andreas Vesalius*. New York: Schuman's, 1943.

Daston, Lorraine, and Katharine Park. *Wonders and the Order of Nature, 1150–1750*. New York: Zone Books, 1998.

David-Peyre, Yvonne. "La alegoría del cuerpo humano en el *Criticón* de B. Gracián." *Asclepio* 26–7 (1974–5): 141–56.

Davis, Charles. "El tacitismo político español y la metáfora del cuerpo humano." In *Le corps comme métaphore dans l'Espagne des XVI^E et XVII^E siècles*, ed. Augustin Redondo, 31–9. Paris: Publications de la Sorbonne, 1992.

Daza Chacón, Dionisio. *Práctica y theórica de cirugía en romance y en latín*. Valladolid: Bernardino de Sancto Domingo, 1582.

De Armas, Frederick A. "'En dos pechos repartidos': Felipe II y su privado en *Cómo ha de ser el valido*." *Hispanófila* 140 (2004): 9–21.

– *Quixotic Frescoes: Cervantes and Italian Renaissance Art*. Toronto: University of Toronto Press, 2006.

De Ros, Fidel. "Los místicos del Norte y Fray Luis de Granada." *Archivo ibero americano* 25 and 26 (1947): 6–30 and 145–65.

Demonet, Marie-Luce. "Le *skeletos* de Montaigne ou la leçon d'anatomie." In *Théâtre de l'anatomie et corps en spectacle: Fondements d'une science de la Renaissance*, ed. Ilana Zinguer and Isabelle Martin, 63–88. Bern: Peter Lang, 2006.

Denery, Dallas G. *Seeing and Being Seen in the Later Medieval World: Optics, Theology and Religious Life*. Cambridge: Cambridge University Press, 2005.

Derville, André, and Aimé Solignac. "Homme intérieur." In *Dictionnaire de spiritualité ascétique et mystique*, ed. Marcel Viller, vol. 7, cols. 650–74. Paris: Beauchesne, 1969.

Des Chen, Dennis. *Life's Form: Late Aristotelian Conceptions of the Soul*. Ithaca: Cornell University Press, 2000.

Descargues, Pierre. *Perspective*. Trans. I. Mark Paris. New York: Harry N. Abrams, 1977.

Descartes, René. *Oeuvres*. 11 vols. Ed. Charles Adam and Paul Tannery. Paris: Vrin, 1964–71.

Díaz-Plaja, Fernando. *La historia de España en sus documentos: El siglo XVII*. Madrid: Instituto de Estudios Políticos, 1957.

Díaz-Plaja, Guillermo. "El retablo de Maese Pedro." *Ínsula* 204 (1963): 1, 12.

Donne, John. *The Complete Poetry and Selected Prose of John Donne*. Ed. Charles M. Coffin. New York: Modern Library, 1952.

Dopico Black, Georgina. *Perfect Wives, Other Women: Adultery and Inquisition in Early Modern Spain*. Durham, NC: Duke University Press, 2001.

Doueihi, Milad. *A Perverse History of the Human Heart*. Cambridge, MA: Harvard University Press, 1997.

Draaisma, Douwe. *Metaphors of Memory: A History of Ideas about the Mind*. Trans. Paul Vincent. Cambridge: Cambridge University Press, 2000.

Dryden, John, trans. *Ovid's Metamorphoses*. London: Wordsworth Classics, 1998.

Duarte, J. Enrique. "Presencias diabólicas en Quevedo." *La perinola* 8 (2004): 125–53.

Dundas, Judith. "Allegory as a Form of Wit." *Studies in the Renaissance* 11 (1964): 223–33.

Dunn, Peter N. "Cervantes De/Re-Constructs the Picaresque." *Cervantes* 2.2 (1982): 109–31.

– *Spanish Picaresque Fiction: A New Literary History*. Ithaca: Cornell University Press, 1993.

Dunstan, G.R., ed. *The Human Embryo: Aristotle and the Arabic and European Traditions*. Exeter: University of Exeter Press, 1990.

Edgerton, Samuel Y., Jr. *The Renaissance Discovery of Linear Perspective*. New York: Basic Books, 1975.

Edwards, Gwynne. "Cervantes's *El licenciado Vidriera*: Meaning and Structure." *Modern Language Review* 68.3 (1973): 559–68.

Egginton, William. "Gracián and the Emergence of the Modern Subject." In *Rhetoric and Politics: Baltasar Gracián and the New World Order*, ed. Nicholas Spadaccini and Jenaro Talens, 151–69. Minneapolis: University of Minnesota Press, 1997.

– *How the World Became a Stage: Presence, Theatricality, and the Question of Modernity*. Albany: State University of New York Press, 2003.

– "Of Baroque Holes and Baroque Folds." In *Hispanic Baroques: Reading Cultures in Context*, ed. Nicholas Spadaccini and Luis Martín-Estudillo, 55–71. Nashville: Vanderbilt University Press, 2005.

Egido, Aurora. *Las caras de la prudencia y Baltasar Gracián*. Madrid: Editorial Castalia, 2000.

Eisenberg, Daniel. "Un médico examina a Cervantes." *Cervantes* 24.2 (2004): 172–82.

Eisenstein, Elizabeth L. *The Printing Revolution in Early Modern Europe*. Cambridge: Cambridge University Press, 2005.

El Saffar, Ruth S. *Cervantes, El casamiento engañoso and El coloquio de los perros*. London: Grant and Cutler, 1976.

– *Novel to Romance: A Study of Cervantes's Novelas ejemplares*. Baltimore: Johns Hopkins University Press, 1974.

– "Tracking the Trickster in the Works of Cervantes." *Symposium* 37.2 (1983): 106–24.

Elliott, J.H. *The Count-Duke of Olivares: The Statesman in an Age of Decline*. New Haven: Yale University Press, 1986.

– "The Court of the Spanish Habsburg: A Peculiar Institution?" In *Politics and Culture in Early Modern Europe: Essays in Honor of H.G. Koenigsberger*, ed. Margaret C. Jacob and Phyllis Mack, 5–24. Cambridge: Cambridge University Press, 1987.

– "Introduction." In *The World of the Favourite*, ed. L.W.B. Brockliss and J.H. Elliott, 1–25. New Haven: Yale University Press, 1999.

– "Quevedo and the Count-Duke of Olivares." In *Quevedo in Perspective: Eleven Essays for the Quadricentennial*, ed. James Iffland, 227–61. Newark, DE: Juan de la Cuesta, 1980.

– *Richelieu and Olivares*. Cambridge: Cambridge University Press, 1984.

– "Staying in Power: The Count-Duke of Olivares." In *The World of the Favourite*, ed. J.H. Elliott and L.W.B. Brockliss, 112–22. New Haven: Yale University Press, 1999.

End, Adelheid, and Ernst Wolner. "The Heart: Location of the Human Soul, Site of Surgical Intervention." *Journal of Cardiac Surgery* 8.3 (1993): 398–403.

Erickson, Robert A. *The Language of the Heart, 1600–1750*. Philadelphia: University of Pennsylvania Press, 1997.

Estienne, Charles. *De dissectione partium corporis humani*. Paris: Simon de Colines, 1545.

Ettinghausen, Henry. *Francisco de Quevedo and the Neostoic Movement*. Oxford: Oxford University Press, 1972.

– "Quevedo, ¿un caso de doble personalidad?" In *Homenaje a Quevedo*, ed. Víctor García de la Concha, 27–44. Salamanca: Caja de Ahorros y Monte de Piedad de Salamanca, 1982.

Evennett, H. Outram. "Counter-Reformation Spirituality." In *The Counter-Reformation: Essential Readings*, ed. David M. Luebke, 48–63. Oxford: Blackwell, 1999.

Ferenczi, Sándor. *Further Contributions to the Theory and Technique of Psychoanalysis*. Trans. Isabel Suttie. New York: Boni and Liveright, 1927.

Fernández, Enrique. "Fragmentación corporal y exégesis política en Quevedo." *La perinola* 14 (2010): 305–19.

– "La grotesca interioridad de Richelieu anatomizada por Quevedo." *Bulletin hispanique* 105 (2003): 215–29.

– "'Sola una de vuestras hermosas manos': Desmembramiento petrarquista y disección anatómica en la venta (*DQ* I, 43)." *Cervantes* 21.2 (2001): 27–49.

Fernández de Oviedo, Gonzalo. *Historia general y natural de las Indias*. Ed. Juan Pérez de Tudela Bueso. Vol. 117. Madrid: BAE, 1959.

Fernández-Santamaría, J.A. *Reason of State and Statecraft in Spanish Political Thought 1595–1640*. Lanham, MD: University Press of America, 1983.

– *The State, War and Peace: Spanish Political Thought in the Renaissance, 1516–1559*. Cambridge: Cambridge University Press, 1977.

Fernández Suárez, José Ramón. "Popularidad de Fray Luis de Granada en Inglaterra: Valoración de su persona y de sus escritos." In *Fray Luis de Granada, su obra y su tiempo. Actas del congreso internacional, Granada 27–30 septiembre 1988*, ed. Urbano Alonso del Campo and Antonio García del Moral, vol. 2, 207–26. Granada: Universidad de Granada, 1993.

Feros, Antonio. "Images of Evil, Images of Kings: The Contrasting Faces of the Royal Favourite and the Prime Minister in Early Modern European Political Literature, c. 1580–1650." In *The World of the Favourite*, ed. L.W.B. Brockliss and J.H. Elliott, 205–22. New Haven: Yale University Press, 1999.

– "Twin Souls: Monarchs and Favourites in Early Seventeenth-Century Spain." In *Spain, Europe, and the Atlantic World: Essays in Honour of John H. Elliott*, ed. Geoffrey Parker and Richard Kagan, 27–47. Cambridge: Cambridge University Press, 1995.

Ferrari, Giovanna. "Public Anatomy Lessons and the Carnival: The Anatomy Theatre of Bologna." *Past and Present* 117 (1987): 50–106.

Ferreras, Jacqueline. "Didacticismo y arte literario en el diálogo humanístico del siglo XVI." *Criticón* 58 (1993): 95–102.

Ferry, Anne. *The Inward Language: Sonnets of Wyatt, Sidney, Shakespeare, Donne*. Chicago: University of Chicago Press, 1983.

Finkelstein, David H. *Expression and the Inner*. Cambridge, MA: Harvard University Press, 2003.

Flacius, Matthias. *Catalogus testium veritatis*. Basel: Oporinus, 1556.

Flor, Fernando R. de la. *Pasiones frías: secreto y disimulación en el barroco hispano*. Madrid: Marcial Pons, 2005.

Forastieri Braschi, Eduardo. "Baltasar Gracián y el *theatrum mundi*." In *Actas del V Congreso Internacional de Hispanistas*, ed. François López, Joseph Pérez,

Noël Salomon, and Maxime Chevalier, vol. 1, 393–400. Bordeaux: Instituto de Estudios Ibéricos e Iberoamericanos, Université de Bordeaux III, 1977.

Forcione, Alban K. *Cervantes and the Humanist Vision: A Study of Four Exemplary Novels*. Princeton: Princeton University Press, 1982.

– *Cervantes and the Mystery of Lawlessness: A Study of* El casamiento engañoso *and* El coloquio de los perros. Princeton: Princeton University Press, 1984.

Foucault, Michel. "Governmentality." Trans. Rosi Braidotti. In *The Foucault Effect: Studies in Governmentality*, ed. Graham Burchell, Colin Gordon, and Peter Miller, 87–104. Chicago: University of Chicago Press, 1991.

– *The History of Sexuality*. Trans. Robert Hurley. Vol. 1. New York: Pantheon Books, 1978.

– *Les mots et les choses; une archéologie des sciences humaines*. Paris: Gallimard, 1966.

Fowler, Chris. *The Archeology of Personhood: An Anthropological Approach*. London: Routledge, 2004.

Foxe, John. *Book of Martyrs (Acts and Monuments)*. London: John Day, 1554.

Freud, Sigmund. "Anxiety and Instinctual Life." In *The Standard Edition of the Complete Psychological Works of Sigmund Freud*, ed. James Strachey, vol. 22, 81–111. London: The Hogarth Press and the Institute of Psycho-Analysis, 1930.

– "Inhibitions, Symptoms, and Anxieties." In *The Standard Edition of the Complete Psychological Works of Sigmund Freud*, ed. James Strachey, vol. 20, 75–171. London: The Hogarth Press and the Institute of Psycho-Analysis, 1926.

– "A Neurosis of Demonical Possession in the Seventeenth Century." Trans. Joan Riviere. In *Collected Papers*, ed. Ernest Jones, vol. 4, 436–72. London: The Hogarth Press and the Institute of Psycho-Analysis, 1948.

Frye, Northrop. *Anatomy of Criticism: Four Essays*. Princeton: Princeton University Press, 1971.

Ganelin, Charles V. "Bodies of Discovery: Vesalian Anatomy and Luis Barahona de Soto's *Las lágrimas de Angélica*." *Calíope* 6.1–2 (2000): 295–308.

García Ballester, Luis. *Historia social de la medicina en la España de los siglos XIII al XVI*. Vol. 1. Madrid: Akal, 1976.

García Barreno, Pedro. "La medicina en *El Quijote* y su entorno." In *La ciencia y El Quijote*, ed. José Manuel Sánchez Ron, 155–79. Barcelona: Crítica, 2005.

García-Bryce, Ariadna. *Transcending Textuality: Quevedo and Political Authority in the Age of Print*. University Park: Pennsylvania State University Press, 2011.

García-Diego, José A. *Los relojes y autómatas de Juanelo Turriano*. Madrid: Albatros, 1982.

García Lorca, Francisco. "*El licenciado Vidriera* y sus nombres." *Revista hispánica moderna* 31 (1965): 159–68.

García Sánchez, María Dolores, ed. *Información y curación de la peste de Zaragoza y praeservación contra peste en general, Joan Tomás Porcell (1565)*. Caligari: Centro di Studi Filologici Sardi, 2009.

García Tapia, Nicolás. "Los molinos en *El Quijote* y la técnica española en la época." In *La ciencia y* El Quijote, ed. José Manuel Sánchez Ron, 209–26. Barcelona: Crítica, 2005.

– *Tecnología e imperio: Ingenios y leyendas del Siglo de Oro, Turriano, Lastanosa, Herra, Ayanz*. Tres Cantos, Madrid: Nivola, 2002.

Gaylord, Mary Malcolm. "Pulling Strings with Master Peter's Puppets: Fiction and History in *Don Quixote*." *Cervantes* 18.2 (1998): 117–47.

– "The Whole Body of Fable with All of Its Members: Cervantes, Pinciano, Freud." In *Quixotic Desire: Psychoanalitic Perspectives on Cervantes*, ed. Ruth Anthony El Saffar and Diana de Armas Wilson, 117–34. Ithaca: Cornell University Press, 1993.

Germain, Gilbert G. *A Discourse on Disenchantment: Reflections on Politics and Technology*. Albany: State University of New York Press, 1993.

*Gesta Romanorum*. Trans. Charles Swan. Ed. Wynnard Hooper. Bohn Library Edition 1876. New York: Dover, 1959.

Gierke, Otto Friedrich von. *Political Theories of the Middle Age*. Boston: Beacon Press, 1959.

Gil Encabo, Fermín. "Del objeto prodigioso al prestigio literario: El coleccionismo pautado de Vincencio Juan de Lastanosa, mecenas de Gracián." *L'objet de main en main*, special issue of *Mélanges de la Casa de Velázquez* 40.1 (2010): 99–122.

Girard, René. *A Theater of Envy: William Shakespeare*. New York: Oxford University Press, 1991.

González Fernández de Sevilla, José Manuel. "La poesía metafísica de John Donne y Francisco de Quevedo." *Neophilologus* 75 (1991): 548–61.

Gougaud, Louis. *Devotional and Ascetic Practices in the Middle Ages*. London: Burns Oates and Washbourne, 1927.

Goytisolo, Juan. "El mundo erótico de María de Zayas." In *Disidencias*, 63–115. Barcelona: Seix Barral, 1978.

– "Quevedo: La obsesión excremental." In *Disidencias*, 117–35. Barcelona: Seix Barral, 1978.

Grabes, Herbert. *The Mutable Glass: Mirror-Imagery in Titles and Texts of the Middle Ages and English Renaissance*. Cambridge: Cambridge University Press, 1982.

Gracián y Morales, Baltasar. *The Complete Gentleman* (Trans. of *El Discreto*). Trans. Saldkeld. Dublin: W. Whitestone, 1776.

– *The Courtier's Manual Oracle or the Art of Prudence*. Trans. Anonymous. London: M. Flesher, 1685.

– *The Hero*. Trans. J. de Courbeville. London: James and John Knapton, 1726.

– *Obras completas*. Ed. Santos Alonso. Madrid: Cátedra, 2011.

Grafton, Anthony. *Magic and Technology in Early Modern Europe*. Washington, DC: Smithsonian Institution Libraries, 2005.

Granada, Fray Luis de. *Historia de Sor María de la Visitación y sermón de las caídas públicas*. Ed. Álvaro Huerga. Barcelona: J. Flors, 1962.

– *Introducción del símbolo de la fe*. Ed. José María Balcells. Madrid: Cátedra, 1989.

– *Obras del V.P.M. Fray Luis de Granada, con un prólogo y la vida del autor por Don José Joaquín de Mora*. 3 vols. Madrid: BAE, 1944–5.

Granjel, Luis. *Historia general de la medicina española II: La medicina española del Renacimiento*. Salamanca: Ediciones Universidad de Salamanca, 1981.

Grant, Helen F. "El mundo al revés." In *Hispanic Studies in Honour of Joseph Manson*, ed. Anthony H. Clarke and Dorothy M. Atkinson, 119–37. Oxford: Dolphin Book, 1972.

Greenblatt, Stephen. *Renaissance Self-Fashioning: From More to Shakespeare*. Chicago: University of Chicago Press, 1980.

Greene, Thomas. "The Flexibility of the Self in Renaissance Literature." In *The Disciplines of Criticism*, ed. Peter Demetz, Thomas Greene, and Lowry Nelson, 241–64. New Haven: Yale University Press, 1968.

Greenfield, Matthew. "Christopher Marlowe's Wound Knowledge." *PMLA* 119.2 (2004): 233–46.

Greer, Margaret Rich. *María de Zayas Tells Baroque Tales of Love and the Cruelty of Men*. University Park: Pennsylvania State University Press, 2000.

Greer, Margaret Rich, and Elizabeth Rhodes, eds. and trans. *Exemplary Tales of Love and Tales of Disillusion (María de Zayas y Sotomayor)*. Chicago: University of Chicago Press, 2009.

Gregory, Brad S. *Salvation at Stake: Christian Martyrdom in Early Modern Europe*. Cambridge, MA: Harvard University Press, 1999.

Grieve, Patricia E. "Embroidering with Saintly Threads: María de Zayas Challenges Cervantes and the Church." *Renaissance Quarterly* 44.1 (1991): 86–106.

Groebner, Valentin. *Who Are You? Identification, Deception, and Surveillance in Early Modern Europe*. Brooklyn, NY: Zone Books, 2007.

Gross, Charles G. "Rembrandt's *The Anatomy Lesson of Dr. Joan Deijman*." *Trends in Neurosciences* 21.6 (1998): 237–40.

Guevara, Antonio de. *Reloj de príncipes*. Valladolid: Nicolas Thierry, 1529.

Guillén, Claudio. "On the Concept of Metaphor of Perspective." In *Literature as System: Essays Toward the Theory of Literary History*, 283–371. Princeton: Princeton University Press, 1971.

Haggerty, Kevin D., and Richard V. Ericson. "The Surveillant Assemblage." *British Journal of Sociology* 51.4 (2000): 605–22.

Hale, David George. *The Body Politic: A Political Metaphor in English Literature*. The Hague: Mouton, 1971.

Haley, George. "The Narrator in *Don Quijote*: Maese Pedro's Puppet Show." *Modern Language Notes* 80.2 (1965): 145–65.

Hankison, R.J. "Stoicism and Medicine." In *The Cambridge Companion to the Stoics*, ed. Brad Inwood, 295–309. Cambridge: Cambridge University Press, 2003.

Hanson, Elizabeth. *Discovering the Subject in Renaissance England*. Cambridge: Cambridge University Press, 1998.

Harris, Jonathan Gil. *Foreign Bodies and the Body Politic: Discourses of Social Pathology in Early Modern England*. Cambridge: Cambridge University Press, 1998.

Hart, Thomas R. "Renaissance Dialogue into Novel: Cervantes's *Coloquio*." *Modern Language Notes* 105 (1990): 191–202.

Harvey, E. Ruth. *The Inward Wits: Psychological Theory in the Middle Ages and the Renaissance*. London: The Warburg Institute, University of London, 1975.

Haydn, Hiram Collins. *The Counter-Renaissance*. New York: Harcourt, 1950.

Heiple, Daniel L. *Mechanical Imagery in Golden Age Spain*. Madrid: José Porrúa Turanza, 1983.

Hektoen, Ludwig. "Early Postmortem Examinations by Europeans in America." *Journal of the American Medical Association* 86 (1926): 576–7.

Heninger, S.K., Jr. *The Cosmographical Glass: Renaissance Diagrams of the Universe*. San Marino, CA: The Huntington Library, 1977.

– *Touches of Sweet Harmony: Pythagorean Cosmology and Renaissance Poetics*. San Marino, CA: The Huntington Library, 1974.

Hernández Morejón, Antonio. *Bellezas de medicina práctica, descubiertas por Antonio Hernández Morejón en* El Ingenioso Caballero Don Quijote de la Mancha, *compuesto por Miguel de Cervantes Saavedra*. Madrid: Tomás Jordán, 1836.

Herrero García, Miguel. *El reloj en la vida española*. Madrid: Roberto Carbonell Blasco, 1955.

Herrlinger, Robert. *History of Medical Illustration: From Antiquity to AD 1600*. Nijkerk, Holland: Pitman Medical & Scientific Publishing, 1970.

Hillman, David. "The Inside History." In *Historicism, Psychoanalysis and Early Modern Culture*, ed. Carla Mazzio and Douglas Trevor, 299–324. New York: Routledge, 2000.

– *Shakespeare's Entrails: Belief, Scepticism and the Interior of the Body*. Hampshire: Palgrave Macmillan, 2007.

– "Visceral Knowledge." In *The Body in Parts: Fantasies of Corporeality in Early Modern Europe*, ed. David Hillman and Carla Mazzio, 81–106. New York: Routledge, 1997.

Hillman, David, and Carla Mazzio. "Introduction: Individual Parts." In *The Body in Parts: Fantasies of Corporeality in Early Modern Europe*, ed. David Hillman and Carla Mazzio, xi–xxix. New York: Routledge, 1997.

Hirsch, D.A. Hedrich. "Donne's Atomies and Anatomies: Deconstructed Bodies." *Studies in English Literature* 31.1 (1991): 69–95.

*Holy Bible, King James Version, Standard Edition*. Cambridge: Cambridge UP, 1995.

Homer. *The Iliad*. Trans. A.T. Murray. Cambridge, MA: Harvard University Press, 1954.

Honig, Edwin. *Calderón and the Seizures of Honor*. Cambridge, MA: Harvard University Press, 1974.

Hoover, L. Elaine. *John Donne and Francisco de Quevedo: Poets of Love and Death*. Chapel Hill: University of North Carolina Press, 1978.

Huarte de San Juan, Juan. *Examen de ingenios para las ciencias*. Buenos Aires: Espasa-Calpe, 1946.

Huerga, Álvaro. "Fray Luis de Granada entre mística, alumbrados e inquisición." In *Fray Luis de Granada, su obra y su tiempo. Actas del congreso internacional, Granada 27–30 septiembre 1988*, ed. Urbano Alonso del Campo and Antonio García del Moral, vol. 2, 289–305. Granada: Universidad de Granada, 1993.

– *Fray Luis de Granada: Una vida al servicio de la Iglesia*. Madrid: Biblioteca de Autores Cristianos, 1988.

– "La vida seudomística y el proceso inquisitorial de Sor María de la Visitación." *Hispania sacra* 12 (1959): 35–130.

Hume, D. *A Treatise of Human Nature*. Ed. L.A. Selby-Bigge and P.H. Nidditch. Oxford: Oxford University Press, 1973.

Hyma, Albert. *The Christian Renaissance: A History of the "Devotio Moderna."* Grand Rapids, MI: The Reformed Press, 1924.

Iffland, James. *Quevedo and the Grotesque*. 2 vols. London: Tamesis, 1978.

Iglesias, Rafael. "El imposible equilibrio entre el encomio cortesano y la reprimenda política: Hacia una nueva interpretación de *Cómo ha de ser el privado* de Quevedo." *La perinola* 9 (2005): 267–97.

– "Las fuentes literarias de *Cómo ha de ser el privado* de Don Francisco de Quevedo." *Bulletin of the Comediantes* 57.2 (2005): 365–406.

Imirizaldu, Jesús. *Monjas y beatas embaucadoras*. Madrid: Editora Nacional, 1977.

Impey, O.R., and Arthur MacGregor. *The Origins of Museums: The Cabinet of Curiosities in Sixteenth- and Seventeenth-Century Europe*. Oxford: Clarendon Press, 1985.

Isidore of Seville, Saint. *Isidori Hispalensis Episcopi etymologiarum sive originum libri XX*. Ed. Wallace Martin Lindsay. Oxford: Clarendon Press, 1971.

Jacobs, Fredrika. "(Dis)assembling: Marsyas, Michelangelo, and the *Accademia del Disegno*." *Art Bulletin* 84.3 (2002): 426–49.

Jager, Eric. "The Word in the 'Breost': Interiority and the Fall in Genesis B." *Neophilologus* 75 (1991): 279–90.

Jauralde Pou, Pablo. *Francisco de Quevedo (1580–1645)*. Madrid: Castalia, 1998.

Jehenson, Yvonne, and Marcia L. Welles. "María de Zayas' Wounded Women: A Semiotics of Violence." In *Gender, Identity, and Representation in Spain's Golden Age*, ed. Anita K. Stoll and Dawn L. Smith, 178–202. Lewisburg, PA: Bucknell University Press, 2000.

Jouhaud, Christian. *La main de Richelieu ou le pouvoir du cardinal*. Paris: Gallimard, 1991.

Juan Bautista de la Concepción, Saint (Juan García Gómez). *Algunas penas del justo en el camino de la perfección*. Ed. Juan Pujana. Madrid: Editorial Católica, 1995.

Junquera, Paulina. *Relojería palatina: Antología de la colección real española*. Biblioteca literaria del relojero. Madrid: Roberto Carbonell Blasco, 1956.

Justo, Alberto E. "El desierto interior según Fray Luis de Granada." In *Fray Luis de Granada, su obra y su tiempo. Actas del congreso internacional, Granada 1988*, ed. Urbano Alonso del Campo and Antonio García del Moral, 87–98. Granada: Universidad de Granada, 1993.

Kagan, Richard L. *Lucrecia's Dreams: Politics and Prophecy in Sixteenth-Century Spain*. Berkeley: University of California Press, 1990.

– "Politics, Prophecy, and the Inquisition in Late Sixteenth-Century Spain." In *Cultural Encounters: The Impact of the Inquisition in Spain and the New World*, ed. Mary Elizabeth Perry and Anne J. Cruz, 105–26. Berkeley: University of California Press, 1991.

Kaimal, Padma. "Shiva Nataraja: Shifting Meanings of an Icon." *The Art Bulletin* 81.3 (1999): 390–419.

Kamen, Henry. *Inquisition and Society in Spain in the Sixteenth and Seventeenth Centuries*. Bloomington: Indiana University Press, 1985.

- *The Iron Century: Social Change in Europe 1550–1660*. New York: Praeger, 1971.
- *Philip of Spain*. New Haven: Yale University Press, 1997.
- *The Spanish Inquisition*. London: Weidenfeld and Nicolson, 1965.
- "Toleration and Dissent in Sixteenth Century Spain: The Alternative Tradition." *Sixteenth Century* 19 (1988): 3–23.

Kearns, Michael S. *Metaphors of Mind in Fiction and Psychology*. Lexington: University Press of Kentucky, 1987.

Kellett, C.E. "A Note on Rosso and the Illustrations to Charles Estienne's *De dissectione*." *Journal of the History of Medicine and Allied Sciences* 12.7 (1957): 325–36.

King, Helen. *Hippocrates' Woman: Reading the Female Body in Ancient Greece*. London: Routledge, 1998.

Kurtz, Barbara. "The *Agricultura cristiana* of Juan de Pineda in the Context of Renaissance Mythography and Encyclopedism." *Inti* 24–5 (1986–7): 191–202.

Lactantius, Lucius Caecilius Firmianus. *De opificio Dei: la création de dieu*. Ed. Béatrice Bakhouche. Turnhout: Brepols, 2009.

Laguna, Andrés. *Pedacio Dioscórides Anazarbeo, acerca de la materia medicinal y de los venenos mortíferos*. Antwerp: Juan Latio, 1555.

Laín Entralgo, Pedro. *La antropología en la obra de Fray Luis de Granada*. Madrid: CSIC, 1988.

Lakoff, George. *Metaphors We Live By*. Chicago: University of Chicago Press, 1980.

Lakoff, George, and Mark Johnson. *Philosophy in the Flesh: The Embodied Mind and Its Challenge to Western Thought*. New York: Basic Books, 1999.

Laplana Gil, José Enrique. "Gracián y la fisiognomía." *Alazet: Revista de filología* 9 (1997): 103–24.

Laqueur, Thomas. "Orgasm, Generation, and the Politics of Reproductive Biology." In *The Making of the Modern Body: Sexuality and Society in the Nineteenth Century*, ed. Thomas Laqueur and Catherine Gallagher, 1–41. Berkeley: University of California Press, 1987.

Larson, Donald R. *The Honor Plays of Lope de Vega*. Cambridge, MA: Harvard University Press, 1977.

Le Breton, David. *Anthropologie du corps et modernité*. Paris: Presses Universitaires de France, 1990.

- *Corps et sociétés: Essai de sociologie et d'anthropologie du corps*. Paris: Méridiens Klincksieck, 1991.
- "Dualism and Renaissance: Sources for a Modern Representation of the Body." *Diogenes* 142 (1988): 47–69.

Lea, Henry Charles. *A History of Auricular Confession and Indulgences in the
    Latin Church*. 3 vols. New York: Greenwood Press, 1968.
– *A History of the Inquisition of Spain*. 4 vols. London: Macmillan, 1922.
Leary, Mark R. *The Curse of the Self*. Oxford: Oxford University Press, 2004.
Lemay, Helen Rodnite. *Women's Secrets: A Translation of Pseudo-Ablertus
    Magnus* De secretis mulierum *with Commentaries*. New York: State
    University of New York Press, 1992.
Levisi, Margarita. "La crueldad en los *Desengaños amorosos* de María de
    Zayas." In *Estudios literarios de hispanistas norteamericanos dedicados a Helmut
    Hatzfeld con motivo de su 80 aniversario*, ed. Josep M. Sola-Sole and Helmut
    Anthony Hatzfeld, 447–56. Barcelona: Hispam, 1974.
– "La interioridad visualizable en Garcilaso." *Hispanófila* 73 (1981): 11–20.
– "Las figuras compuestas en Arcimboldo y Quevedo." *Comparative Literature*
    20 (1968): 217–35.
Lewis, C.S. *The Discarded Image*. Cambridge: Cambridge University Press, 1964.
Lewis, Ewart. "Organic Tendencies in Medieval Political Thought." *The
    American Political Science Review* 32.5 (1938): 849–76.
Lipsius, Justus. *Epistolario de Justo Lipsio y los españoles, 1577–1606*. Ed.
    Alejandro Ramírez. Madrid: Editorial Castalia, 1966.
Lobera de Ávila, Luis. *Remedio de cuerpos humanos (libro de anatomía)*. Alcalá de
    Henares: Juan de Brocar, 1542.
López Alonso, Antonio. *Cervantes, manco y bien manco*. Alcalá de Henares:
    Universidad de Alcalá de Henares, 1997.
López de Úbeda, Francisco. *La pícara Justina*. Ed. Antonio Rey Hazas. 2 vols.
    Madrid: Editorial Nacional, 1977.
López Piñero, José María. "The Vesalian Movement in Sixteenth-Century
    Spain." *Journal of the History of Biology* 12.1 (1997): 45–81.
López Piñero, José María, and Francisco Calero. *Los temas polémicos de la
    medicina renacentista: Las* Controversias *(1586) de Francisco Vallés*. Madrid:
    CSIC, 1988.
López Piñero, José María, and María Luz Terrada Ferrandis. *La obra de Juan
    Tomás Porcell (1565) y los orígenes de la anatomía patológica moderna*. Barcelona:
    Editorial Rocas, 1963.
López-Ríos Moreno, Fernando, and Fernando López-Ríos Fernández.
    "Las primeras disecciones anatómicas en el nuevo mundo." In *Congreso
    Internacional de Historia de la Medicina, Granada 1992*, 215–22. Sevilla:
    Sociedad Española de Historia de la Medicina, 1994.
Lord, Susan, and Annette Burfoot, eds. *Killing Women: The Visual Culture of
    Gender and Violence*. Waterloo, ON: Wilfrid Laurier University Press, 2006.

Los, Maria. "Looking into the Future: Surveillance, Globalization and the Totalitarian Potential." In *Theorizing Surveillance: The Panopticon and Beyond*, ed. David Lyon, 69–94. London: William Publishing, 2006.

Lubac, Henri de. *Corpus Mysticum, l'Eucharistie et l'Église au Moyen Âge, étude historique*. Paris: Aubier, 1949.

Lucian of Samosata. "A True Story." In *Lucian Works*, ed. A.M. Harmon, vol. 1, 248–357. London: The Loeb Classical Library, 1921.

Lucretius Carus, Titus. *De rerum natura libri sex*. Ed. Cyri Bailey. 3 vols. Oxford: Clarendon Press, 1966.

Lynch, John. *Spain 1516–1598: From Nation State to World Empire*. Oxford: Blackwell, 1992.

MacCurdy, Raymond R. *The Tragic Fall: Don Álvaro de Luna and Other Favourites in Spanish Golden Age Drama*. Chapel Hill: University of North Carolina Press, 1978.

MacInnes, Ian. "Stigmata on Trial: The Nun of Portugal and the Politics of the Body." *Viator* 30 (2000): 381–97.

Malpas, Jeff. "Finding Place: Speciality, Locality and Subjectivity." In *Philosophy and Geography III: Philosophies of Place*, ed. Jonathan M. Smith and Andrew Light, 21–43. Lanham, MD: Rowman & Littlefield, 1998.

Mansberger Amorós, Roberto. "Un capítulo de la lucha y reforma de las ideas de la España ilustrada: La traducción de la *Retórica eclesiástica* de Fray Luis de Granada." *Documentos A* 4 (1992): 62–70.

Marañón, Gregorio. *El conde-duque de Olivares: La pasión de mandar*. Madrid: Espasa-Calpe, 1959.

Maravall, José Antonio. *Culture of the Baroque: Analysis of a Historical Structure*. Trans. Terry Cochran. Manchester: Manchester University Press, 1986.

– *Estudios de historia del pensamiento español*. Madrid: Ediciones Cultura Hispánica, 1983.

– *La teoría española de estado en el siglo XVII*. Madrid: Instituto de Estudios Políticos, 1944.

– "The Origins of the Modern State." *Cahiers d'histoire mondiale* 6.4 (1961): 789–808.

– *Poder, honor y élites en el siglo XVII*. Madrid: Siglo Veintiuno de España, 1979.

– "Sobre el pensamiento social y político de Quevedo (una revisión)." In *Homenaje a Quevedo*, ed. Víctor García de la Concha, 69–132. Salamanca: Caja de Ahorros y Monte de Piedad de Salamanca, 1982.

Mariscal, George. *Contradictory Subjects: Quevedo, Cervantes and Seventeenth-Century Spanish Culture*. Ithaca: Cornell University Press, 1991.

Mariscal y García, Nicasio. *El doctor Juan Thomas Porcell y la peste de Zaragoza de 1564*. Madrid: Instituto de España, Real Academia Nacional de Medicina, 1914.

Márquez, Antonio. *Los alumbrados: Orígenes y filosofía, 1525–1559*. Madrid: Taurus, 1972.

Marshall, Patricia A. *Anatomía y escenificación: La representación del cuerpo humano en el teatro de Calderón de la Barca*. New York: Peter Lang, 2003.

Martín, Adrienne Laskier. *Cervantes and the Burlesque Sonnet*. Berkeley: University of California Press, 1991.

Martin, Dale B. *The Corinthian Body*. New Haven: Yale University Press, 1995.

Martín Santos, Luis. *Barberos y cirujanos de los siglos XVI y XVII*. Salamanca: Junta de Castilla y León, 2000.

Marvick, Elizabeth Wirth. "Favourites in Early Modern Europe: A Recurring Psychopolitical Role." *Journal of Psychohistory* 10 (1983): 463–89.

Matos-Nin, Ingrid E. *Las novelas de María de Zayas, 1590–1650: Lo sobrenatural y lo oculto en la literatura femenina española del siglo XVII*. Lewiston, NY: Edwin Mellen Press, 2010.

Maus, Katharine Eisaman. *Inwardness and Theater in the English Renaissance*. Chicago: University of Chicago Press, 1995.

Mayr, Otto. *Authority, Liberty, and Automatic Machinery in Early Modern Europe*. Baltimore: Johns Hopkins University Press, 1986.

Mechoulan, Henry. "Luis de Granada en ayuda de la ortodoxia judía en Ámsterdam en el siglo XVII: La utilización de Luis de Granada en *La certeza del camino* de Abraham Pereyra." In *Fray Luis de Granada, su obra y su tiempo. Actas del congreso internacional, Granada 27–30 septiembre 1988*, ed. Urbano Alonso del Campo and Antonio García del Moral, 307–20. Granada: Universidad de Granada, 1993.

Melzack, Ronald. "Phantom Limbs, the Self, and the Brain: The D.O. Hebb Memorial Lecture." *Canadian Psychology* 30 (1989): 1–16.

Menéndez Pelayo, Marcelino. *Historia de los heterodoxos españoles*. Madrid: Librería Católica de San José, 1880.

Merola, Jerónimo. *Historia general del cuerpo humano*. Barcelona: Pedro Malo, 1587.

Meseguer Fernández, Juan. "Introducción a Juan de Pineda." In *Diálogos familiares de la agricultura cristiana de Juan de Pineda*, vol. 161, vii–cxiv. Madrid: BAE, 1963.

Miles, Margaret Ruth. *Augustine on the Body*. Missoula, MT: Scholars Press, 1979.

Mitchell, Peter. *The Purple Island and Anatomy in Early Seventeenth-Century Literature, Philosophy, and Theology*. Madison, NJ: Fairleigh Dickinson University Press, 2007.

Molina, Tirso de. *Cigarrales de Toledo*. Ed. Luis Vázquez. Madrid: Castalia, 1996.

Mondino de Luzzi (Mundinus). *Anathomia Mondini*. Leipzig: Martin Pollick van Mellerstadt, 1493.

– *Anathomia Mundini*. Ed. Johann Dryander. Marpurgi: Christiani Egenolphi, 1541.

Montaigne, Michel de. *The Complete Essays*. Ed. and trans. M.A. Screech. London: Penguin, 2003.

Montaña de Monserrate, Bernardino. *Libro de la anothomia del hombre nuevamente compuesto por Bernardino Montaña de Monserrate ... juntamente con una declaracion de un sueño que soño ... Luys Hurtado de Mendoça Marques de Mondejar*. Valladolid: Sebastián Martínez, 1551.

Montañés Fontenla, Luis, ed. *Biblioteca literaria del relojero*. 6 vols. Madrid: Roberto Carbonell Blasco, 1953–8.

– *Capítulos de la relojería en España*. Biblioteca literaria del relojero. Madrid: Roberto Carbonell Blasco, 1954.

Moore, John A. *Fray Luis de Granada*. Boston: Twayne, 1977.

Moore, Roger, and Clare Moore. "Quevedo Biography." 2000. http://moore.lib.unb.ca/bibliog/bibframe.htm.

Moreno Castillo, Enrique. "Anotaciones a la silva *Sermón estoico de censura moral* de Francisco de Quevedo." *La perinola* 11 (2007): 131–83.

Morreale, Margarita. "Luciano y Quevedo: La humanidad condenada." *Revista de literatura* 8 (1955): 213–27.

Morris, Colin. *The Discovery of the Individual 1050–1200*. New York: Harper & Row, 1972.

Mujica, Barbara L. "María Zayas y Sotomayor: ¿Protofeminista o *marketing genius* por excelencia?" In *Women Writers of Early Modern Spain: Sophia's Daughters*, ed. Barbara L. Mujica, 126–36. New Haven: Yale University Press, 2004.

Munguía García, Víctor Eduardo. "*El licenciado Vidriera* y Don Quijote." *Anales cervantinos* 30 (1992): 157–63.

Muñoz Palomares, Antonio. *El teatro de Mira de Amescua: Para una lectura política y social de la comedia áurea*. Pamplona: Universidad de Navarra, 2007.

Myers, Davie W. *"Poor Sinning Folk": Confessions and Conscience in Counter Reformation Germany*. Ithaca: Cornell University Press, 1994.

Nebrija, Antonio de. *Dictionarium Hispano-Latinum*. Ed. John O'Neill. New York: Electronic Texts and Concordances of the Madison Corpus of Early Spanish Manuscripts and Printings, 1999.

Nédoncelle, Maurice. "Intériorité." In *Dictionnaire de spiritualité ascétique et mystique*, ed. Marcel Viller, vol. 7, cols. 1877–903. Paris: Beauchesne, 1937.

Nelson, Bradley J. *The Persistence of Presence: Emblem and Ritual in Baroque Spain.* Toronto: University of Toronto Press, 2010.

Neumeister, Sebastian. "La observación del otro y de sí mismo en Gracián." *Ínsula* 655–6 (2001): 37–9.

Nieman, Meghan. "Foxe's Female Martyrs and the Utility of Interiority." *The Dalhousie Review* 85.2 (2005): 295–305.

Nolting-Hauff, Ilse. *Visión, sátira y agudeza en los* Sueños *de Quevedo.* Madrid: Gredos, 1974.

O'Brien, Eavan. *Women in the Prose of María de Zayas.* Woodbridge, UK: Tamesis, 2010.

Oechselin, R.L. *Louis of Granada.* London: B. Herder, 1962.

Oestreich, Gerhard. *Neostoicism and the Early Modern State.* Trans. David McLintock. Cambridge: Cambridge University Press, 1982.

Olivares, Julián. "Introducción." In *Novelas amorosas y ejemplares*, ed. Julián Olivares, 9–147. Madrid: Cátedra, 2010.

Oliver, Antonio. "La filosofía en *El licenciado Vidriera.*" *Anales cervantinos* 4 (1954): 227–38.

O'Malley, C.D. *Andreas Vesalius of Brussels, 1514–1564.* Berkeley: University of California Press, 1964.

Onians, Richard Broxton. *The Origins of European Thought about the Body, the Mind, the Soul, the World, Time, and Fate.* Cambridge: Cambridge University Press, 1954.

Orgel, Stephen. *The Illusion of Power: Political Theater in the English Renaissance.* Berkeley: University of California Press, 1975.

Ovid, P. *Ovidi Nasonis Metamorphoses.* Ed. R.J. Tarrant. Oxford: Oxford University Press, 2008.

Paige, Nicholas D. *Being Interior: Autobiography and the Contradictions of Modernity in Seventeenth-Century France.* Philadelphia: University of Pennsylvania Press, 2001.

Pando Canteli, María. "'One Like None, and Lik'd of None': John Donne, Francisco de Quevedo, and the Grotesque Representation of the Female Body." *John Donne Journal* 12.1–2 (1993): 1–15.

Panichi, Nicola. "Montaigne et 'l'anatomie de la philosophie.'" In *Théâtre de l'anatomie et corps en spectacle: Fondements d'une science de la Renaissance*, ed. Ilana Zinguer and Isabelle Martin, 89–122. Bern: Peter Lang, 2006.

Panofsky, Erwin. *Perspective as Symbolic Form.* New York: Zone Books, 1991.

Pardo Tomás, José, and Alvar Martínez Vidal. "Los orígenes del teatro anatómico de Madrid (1689–1728)." *Asclepio* 49.1 (1997): 5–38.

Paré, Ambroise. *La manière de traicter les playes faictes tant par hacquebutes, que par flèches, etc.* Paris: Arnoul l'Angelié, 1552.

Park, Katharine. "Dissecting the Female Body: From Women's Secrets to the Secrets of Nature." In *Crossing Boundaries: Attending to Early Modern Women*, ed. Jane Donawerth and Adel Seeff, 29–47. Newark: University of Delaware Press, 2000.

– *Secrets of Women: Gender, Generation, and the Origins of Human Dissection.* New York: Zone Books, 2006.

Parker, Geoffrey. *Europe in Crisis, 1598–1648.* London: Fontana, 1979.

– *The Grand Strategy of Philip II.* New Haven: Yale University Press, 1998.

– *Philip II.* London: Hutchinson & Co., 1979.

Paster, Gail Kern. *The Body Embarrassed: Drama and the Disciplines of Shame in Early Modern England.* Ithaca: Cornell University Press, 1993.

Paster, Gail Kern, Katherine Rowe, and Mary Floyd-Wilson, eds. *Reading the Early Modern Passions: Essays in the Cultural History of Emotion.* Philadelphia: University of Pennsylvania Press, 2004.

Paun de García, Susan. "Magia y poder en María de Zayas." *Cuadernos de ALDEUU* 9.1 (1992): 43–54.

Peers, Allison. *Studies of the Spanish Mystics.* Vol. 1. New York: Macmillan, 1951.

Peña Chavarria, A., and P.G. Shipley. "The Siamese Twins of Española: The First Known Post-Mortem Examination in the New World." *Medical History* 6 (1924): 297–302.

Peraita, Carmen. "La oreja, lengua, voz, el grito y las alegorías del acceso al rey: Elocuencia sacra y afectos políticos en *Política de Dios* de Quevedo." *La perinola* 5 (2001): 185–205.

– "Mapas de lectura, diálogos con los textos: La 'Carta al rey Luis XIII' y las anotaciones en el ejemplar de la *Utopía* de Quevedo." *La perinola* 8 (2004): 322–41.

Pérez, Joseph. *The Spanish Inquisition: A History.* New Haven: Yale University Press, 2005.

Pérez Fadrique, Juan Eulogio. *Moda práctica de embalsamar cuerpos defunctos para preservarlos incorruptos y eternizarlos en lo posible.* Seville: Thomé de Dios Miranda, 1666.

Pérez Villanueva, Joaquín, and Bartolomé Escandell Bonet. *Historia de la Inquisición en España y América.* 3 vols. Madrid: BAE, 1984.

Petrarch, Francesco. *Petrarch's Lyric Poems: The Rime Sparse and Other Lyrics.* Ed. and trans. Robert M. Durling. Cambridge, MA: Harvard University Press, 1976.

Pico della Mirandola, Giovanni Francesco. *On the Dignity of Man.* Trans. Charles Glenn Wallis. Indianapolis: Bobbs-Merrill Company, 1965.

Pineda, Juan de. *Diálogos familiares de la agricultura cristiana*. Vols. 161–4. Madrid: BAE, 1963.

Pinto Crespo, Virgilio. "Censorship: A System of Control and an Instrument of Action." Trans. Esther da Costa-Frankel. In *The Spanish Inquisition and the Inquisitorial Mind*, ed. Ángel Alcalá, 303–19. Highland Lake, NJ: Atlantic Research and Publications, 1987.

– *Inquisición y control ideológico en la España del siglo XVI*. Madrid: Taurus, 1983.

Porcell, Joan Tomás. *Información y curación de la peste de Zaragoza y preservación contra la peste en general*. Zaragoza: Viuda de Bartolomé de Nájera, 1565.

Porres Martín-Cleto, Julio. *Historia de las calles de Toledo*. Toledo: Diputación Provincial, 1971.

Prieto Carrasco, Casto. *Dos estudios sobre la enseñanza de la medicina en la universidad de Salamanca*. Salamanca: Ediciones Universidad de Salamanca, 1986.

Puerto, Javier. "La materia médica de Dioscórides, Andrés Laguna y *El Quijote*." In *La ciencia y* El Quijote, ed. José Manuel Sánchez Ron, 141–54. Barcelona: Crítica, 2005.

Quevedo, Francisco de. *La vida del Buscón llamado Don Pablos*. Ed. Domingo Ynduráin. Madrid: Cátedra, 1998.

– *Obras completas*. Ed. Felicidad Buendía. 2 vols. Madrid: Aguilar, 1961.

Quiñones de Benavente, Luis. "Entremés de los ladrones y el reloj." In *Nuevos entremeses atribuidos a Luis Quiñones Benavente*, ed. Abraham Madroñal Durán, 201–14. Kassel: Reichenberger, 1996.

Real Academia Española. *Diccionario de autoridades*. Madrid: Francisco del Hierro, 1726.

Redondo, Augustin. "La folie du Cervantin Licencié de Verre." In *Visages de la folie, 1500–1650, domaine hispano-italien*, ed. André Rochon and Augustin Redondo, 33–44. Paris: Publications de la Sorbonne, 1981.

Reed, Cory. "Ludic Revelations in the Enchanted Head Episode in *Don Quijote* (II, 62)." *Cervantes* 24.1 (2004): 189–216.

Reichenberger, Kurt. *Cervantes and the Hermeneutics of Satire*. Kassel: Edition Reichenberger, 2005.

Reiss, J. *Mirages of the Self: Patterns of Personhood in Ancient and Early Modern Europe*. Stanford: Stanford University Press, 2003.

Resina Rodrigues, Maria Idalina. *Fray Luis de Granada y la literatura de espiritualidad en Portugal (1554–1632)*. Trans. María Victoria Navas. Madrid: Universidad Pontificia de Salamanca, 1988.

Rhodes, Elizabeth. *Dressed to Kill: Death and Meaning in Zayas's Desengaños*. Toronto: University of Toronto Press, 2011.

- "El *Libro de oración* como el best-seller del Siglo de Oro." In *Actas del X Congreso de la Asociación Internacional de Hispanistas, Barcelona 21–26 de agosto de 1989*, ed. Antonio Vilanova, 525–32. Barcelona: Promociones y Publicaciones Universitarias, 1992.

Riandière la Roche, Josette. "Corps politique et corps mystique dans *La política de Dios* de Quevedo." In *Le corps comme métaphore dans l'Espagne des XVI$^E$ et XVIII$^E$ siècle*, ed. André Rochon and Augustin Redondo, 115–34. Paris: Publications de la Sorbonne, 1992.

-, ed. "Francisco de Quevedo y Villegas: Visita y anatomía del eminentísimo cardenal Armando Richelieu." *Criticón* 25 (1984): 19–113.

- "La folie médicale et son utilisation dans la satire politique: Étude d'un pamphlet de Quevedo." In *Visages de la folie, 1500–1650, domaine hispano-italien*, ed. André Rochon and Augustín Redondo, 155–68. Paris: Publications de la Sorbonne, 1981.

Ribera, José de. *Apollo Flaying Marsyas*. 1637. Musées royaux des Beaux-Arts de Belgique, Brussels. Another version at the Museo Nazionale di Capodimonte, Naples.

Ricapito, Joseph V. *Cervantes's Novelas ejemplares: Between History and Creativity*. West Lafayette: Purdue University Press, 1996.

- "Los 'pasteles de a cuatro': Quevedo y la antropofagia." *Letras de Deusto* 17.37 (1987): 161–7.

Richardson, Ruth. *Death, Dissection and the Destitute*. London: Routledge and Kegan Paul, 1987.

Rico, Francisco. *El pequeño mundo del hombre: Varia fortuna de una idea en la cultura española*. Madrid: Alianza Editorial, 1986.

Riley, E.C. "Cervantes and the Cynics (*El licenciado Vidriera* and *El coloquio de los perros*)." *Bulletin of Hispanic Studies* 53.3 (1976): 189–99.

Rivadeneira, Pedro de. *Flos sanctorum*. 2 vols. Madrid: Luis Sánchez, 1599–1601.

- *Tratado de la religión y virtudes que debe tener el príncipe cristiano para gobernar sus estados*. In *Obras escogidas del Padre de Rivadeneira de la Compañía de Jesús*, ed. Vicente de la Fuente, 449–587. 1595; Madrid: Atlas, 1952.

Robres Lluch, Ramón, and José Ramón Ortola. *La monja de Lisboa: Epistolario inédito entre Fray Luis de Granada y el Patriarca Ribera*. Castellón de la Plana: Sociedad Castellonense de Cultura, 1947.

Rodríguez de la Flor, Fernando. "Las sedes del alma: La figuración interior en la literatura y el arte." In *La península metafísica: Arte, literatura y pensamiento en la España de la Contrarreforma*, 201–31. Madrid: Biblioteca Nueva, 1999.

Rorty, Richard. *Philosophy and the Mirror of Nature*. Princeton: Princeton University Press, 1979.

Rowe, Katherine. "Humoral Knowledge and Liberal Cognition in Davenant's *Macbeth*." In *Reading the Early Modern Passions: Essays in the Cultural History of Emotion*, ed. Gail Kern Paster, Katherine Rowe, and Mary Floyd-Wilson, 169–91. Philadelphia: University of Pennsylvania Press, 2004.

Ruan, Felipe. "Carta de guía, carto-grafía: Fallas y fisuras en *El licenciado Vidriera*." *Cervantes* 20.2 (2000): 151–62.

Rufo, Juan. *Las seiscientas apotegmas*. Ed. Alberto Blecua. Madrid: Espasa-Calpe, 1972.

Ruiz, Juan, Arcipreste de Hita. *Libro de buen amor*. Ed. Julio Cejador y Frauca. Vol. 1. Madrid: Espasa-Calpe, 1931.

Rupp, Stephen James. *Allegories of Kingship: Calderón and the Anti-Machiavellian Tradition*. University Park: Pennsylvania State University Press, 1996.

Russell, K.F. "Ivory Anatomical Manikins." *Medical History* 16.2 (1972): 131–42.

Saavedra Fajardo, Diego de. *Idea de un príncipe político-cristiano representada en cien empresas*. Ed. Vicente García de Diego. Madrid: Espasa-Calpe, 1946.

Sabean, David Warren. "Production of the Self during the Age of Confessionalism." *Central European History* 29.1 (1996): 1–18.

Sabuco, Miguel, and Oliva Sabuco. *Nueva filosofía de la naturaleza del hombre*. Madrid: P. Madrigal, 1588.

San José Salazar, María de, Alison Weber, and Amanda Powell, eds. *Book for the Hour of Recreation*. Chicago: Chicago University Press, 2002.

Sánchez, Galo. "Datos jurídicos acerca de la venganza del honor." *Revista de filología española* 4 (1917): 292–5.

Sánchez Valdés de la Plata, Iván. *Coronica y historia general del hombre*. Madrid: Luis Sánchez, 1598.

Sandnes, Karl Olav. *Belly and Body in the Pauline Epistles*. Cambridge: Cambridge University Press, 2002.

Saunders, J.B., and Charles D. O'Malley. *The Illustrations from the Works of Andreas Vesalius of Brussels*. Cleveland: The World Publishing Company, 1950.

Saunders, Jason Lewis. *Justus Lipsius: The Philosophy of Renaissance Stoicism*. New York: Liberal Arts Press, 1955.

Sawday, Jonathan. *The Body Emblazoned: Dissection and the Human Body in Renaissance Culture*. London: Routledge, 1995.

– *Engines of the Imagination: Renaissance Culture and the Rise of the Machine*. London: Routledge, 2007.

– "The Fate of Marsyas: Dissecting the Renaissance Body." In *Renaissance Bodies: The Human Figure in English Culture c. 1540–1660*, ed. Lucy Gent and Nigel Llewellyn, 111–35. London: Reaktion Books, 1990.

Schiebinger, Londa L. "Skeletons in the Closet: The First Illustrations of the Female Skeleton in Eighteenth-Century America." In *The Making of the Modern Body: Sexuality and Society in the Nineteenth Century*, ed. Thomas Laqueur and Catherine Gallagher, 42–82. Berkeley: University of California Press, 1987.

Schiffman, Zachary. "Montaigne and the Problem of Machiavellism." *Journal of Medieval and Renaissance Studies* 12.1 (1982): 237–58.

Schlanger, Judith E. *Les métaphores de l'organisme*. Paris: Vrin, 1971.

Schleiner, Winfried. "The Glass Graduate and the Aphrodisiac that Went Wrong: New Lights from Old Texts." *Forum for Modern Languages Studies* 27.4 (1991): 370–81.

Schmidt, G.D. *The Iconography of the Mouth of Hell: Eighth-Century Britain to the Fifteenth Century*. Selinsgrove, PA: Susquehanna University Press, 1995.

Schmidt, Rachel. *Forms of Modernity: Don Quixote and Modern Theories of the Novel*. Toronto: University of Toronto Press, 2011.

Schoenfeldt, Michael. *Bodies and Selves in Early Modern England: Physiology and Inwardness in Spenser, Shakespeare, Herbert, and Milton*. Cambridge: Cambridge University Press, 1999.

– "Fables of the Belly in Early Modern England." In *The Body in Parts: Fantasies of Corporeality in Early Modern Europe*, ed. David Hillman and Carla Mazzio, 243–62. New York: Routledge, 1997.

Schopenhauer, Arthur. *Sämtliche Werke*. Ed. Eduard Grisebach. Vol. 1. Leipzig: Philip Reclam, 1920.

Selleck, Nancy. "Donne's Body." *Studies in English Literature* 41.1 (2001): 149–74.

Seneca, Lucius Annaeus. *Moral Essays: De providentia, De constantia, De ira, De clementia*. 3 vols. Trans. John. W. Basore. London: Loeb Classical Library, 1928.

Serrano Poncela, Segundo. "Formas de vida hispánica (Garcilaso, Quevedo, Godoy y los ilustrados)." In *Formas de vida hispánica (Garcilaso, Quevedo, Godoy y los ilustrados)*, ed. Segundo Serrano Poncela, 64–123. Madrid: Gredos, 1963.

– "Quevedo, hombre político, análisis de un resentimiento." *La torre* 6 (1958): 55–95.

Shapin, Steven. *The Scientific Revolution*. Chicago: University of Chicago Press, 1996.

Shipley, George. "Vidriera's Blather." *Cervantes* 22.2 (2002): 49–124.

Shuger, Debora Kuller. *Habits of Thought in the English Renaissance: Religion, Politics, and the Dominant Culture*. Berkeley: University of California Press, 1990.

Singer, Charles. *A Short History of Anatomy from the Greeks to Harvey*. New York: Dover Publications, 1957.

Solomon, Howard M. *Public Welfare, Science and Propaganda in Seventeenth Century France: The Innovations of Théophraste Renaudt*. Princeton: Princeton University Press, 1972.

Somers, Melvina. "Quevedo's Ideology in *Cómo ha de ser el privado*." *Hispania* 39.3 (1956): 261–8.

Sontag, Susan. *Illness as Metaphor, and AIDS and Its Metaphors*. New York: Picador, 2001.

Speak, Gill. "*El licenciado Vidriera* and the Glass Men of Early Modern Europe." *Modern Language Review* 85 (1990): 850–65.

Spitzer, Leo. "Sobre el arte de Quevedo en el *Buscón*." In *Francisco de Quevedo*, ed. Gonzalo Sobejano, 123–84. Madrid: Taurus, 1978.

Stallybrass, Peter. "Patriarchal Territories: The Body Enclosed." In *Rewriting the Renaissance: The Discourse of Sexual Difference in Early Modern Europe*, ed. Margaret W. Ferguson, Maureen Quilligan, and Nancy J. Vickers, 123–42. Chicago: University of Chicago Press, 1986.

Stark, Werner. *The Fundamental Forms of Social Thought*. New York: Fordham University Press, 1963.

Starobinski, Jean. "The Inside and the Outside." *The Hudson Review* 28.3 (1975): 333–51.

Stephens, Elizabeth. *Anatomy as Spectacle: Public Exhibitions of the Body from 1700 to the Present*. Liverpool: Liverpool University Press, 2011.

Stevens, Scott Manning. "Sacred Heart and Secular Brain." In *The Body in Parts: Fantasies of Corporeality in Early Modern Europe*, ed. David Hillman and Carla Mazzio, 263–84. New York: Routledge, 1997.

Strosetzki, Christoph. "Aristóteles y el orden de las cosas en Fray Luis de Granada, Francisco Sánchez, Huarte de San Juan y Antonio de Torquemada." In *Fantasía y literatura en la Edad Media y los Siglos de Oro*, ed. Nicasio Salvador Miguel, Santiago López-Ríos, and Esther Borrego Gutiérrez, 337–60. Madrid and Frankfurt am Main: Iberoamericana-Vervuert, 2004.

Stroud, Matthew D. *Fatal Union: A Pluralistic Approach to the Spanish Wife-Murder Comedias*. Lewisburg, PA: Bucknell University Press, 1990.

Sutton, John. *Philosophy and Memory Traces: Descartes to Connectionism*. Cambridge: Cambridge University Press, 1998.

Tato Puigcerver, José Julio. "Sobre la 'Visita y anatomía de la cabeza del cardenal Richelieu,' de Francisco de Quevedo." *Espéculo* 39 (2008). http://www.ucm.es/info/especulo/numero39/cardrich.html

Taylor, Scott K. *Honor and Violence in Golden Age Spain*. New Haven: Yale University Press, 2008.

Tentler, Thomas N. "The Summa for Confessors as an Instrument of Social Control." In *The Pursuit of Holiness in Late Medieval and Renaissance Religion*, ed. Heiko A. Oberman and Charles Trinkaus, 103–26. Leiden: Brill, 1972.

Thompson, C.J.S. "Anatomical Manikins." *Journal of Anatomy* 59.4 (1925): 442–5.

Thompson, Colin. "Eutrapelia and Exemplarity in the *Novelas ejemplares*." In *A Companion to Cervantes's* Novelas ejemplares, ed. Stephen Boyd, 261–82. London: Tamesis, 2005.

Tierno Galván, Enrique. "Quevedo." In *Francisco de Quevedo*, ed. Gonzalo Sobejano, 29–33. Madrid: Taurus, 1978.

Timoneda, Juan de. *Buen aviso y portacuentos*. Ed. María Pilar Cueto and Maxime Chevalier. Madrid: Espasa-Calpe, 1990.

Tomás y Valiente, Francisco. *Los validos en la monarquía española del siglo XVII: Estudio institucional*. Madrid: Siglo XXI, 1982.

Traub, Valerie. "Gendering Mortality in Early Modern Anatomies." In *Feminist Readings of Early Modern Culture: Emerging Subjects*, ed. Valerie Traub, M. Lindsay Kaplan, and Dympna Callaghan, 44–92. Cambridge: Cambridge University Press, 1996.

Vaillo, Carlos. "'El mundo al revés' en la poesía satírica de Quevedo." *Cuadernos hispanoamericanos* 380 (1982): 364–93.

Valdés, Ramón. "Quevedo: Metáforas tópicas, motivos y modelo de la 'Visita y anatomía de la cabeza del cardenal Richelieu.'" *Rivista di filologia e letterature ispaniche* 1 (1998): 129–42.

Valle Lersundi, Fernando del. "Testamento de Fernando de Rojas, autor de *La Celestina*." *Revista de filología española* 16 (1929): 385–96.

Valverde de Amusco, Juan. *Anatomía del corpo humano*. Rome: Ant. Salamanca and Antonio Lafrery, 1560.

Varey, J.E. *Historia de los títeres en España (desde sus orígenes hasta mediados del siglo XVIII)*. Madrid: Revista de Occidente, 1957.

Vega Carpio, Lope de. *Servir a buenos*. In *Comedias escogidas de Lope de Vega Carpio*, ed. Juan Eugenio Hartzenbusch, 425–42. Madrid: Atlas, 1950.

Vesalius, Andreas. *De humani corporis fabrica*. Basilea: J. Oporinus, 1543.

Vilar, Jean. "Judas según Quevedo (un tema para una biografía)." In *Francisco de Quevedo*, ed. Gonzalo Sobejano, 106–19. Madrid: Taurus, 1975.

Villalón, Cristóbal de. *Ingeniosa comparación entre lo antiguo y lo presente*. Ed. M. Serrano y Sanz. Madrid: Sociedad de Bibliófilos Españoles, 1908.

Virz, Evelyn Birge. *Medieval Narrative and Modern Narratology*. New York: New York University Press, 1989.

Vollendorf, Lisa. *Reclaiming the Body: María de Zayas's Early Modern Feminism.* Chapel Hill: University of North Carolina Press, 2001.

von Bertele, H. "Precision Timekeeping in the Pre-Huygens Era." *The Horological Journal* 95 (1953): 794–816.

Voros, Sharon D. "Fashioning Femenine Wit in María de Zayas, Ana Caro, and Leonor de la Cueva." In *Gender, Identity, and Representation in Spain's Golden Age*, ed. Anita K. Stoll and Dawn L. Smith, 156–77. Lewisburg, PA: Bucknell University Press, 2000.

Waley, Pamela. "The Unity of the *Casamiento engañoso* and the *Coloquio de los perros*." *Bulletin of Hispanic Studies* 34 (1957): 201–12.

Wardropper, Bruce. "La eutrapelia en las *Novelas ejemplares* de Cervantes." In *Actas del séptimo congreso de la Asociación Internacional de Hispanistas, celebrado en Venecia del 25 al 30 de agosto de 1980*, ed. Giuseppe Bellini, vol. 1, 153–69. Rome: Bulzoni, 1982.

Warner, Marina. *Alone of All Her Sex: The Myth and Cult of the Virgin Mary.* London: Picador, 1976.

Weber, Alison. *Theresa of Avila and the Rhetoric of Femininity.* Princeton: Princeton University Press, 1990.

Weber, Max. *The Sociology of Religion.* Boston: Beacon, 1993.

Weiss, Geil, and Honi F. Haber. "Introduction." In *Perspectives on Embodiment: The Intersections of Nature and Culture*, ed. G. Weiss and H.F. Haber, xiii–xvii. New York: Routledge, 1999.

Welles, Marcia L. "María de Zayas y Sotomayor and Her 'novela cortesana': A Re-evaluation." *Bulletin of Hispanic Studies* 55 (1978): 301–10.

Wells, L.H. "A Note on the Valverde Muscle Man." *Medical History* 3.3 (1959): 212–14.

Whitenack, Judith A. "'Lo que ha menester': Erotic Enchantment in 'La inocencia castigada.'" In *María de Zayas: The Dynamics of Discourse*, ed. Amy R. Williamsen and Judith A. Whitenack, 170–91. Madison, NJ: Fairleigh Dickinson University Press, 1995.

Wiener, Philip P., ed. *Dictionary of the History of Ideas: Studies of Selected Pivotal Ideas.* 5 vols. New York: Scribner, 1973.

Williams, Robert Haden. "Boccalini in Spain: A Study of His Influence on Prose Fiction of the Seventeenth Century." PhD thesis, Columbia University, 1946.

Williamsen, Amy R. "'Death Becomes Her': Fatal Beauty in María de Zayas's 'Mal presagio casar lejos.'" *Romance Languages Annual* 6 (1994): 619–23.

Wilson, Eric G. *The Spiritual Science of Ice: Romanticism, Science, and the Imagination.* New York: Palgrave Macmillan, 2003.

Wilson, Luke. "William Harvey's *Prelectiones:* The Performance of the Body in the Renaissance Theater of Anatomy." *Representations* 17 (1987): 62–95.

Winkler, Mary G. "The Anatomical Theater." *Literature and Medicine* 12.1 (1993): 65–80.

Winstead, Karen A. *Virgin Martyrs: Legends of Sainthood in Late Medieval England*. Ithaca: Cornell University Press, 1997.

Wittgenstein, Ludwig. *Philosophical Investigations*. Trans. G.E.M. Anscombe. Oxford: Blackwell, 1997.

Wolfe, Jessica. *Humanism, Machinery, and Renaissance Literature*. Cambridge: Cambridge University Press, 2004.

Wolman, Benjamin B. "Anxiety, Fear, and Depression." In *Encyclopedia of Psychiatry, Psychology, and Psychoanalysis*, ed. Benjamin B. Wolman, 43–4. New York: Aesculapius, 1996.

Woodward, L.J. "*El casamiento engañoso* y *El coloquio de los perros*." *Bulletin of Hispanic Studies* 36 (1959): 80–7.

Yllera, Alicia. "Introducción." In *Parte segunda del Sarao y entretenimiento honesto (Desengaños amorosos)*, ed. Alicia Yllera, 9–112. Madrid: Cátedra, 2009.

Zagorin, Perez. *Ways of Lying: Dissimulation, Persecution, and Conformity in Early Modern Europe*. Cambridge, MA: Harvard University Press, 1990.

Zahavi, Dan. *Subjectivity and Selfhood*. Cambridge, MA: MIT Press, 2005.

Zappala, Michael. "Cervantes and Lucian." *Symposium* 33.1 (1979): 65–82.

Zayas y Sotomayor, María de. *The Disenchantments of Love: A Translation of the Desengaños amorosos*. Trans. H. Patsy Boyer. Albany: State University of New York Press, 1997.

– *Exemplary Tales of Love and Tales of Disillusion*. Trans. Margaret Rich Greer and Elizabeth Rhodes. Chicago: University of Chicago Press, 2009.

– *Novelas amorosas y ejemplares*. Ed. Julián Olivares. Madrid: Cátedra, 2010.

– *Parte segunda del Sarao y entretenimiento honesto (Desengaños amorosos)*. Ed. Alicia Yllera. Madrid: Cátedra, 2009.

Ziolkowski, Eric J. *The Sanctification of Don Quixote: From Hidalgo to Priest*. University Park: Pennsylvania State University Press, 1991.

# Index

# TORONTO IBERIC

CO-EDITORS: Robert Davidson (Toronto) and Frederick A. de Armas (Chicago)

EDITORIAL BOARD: Josiah Blackmore (Harvard); Marina Brownlee (Princeton); Anthony J. Cascardi (Berkeley); Emily Francomano (Georgetown); Justin Crumbaugh (Mt Holyoke); Jordana Mendelson (NYU); Joan Ramon Resina (Stanford); Kathleen Vernon (SUNY Stony Brook)

1  Anthony J. Cascardi, *Cervantes, Literature, and the Discourse of Politics*
2  Jessica A. Boon, *The Mystical Science of the Soul: Medieval Cognition in Bernardino de Laredo's Recollection Method*
3  Susan Byrne, *Law and History in Cervantes' Don Quixote*
4  Mary E. Barnard and Frederick A. de Armas (eds), *Objects of Culture in the Literature of Imperial Spain*
5  Nil Santiáñez, *Topographies of Fascism: Habitus, Space, and Writing in Twentieth-Century Spain*
6  Nelson Orringer, *Lorca in Tune with Falla: Literary and Musical Interludes*
7  Ana M. Gómez-Bravo, *Textual Agency: Writing Culture and Social Networks in Fifteenth-Century Spain*
8  Javier Irigoyen-García, *The Spanish Arcadia: Sheep Herding, Pastoral Discourse, and Ethnicity in Early Modern Spain*
9  Stephanie Sieburth, *Survival Songs: Conchita Piquer's* Coplas *and Franco's Regime of Terror*
10  Christine Arkinstall, *Spanish Female Writers and the Freethinking Press, 1879-1926*
11  Margaret Boyle, *Unruly Women: Performance, Penitence, and Punishment in Early Modern Spain*

Printed and bound by CPI Group (UK) Ltd, Croydon, CR0 4YY

09/06/2025

14685788-0001